Body and personality

BODY AND PERSONALITY

Brian W. P. Wells

LONGMAN
London and New York

LONGMAN GROUP LIMITED
Longman House, Burnt Mill, Harlow
Essex CM20 2JE, England
Associated companies throughout the world

Published in the United States of America
by Longman Inc., New York

First published 1983

BRITISH LIBRARY CATALOGUING IN PUBLICATION DATA

Wells, Brian W. P.
Body and personality.
1. Mind and body
I. Title
128′.2 BF161

ISBN 0-582-29596-3

LIBRARY OF CONGRESS CATALOGING IN PUBLICATION DATA

Wells, Brian.
Body and personality.

Bibliography: p.
Includes index.
1. Personality. 2. Mind and body. I. Title.
BF698.W43 1983 155.2 82-17947
ISBN 0-582-29596-3

Set in 10/11 pt Linotron 202 Plantin

Printed in Singapore by
Huntsmen Offset Printing Pte Ltd.

CONTENTS

Preface vi

1. Form, bearing and personality 1
2. Body image and self-esteem 34
3. Sex and sexuality: general 63
4. Sex and sexuality: specifics 90
5. Personality and physical malfunction 119
6. Ageing and dying 146
7. Mind over matter 170
8. Healthy body and healthy mind 204

Coda 239

References and further reading 246
Index 256

PREFACE

Though they appear at the beginning, prefaces are usually the last thing to be written, and this one is no exception. In many respects, they are an indulgence, a refreshment after the work is done, and a time to look back and ask what one has tried to do, and why. Of course, rationalization must play its part; one's motives and ideas are never static, and the mere act of writing a book is guaranteed to shake them up more than usual. Yet, whatever else may have changed in the course of writing, my main reason for beginning remains quite clear – it was simply an overwhelming feeling that psychology was becoming far too metaphysical, and that a case made on behalf of the physical self might do something to offset what I felt to be an increasingly, and perilously, abstract view of psychology. After all, the body is the channel through which everything beyond the skin is experienced; it is the palpable presence by which we are known to others, and it is the instrument upon which we must largely depend in order to influence the world beyond ourselves. Without a body there is no mind, no person, no personality. And because the body is not neutral, either in its functioning or in the limitations, opportunities and social effects it creates, a good case can be made for considering the physical self as the essential starting point for all psychological understanding.

Yet the effect of physical variables continues to receive surprisingly little attention, either in research or attempts to develop theoretical syntheses. Instead, there is much more concern with idealizations of the processes of learning and perceiving, and a taste for theoretical analogies with cybernetic gadgets, computers, or the like, in order to create the 'models' intended to simplify our understanding of people. But, valuable as these approaches may be sometimes, the very fact we are made of flesh and blood rather than transistors and wires; that we develop and continually refine our own 'data banks' and 'logic circuits'; are driven by very variable and fluctuating energy sources, and are all constructed and regulated slightly differently by our genetic control mechanisms, introduces a diversity and complexity we are sometimes tempted to overlook in our haste to find simple principles to explain both behavioural and mental phenomena.

Recently though, research findings from psychophysiology and psychogenetics have begun to be taken more seriously. Whether of a genetic origin or not, it is now very apparent that individual differences in nervous system and endocrine functioning profoundly affect responses to experimental situations ranging from those connected with learning and perception to those concerning coping and other adjustive behaviour. As a result, experimental investigations are now, at least marginally, more likely to allow for the effect of physiologically-based differences within the groups they study. However, though there will be some discussion of the way personality is affected by bodily events at this level, the case to be made involves rather more emphasis on outer than inner aspects of the physical self, even though such a distinction is frequently more notional than actual.

So, with this firmly in mind, most of what follows concerns the way we regard our own bodies; how we react to the changes which inevitably take place in them; how we respond to the bodies of others, and they to ours. Healthy or disabled, young or old, beautiful or ugly, the physical self is always an important element in our previous history, present self-perception, and future expectations. It may not always be a foreground factor, though it often is, but it is seldom a completely irrelevant term in the equations of either social or psychological adjustment.

Unfortunately, recognition or direct experience of this fact is usually most acute where there is disease or deformity, even though the body's influence on mental states is in no way limited to negative effects. Nevertheless, a somewhat pessimistic view of the body's contribution to mental life is hard to escape. Young lovers, athletes, or artists, may rejoice in the body and celebrate its positive qualities but, more frequently, we regard it as something essentially 'medical'; an object whose shortcomings and infirmities of age or illness will inevitably lead to our future distress and final destruction. But though this is true, and an important consideration in determining the way we approach the whole question of body-mind relationships, it is only part of the truth.

Of course, an exhaustive listing, let alone treatment, of all the interrelationships involved is out of the question and, while attempting to cast the net as widely as possible, practical considerations must inevitably result in some selection of material. For example, topics such as ethnic differences, hermaphroditism and transexualism, are obvious candidates for inclusion in any book dealing with body-mind interactions. But, rather than include these, I have chosen instead to allow a more extended treatment of subjects which would otherwise have been even more abbreviated than they already are. On the whole, I have attempted to emphasize normality rather than pathology, and adult rather than childhood developmental themes. Each is there in some measure, though rather than attempting inclusiveness, I have simply tried to develop a more limited case for bodily structures being treated as basic to the understanding of personality.

But, while some topics have had to be restricted, others may seem to have received more than their fair share of attention. Sexuality, for example, despite the many cuts that have had to be imposed on it too, has been allowed two whole chapters dealing with different themes. Others may well have given less prominence to sex-related material than it received here, but the fact that personality psychologists from the time of Freud to the present have always been inclined to see it as a major factor, while contemporary thinking from ethology to feminism continues to highlight the question of male-female differences, seemed to justify the more extended treatment.

No doubt many will also disagree with my choice of emphasis, subject matter, and conclusions. To this I have no answer except to say that while some topics, like giantism or hermaphroditism, have been omitted because they are so uncommon, others – such as ethnic differences – have been left out because it would be impossible to do them justice in the present context. For, though such physical characteristics as skin pigmentation may be easy to identify, and may even be readily associated with a number of psychosocial differences, the cause-effect relationships involved are almost invariably extremely obscure and controversial, and reach out far beyond the realms of conventional psychological analysis. It all very much depends upon the place, the time, the relative numbers involved and the particular ethnic groups concerned. History, politics and other cultural considerations are always absolutely crucial in shaping outcomes which demand, and have received, libraries devoted to themselves alone.

Colour or other obvious and characteristic ethnic differences are, potentially at least, extremely important factors in determining how we feel about ourselves, how we treat those of other ethnic groups and, consequently, how opportunities and self-regard develop. The psychological significance of having a body which is black, white, yellow, or any other hue can, of course, be anything from neutral to obsessively dominating. Unfortunately however, even where different ethnic groups come into close contact with one another, there is all too often an intensification rather than a reduction of both public and private conflict. Whenever such circumstances occur, and whatever the forces at work promoting and sustaining these feelings, there are always likely to be profound consequences for people's sense of pride or shame, anger or content, belonging or alienation, and the experiences upon which their mental lives and growth largely depend. There seems no end to the possible ramifications of what are, biologically speaking, really quite insignificant differences.

But while acknowledging, and indeed stressing, the great potential influence of such bodily differences on the formation of personality, they would require a much more delicate and comprehensive treatment than they could possibly receive in the present context. Ethnic differences are not just additional or supplementary variables that can be tacked on to a treatment of topics like ageing, illness, sexuality, dying, or any of the other subjects discussed here. And, though deeply relevant in many cases, it seemed wisest not to introduce issues which could not then be given adequate treatment.

Decisions about content were often very hard to make, but they were by no means the only ones encountered: presentation too created its own difficulties. For instance, there is no way of avoiding the purely practical need to divide so vast a subject into chapters and topics, despite the fact that the book is essentially about synthesis rather than analysis, and that any such segmentation is necessarily artificial and somewhat arbitrary. In reality, sexual behaviour cannot be considered independent of age, health and appearance, but it would be quite impossible to handle together all the combinations and permutations of possible interactions without becoming hopelessly confused. On the other hand, there is a real risk that dissecting out attributes in this way will obscure the whole which is so much greater, and more psychologically significant, than its parts. Regrettably, there seems to be no satisfactory solution to this dilemma except, perhaps, to bear in mind that each chapter represents only a facet of four-dimensional reality; our major concern always being the individuals whose integrated lives lie beyond the statistical or otherwise derived generalizations about properties and processes.

Final pronouncements on this book, including an assessment of its undoubtedly great sins of omission and commission must, of course, be left to the reader. My aim – to show how much related to human psychology can be unified under the single rubric of the physical self – was an ambitious one; perhaps too ambitious, in that the book's coverage inevitably stretches its substance extremely thin. This I judged to be unavoidable and, in some respects, even desirable in view of the intention to highlight form rather than detail. And, though these two objectives are not necessarily antithetical – except in so far as they involve competition for limited space in a single volume – such was acutely the case in the present instance.

As a result, what follows is very far from being an inventory of facts or catalogue of recent research findings. Rather, it is a collection of ideas on a single theme, to be supplemented according to taste or need. Anyone interested in a particular aspect of body-mind relationships may not find them well enough developed here – such is not the purpose of this book – but they will be able to find much more relevant material in the works listed under *References and further reading*, where detailed bibliographies will amplify what has been briefly touched upon, and point the reader towards more technical and recondite sources.

But, whether one's interests are scholarly or not, it is hoped the contents of this book will serve an immediate and practical purpose by encouraging a more personal concern with the physical features and attributes of ourselves and others. Through careful observation, it should soon become apparent just how much our daily fortunes depend upon bodily characteristics, and how our very personalities come to be moulded by these experiences. Awareness may not guarantee being able to change things, but the old saw 'knowledge is power' is probably just as true in the present instance as in any other concerning human relationships.

What follows therefore relates to self-understanding and the practicalities of coping just as much as it concerns understanding others from a disinterested or scientific point of view. Yet, whatever the point of view adopted, if what has been attempted is successful, it will show just how much unity of viewpoint can be achieved by taking the physical self as both a starting and a focal point for one's psychological thinking. Without some sort of centring device or solid mooring to attach our abstractions, they tend to drift away from one another, making it all too easy to forget that psychology is about people.

Brian W. P. Wells

Chapter one

FORM, BEARING AND PERSONALITY

A single species we may be, but we are still quite astonishingly varied in our physical forms. Ethnic differences add a good deal to this heterogeneity and have often been used to suggest that some innate temperamental or other personality differences might parallel this physical diversity but, if this is so, scientific endorsement is sadly lacking. The potentially confounding factors involved in cross-cultural research are such as to make deriving unequivocal conclusions from very fallible and generally culture-sensitive tests a very shaky enterprise indeed.

Even at the level of individual differences between members of the same ethnic group, the problems are daunting enough, particularly as we are to begin by exploring the more subtle shades of grey – those relating to people within the normal range of variation – whilst reserving until a later chapter explorations of personality characteristics linked to extreme, damaged, deteriorating, or otherwise exceptional body forms. Interestingly enough though, modern theories linking constitutional and psychological processes were originally developed in the context of serious mental disorder and only later generalized to the normal population.

Naturally, the Greeks had not overlooked even this area of study in their remarkable scientific and philosophical boom of the pre-Christian era. As early as 400 BC a specific number of relationships between temperament and body chemistry were proposed by Hippocrates, the founder of modern medicine, and physical types were also related to particular disease susceptibilities. There has, of course, always been a folklore and literature to reflect people's ideas about the relationship between temperament and bodily type – as with Shakespeare's muscular and action-orientated Harry Hotspur; the rotund and sociable Falstaff; and the lean brooding Cassius. And though these might be summarily dismissed as examples of mere stereotypes, a stereotype nevertheless does represent widely-held beliefs, and ones which have proved durable and convincing enough to survive over very long periods of time. One should be careful, therefore, not to underestimate their psychological and sociological significance. Of course, being so generalized and over-simplified, stereotypes could hardly be expected to serve as trustworthy guides in any particular case but, even allowing for a proportion of failures it does not necessarily follow that they are entirely without foundation. Indeed, as people are quick to tell one, such ideas often reflect not only their own personal experience but also a great deal of accumulated wisdom. In the end though, unless one is content to continue at a pre-scientific level of thinking, all such popular ideas must sooner or later be put to the test of experimental investigation.

However, it was not until the mid- to late nineteenth century, when evolution and other social and religious changes were once again making both the biological analysis of mind and a frank evaluation of the naked human body a practicable undertaking, that empirical studies could be undertaken. And it was not until the beginning of the present century that fully scientific studies, like that of the German psychiatrist Ernst Kretschmer, began to appear.

Kretschmer had noticed, during the course of his hospital work, that the body-build of the, then, two most common categories of mental patient – schizophrenics and manic-depressives – seemed to be markedly different. He referred back to earlier formulations of the body-temperament relationship and adopted what was already a traditional trichotomy – the muscular, the rounded-visceral and the light-slender types – each associated with characteristic qualities of temperament. His careful empirical studies gave a great deal of new impetus to this whole area of research, and though he was to some extent concerned with normal individuals, his non-psychiatric contributions were mainly along the lines of stimulating other workers and refining the methodology.

Using a series of checklists, the bodily characteristics of hospitalized schizophrenics and manic-depressives were carefully described and these were then tabulated against the patient's form of illness. The results were very clear cut: manic-depressives were characterized by what he called a *pyknic* body type – that is, typified by extreme visceral development and the presence of a good deal of extra fat – whereas schizophrenics were typically of the *asthenic* type, that is, thin and narrow and of a light skeletal construction. The basis of this categorization was not, however, as has often been supposed, simply a matter of whether people were thin, muscular, or fat. In addition, the classification also depended upon such non-superficial physical structures as the relative length of thorax to abdomen, rib angle, width or depth of chest, thickness of elbow joints or wrist bones. These, and many more besides, were carefully appraised by Kretschmer and his helpers and, though the degree of sophistication now used when making such measures is far greater, it would be wrong to suppose that this early research was either simplistic or naive in its approach to classifying physical characteristics.

Of course, with all the wisdom of hindsight and the advantage of accumulated experience, it is not difficult to spot a great many weaknesses in Kretschmer's approach. For example, his method involved the search for fairly extreme physical categories, with the result that these rather clear-cut types, one might almost say stereotypes, of physique proved to be applicable to only a minority of cases. Despite the creation of a third major and an additional minor category in the self-explanatory *athletic* and the less obvious *dysplastic* or mixed types, both of which he held to be more frequently connected with epilepsy then could be explained, obvious classificatory problems continued to arise from this sort of pigeon-holding taxonomy. Most individuals are, in the nature of things, average or indeterminate. Nevertheless, of those who were classifiable within one or other of the two main physical types mentioned, two-thirds of the schizophrenics were of the frail asthenic kind, whilst two-thirds of the manic-depressives were pyknic – that is, of a round, heavily built, and fat constitution.

But, though Kretschmer's data showed quite clear-cut results, a serious methodological oversight soon became apparent for insufficient attention had been given to the facts of ageing. Schizophrenia most commonly occurs in young people, or when we are likely to be at our most slender. By contrast, the onset of manic-depressive psychosis is more likely to occur during middle age: that is, at a time when most of us will have begun, and may be all too well advanced, in the process of laying down excess adipose tissue around the waist, neck, hips, buttocks, thighs, and indeed anywhere else that fat can form.

This failure to allow for the processes of ageing has frequently been used in, what has fondly been supposed annihilative, attacks on the whole theory. Certainly it is a serious criticism, but the body-type determinations were by no means dependent upon fat measures alone. Other characteristics upon which classification depended – such things as the relatively longer rib-cage of the asthenic when compared with that of the pyknic type, are not affected by diet, and Kretschmer's findings cannot therefore be dismissed out of hand because of his failure to allow for 'middle-aged spread'. In fact, more recent research in which the age variable has been allowed for, still tends to support Kretschmer's main findings, though the relationships are far less pronounced than in this early series. However, this is something which will be referred to again in Chapter five, where we shall be specifically concerned with mental disorder.

Of course, any theory which seeks to link mind and body in a deterministic fashion is always likely to receive some pretty critical, not to say hostile, attention. So, when Kretschmer extrapolated from his psychiatric studies and asserted that the principles which apply to psychosis also apply to normal people, he was acting not only prematurely but also provocatively. Such a premise seems to assume some sort of continuum between psychosis and normality; an implication that the processes seen in mental disorder are merely revealing exaggerations of normal mental activity. Psychologists like Gordon Allport were quick to respond that such an assumption was neither experimentally nor logically derived. The research findings regarding normal populations were then, as now, far too weak to justify the *schizothymia-cyclothymia* dimension proposed by Kretschmer as a major contributor in normal psychological functioning.

Kretschmer's hypothesis envisaged a continuum which ran from the extremes of pathological schizophrenia at one end to manic-depressive psychosis at the other, with normal people occupying the middle ground. Depending upon one's physical constitution, the normal person was held to develop a bias towards some of the mental characteristics expressed more fully in schizophrenics if he was of an asthenic constitution, and dispositions approximating to those of manic–depressive psychosis if he was of the rotund pyknic build. In other words, the slender and fragile asthenic individual will tend to be schizothymic, or cerebral and introverted, whereas the fat and rounded type is characteristically more likely to be cyclothymic, or extraverted and subject to swings in mood from gaiety to gloom.

The logical objection, as Allport pointed out, was that there is no necessary continuity between pathology and normality: for example, one either has, or does not have, cancer. In the same way, there are many non-continuous divisions within the realms of normal functioning: one cannot be just a little pregnant either. If continuities do exist they must needs be demonstrated by research, not accepted on the basis of arguments which are finally dependent upon *a priori* principles, or on reasoning from carefully selected analogies.

Unfortunately for Kretschmer's theory though, more recent research by Hans Eysenck involving a vast amount of clinical and experimental data deriving from normals, has failed to reveal any such major psychological dimension, despite a most careful statistical treatment of the material.

So, it turned out that both the logical and empirical rebuttals have prevailed but, apart from the way in which Kretschmer proposed his schizothymia-cyclothymia dimension, it is surprising just how well other aspects of the general constitutional theory have held up, in spite of the fact that the original research was done on a very atypical population and with a complete lack of advanced statistical techniques.

Of course, Kretschmer was a pioneer and, as such, is perhaps more to be admired for his insights and stimulating hypotheses than criticized for his shortcomings – many of which were, in any case, soon to be rectified in the work of the American psychologist, William Sheldon, and his collaborators.

While Kretschmer had concentrated on severely abnormal personalities and had done a simple matching of their psychiatric diagnosis with their physical constitution, Sheldon began his work from the other end: categorizing the physical characteristics of normal people and looking for any associated psychological patterns. Nevertheless, Sheldon's indebtedness to Kretschmer is obvious, both methodologically and conceptually, and it would be as easy as it is unnecessary to show how similar are the final versions of both men's conclusions. But, in selecting one or the other for more detailed treatment, the much greater subtlety, quantification and scientific control typical of Seldon's approach make his the more natural choice. Moreover, it is a theory specifically about the normal personality, though it is one which has also led to a certain amount of psychiatric probing, and to the generation of results broadly supportive of Kretschmer's own hypotheses.

Sheldon's work also began with a less than random or typical sample of the population. Of course, if one considers what is involved, it soon becomes apparent that this sort of research is really only practicable in some sort of institutional setting – whether a hospital, military organization, prison or, as in Sheldon's case, a university. Moreover, population sources must be big enough to yield the very large numbers required for the production of norms and distributions: Kretschmer himself had seen several thousand cases and Sheldon launched his own study with the physical examination of some 4,000 male students. Great as this number may seem, it has been added to very substantially over the years: the number of research subjects involved, male and female, now totals tens of thousands.

One of the many novel features of Sheldon's precedure was that his primary data were derived from three photographs – a frontal, side and back view of the nude person – posed in an absolutely standard fashion. Meticulous technique produced identical formats in which each individual was placed before a grid-scale, and from which exact measurements could be made.

Sheldon and his colleagues then analysed the pictures, looking for the most basic, and non-overlapping, descriptive qualities which could be used to characterize every case. They came up with three primary components – *endomorphy*, *mesomorphy* and *ectomorphy* – closely paralleling Kretschmer's pyknic, athletic and asthenic types. Like the pyknic, the endomorph is characterized by being round and generally soft; having a relatively large abdominal cavity, having relatively little muscle development, and a skeletal frame lighter than one might expect in view of the bulk.

By contrast, mesomorphs tend to have a much more massive skeletal development, with heavy bones, broad chest, and a tendency to be strongly muscled: in all respects, the counterpart of Kretchmer's athletic type. The final category, ectomorphy, is quite the opposite: frail, lightly boned and muscled, and with a narrow chest. Whereas endomorphy is associated with above average abdominal to thoracic development, mesomorphy with a more even distribution, ectomorphy is connected with a relative underdevelopment of the visceral cavity and digestive system. The resulting configurations are often represented schematically as shown in Figure 1. Again, it is possible to treat these schema or categories as

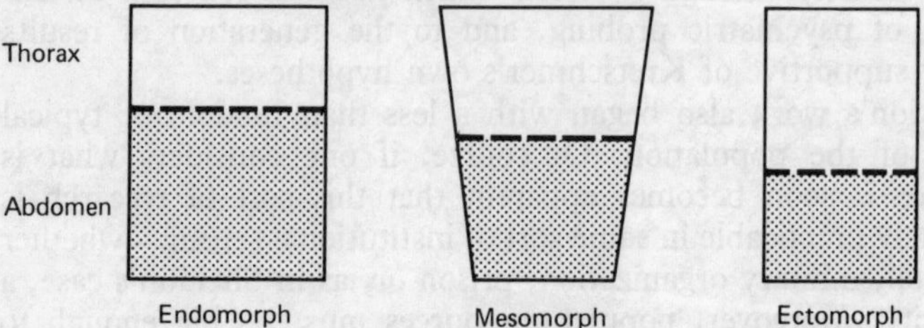

Fig. 1 Trunk development in Sheldon's three categories

single 'types', and indeed some individuals do approximate very closely to one or other of these extremes and can quite accurately be referred to as endomorphs, or whatever. But Sheldon's system differs from that of Kretschmer in that the terms used refer to components of physique, not types. Each of the three can be used to describe each of us, though we may have an absolute minimum of any one, or even two, of them.

For classificatory purposes, each component is rated on a scale of 1–7, in which 1 refers to a minimum and 7 a maximum representation, so that one can be typified by a three-number code. Conventionally, the endomorphic, mesomorphic and ectomorphic ratings are always listed in that sequence. So, for example, a 7–4–1 individual would be extremely endomorphic, with an average degree of mesomorphy and virtually no indications of ectomorphic development. Of course, even more extreme cases, approximating to the 1–1–7 ectomorph do occur, but these are very rare and most of us have a fairly mixed physique, approximating to the 4–4–4 midline.

Sheldon's three-number code expresses what he calls one's *somatotype*, the physical and observable representation of our genetic predispositions. Of course, the genetic pattern can itself never be known directly and completely because all living things reflect the effects of both heredity and environmental interactions. Even so, Sheldon was in no doubt that, under normal conditions of health, exercise and diet, people will express fairly fully their underlying genetic disposition. This presupposes that the body, or rather the somatotype, is a relatively unchanging given, yet our experiences suggest very strongly that this is not so. It is quite evident that overeating or dieting can produce remarkable changes in our appearance, and the effects of training, or living a sedentary life can, just as easily, add or subtract muscle and fat from our bodies, whatever our age.

So how can Sheldon base his ideas of constant relationships on such shifting sand? His answer was to note that starving a mastiff will not produce a poodle: it will simply yield a starved, but quite identifiable, mastiff. In the same way, starving a powerful mesomorph would certainly make him thin, but despite the loss of fat and the wasting of muscles, the underlying physique remains obvious in his shape and proportion, and in his rugged bone structure.

However, the whole question of whether physique is or is not relatively stable is too crucial in such a theory to depend on an analogy. Sheldon's own twelve year follow-up studies, involving several hundred people, confirmed for him his belief that, though muscle and fat may come and go, the diagnostic skeletal conformations are unchanging.

Heavily muscled young sportsmen and women who put on a great deal of fat and become extremely endomorphic in their thirties or forties were as familiar to Sheldon as to ourselves, but his reaction was to underline the difficulties of the procedure, not its failures. Training and the development of powerful muscles, in cases where the fat component is kept in severe check and the original somatotype was known to have both a marked endomorphic and mesomorphic component, can easily result in a misclassification. The problem is one of discrimination and Sheldon later came to realize that detailed life histories – particularly where unusual training, diets, or medical circumstances are involved – are necessary if misclassifications are to be avoided.

So several photographs, taken over a period of time and supplemented by background information, have become the more recent method of choice and Sheldon is satisfied that his measures can now be depended upon to exhibit an extremely high degree of stability over the major part of one's lifetime. However, the period around puberty is acknowledged to be critical: other investigators, such as Lindsay Carter, have also noted that the developmental changes which take place around this time may easily reveal many unsuspected latent tendencies.

Although I have necessarily oversimplified the great technical intricacy of somatotyping, such a relatively simple method of accurately quantifying and categorizing physique opens up the possibility of exploring the most subtle relationships between body and mind – always assuming one can produce an equally reliable and valid categorization of psychological characteristics. And this, of course, was the other half of Sheldon's self-appointed task.

Because the assessment of temperament is so much more time-consuming, being of an altogether more complex nature than physique and much less open to direct inspection, the size of Sheldon's initial programme to establish his basic psychological measures was necessarily on a much reduced scale. Only 33 young university men participated and they were rated, once again using a seven point scale, on the 50 traits which Sheldon and his colleagues had already abstracted from a very overlapping 650 with which they began. But whatever was lost by having so few subjects was, perhaps, gained in the thoroughness with which they were evaluated. Each individual was observed and interviewed by the researchers over the course of a year and the resulting ratings were then statistically treated in the search for clusters of traits which would show high internal correlations and would be negatively correlated with other traits.

The analyses revealed only three such clusters: components of temperament which were named *viscerotonia* – denoting sociability, food and comfort-loving, and even-temperedness; *somatotonia* – designating physical and activity characteristics, particularly aggressiveness, courage, and general delight in competition and muscular activity. *Cerebrotonia*, the third component, is typified by self-consciousness, preference for solitude or small groupings of people, and a generally introverted nature.

Subsequently, the traits used were refined and developed into the 'Scale for Temperament': a checklist which, like the physical scale, utilized the seven point scale and produced scores for each of the three dimensions. Its recommended mode of application might sound somewhat daunting, though reassuringly thorough, in that any rating made must depend upon at least a year's acquaintance with the individual, and at least 20 interviews – each of which should be followed by a rating of all 60 traits which, together, yield the three-fold categorization.

The next step in the research, linking physical and temperamental characteristics thus became very straightforward: simply a matter of matching the two equivalently scaled aspects and asking the ingenuous question of whether there was any statistical relationship between them. Using larger numbers, though still only 200 males for his first major research, Sheldon showed what he had obviously expected, that there is indeed a relationship, and that its magnitude is of a very high order.

No one will be surprised to learn that the fat-rounded endomorphic constitution correlates highly with the viscerotonic love of food, company and comfort; that mesomorphic muscularity also correlates very highly with such somatotonic ways as activity-seeking and competitiveness; or that the frailty of ectomorphy is related to the solitary and reflective nature of the cerebrotonic to an equally high degree.

Common sense, and our familiar stereotypes, combine to make the connections revealed seem highly probable, yet the correlations claimed involved such a close match between the mental and physical components that they seemed to imply a virtually inescapable biological determinism. Now such an assertion is widely regarded as a cardinal ideological crime, and this is particularly so in a discipline like psychology which, since the 1920s has been heavily committed to environmental determination. A swift rejoinder to these findings was therefore entirely to be expected.

Whilst not being able to dismiss the connections claimed, the flurry of research set off by Sheldon's findings nevertheless invariably failed to come up with correlations of anything like the same magnitude as those relating to the numerous studies of men and women, delinquents and the mentally disordered, which Sheldon and his co-workers continued to produce. On the other hand, though Sheldon was criticized for 'loading the dice', consciously or unconsciously, by rating both physique and personality and thereby allowing in the possibility of his preconceptions contaminating the results, many later workers took neither so much trouble in assessing their subjects' personality characteristics, nor in replicating the physical procedures exactly. Even so, the results produced data which many have felt would be difficult to account for without any recourse to biological explanation.

As I have already discussed in an earlier book, *Personality and Heredity*, Sheldon's own causal explanations cover a wide range of possibilities, none of which he seems willing to back wholeheartedly. Nevertheless, the genetic element is implicit in his account of certain embryological events which, purely speculatively, he believes shape our bodily characteristics. Whatever one makes of Sheldon's embryological ideas, and they are generally not well regarded, by the time babies are born they are already of a great variability, and indeed unique in some respects.

Irrespective of developmental conditions, physique certainly does continue to show great variability, so it is not unreasonable to suppose that internal chemistry and the relative development of such psychologically influential structures as the endocrine and nervous systems might also be involved in the more general process of physical differentiation. If so, a direct form of genetic causality might explain the observed relationship between the physical self and temperament. It is, of course, perfectly probable that the sort of individual differences we can easily observe to occur in most parts of the body have their counterparts in all physical systems – including those which are of demonstrable psychological significance.

Another possibility is that psychological characteristics are *indirectly* the result of genetic processes which determine physique. For example, the individual whose genetic endowment disposes him to be light and frail may well find that physically aggressive team games such as rugby football are not only painful but a royal road to failure. As a result, a greater number of ectomorphs might tend to avoid this type of activity and in so doing forgo an activity which incidentally also generates a good deal of extraverted camaraderie and a sense of group membership. Instead, they might tend to develop along more isolated and individualistic lines, perhaps becoming long-distance runners, thus also evolving a psychological life style which is much more individualistic and introverted. As a matter of fact, J. M. Tanner's analysis of the somatotypes of Olympic athletes indicates that those ectomorphs who turn to sport, and do well at it, do indeed tend to gravitate towards individual track events, marathons, jumping, or the like.

Compatible with either a genetic or an environmental point of view, and containing some evidence for both, has been the work of R. W. Parnell, one of Sheldon's more recent successors. His book *Behaviour and Physique* describes research in which the somatotypes of school-children and university students were related to their academic performance and, in the case of students, their choice of subject and profession. Sheldon had already reported a relationship between academic performance and the tendency towards ectomorphy in male university students: a finding which Parnell repeated not only with his university students but also with children in grammar schools. So, it seems that the stereotypically thin academic might have some basis in truth – though whether this is due to some sort of genetic intelligence/physique package, or is due to the indirect effects of selecting to work harder in areas where one is most likely to succeed, is not obvious from the correlational material as such.

It is unfortunate that Parnell's findings regarding university and career choices leave causal connections so much open to speculation but the statistically significant results, based on nearly 3,000 students at the University of Birmingham, are very intriguing. Again, if one was asked to guess at the results, to apply the stereotype, I suppose that most of us would not be too far out. The faculties of medicine, dentistry and mechanical engineering attracted significantly more mesomorphic students whereas those reading for honours arts degrees tended to be much more ectomorphic. Also, fairly predictably, it transpired that the linear ectomorphs avoided subjects like mining. Of course, all these results are based on averages drawn from large numbers: there were also many exceptions, but the mathematical tendencies do require explanation nevertheless.

One last causal possibility for the various apparent connections between body and personality may involve a sort of self-fulfilling prophesy. It is possible that the former universally held stereotypes of the happy sociable endomorph, the direct and aggressive mesomorph, and the secretive and brooding ectomorph are brought to reality by our behaviour. If, for example, we project our expectations towards people often enough, it may be that many will ultimately accept them and fill the social roles we have created. No doubt this sometimes happens, but which cases are the result of which of the several possible causes considered is very difficult to determine.

As we have seen, Parnell, like Sheldon and Kretschmer before him, adopted a system involving three major interfacing mental and physical categories. But, though the data derived in each of these studies seemed to justify the structure adopted, it is still possible to question this apparently solid degree of agreement. One cannot, for example, as Parnell fully realized, completely rule out the possibility of this being due, at least in part, to the existence of a tradition which influences each newcomer to the field.

In this book *The Structure of Human Personality*, the British psychologist, Hans Eysenck, has tabulated 17 different systems and theories of body typing developed over the past 200 years: in every single case, they were based upon three physical types with three temperamental counterparts. Despite the very different terminologies used, the various systems contrive to range from being moderately compatible to virtually overlapping. Jargons proliferated as only they can, though the very earliest of these modern theories, Halle's, used refreshingly plain-language categories – referring to *abdominal*, *muscular* and *cephalic* types. Terminologies, and what they referred to, became ever more complex over the years but, in addition to their underlying generic similarities, until the arrival of Sheldon, they also had in common a more or less archaic pigeonholing approach to classification.

But, even allowing for Sheldon's replacement of types by somatic components, Eysenck argues that this latest of theories is still flawed in the statistical analysis of both the physical and psychological data. His remedy, based largely on the complex factor analysis of data derived from soldiers, normal and neurotic, involves the demonstration that his own favourite dimensions of *neuroticism* and *extraversion* should be treated as major psychological parameters, and that physical dimensions are most parsimoniously described in terms of the two independent factors of height and width. A most persuasive case is worked out for this approach, though field researchers like Parnell have said they still feel the muscle and fat components must be retained in addition to the length and sturdiness factors proposed. This is particularly important if one is adequately to explore differences between individuals of very different appearance who may, none the less, share similar skeletal size and shape.

The emphasis given by Eysenck to general body size did, however, add another aspect to the more usual analysis of shape. From his classification of 1,000 neurotic soldiers, it again turned out that physique could be categorized on a three-fold basis, with statistical criteria for constructing categories of 'above average', 'average', and 'below average' physical largeness. In the subsequent comparison of psychological data with physical category, it transpired that the undersized person was typically less physically aggressive, active and healthy, and that he was more dependent, sexually inhibited and likely to lag behind the physically above average category in education or level of civilian occupation.

It goes without saying that, although other research had previously shown a connection between height and many other social and psychological accomplishments, such findings are not of the sort to be accepted readily. We all know spectacular exceptions in both directions; and even though the conclusions drawn are not related to individual destinies but to broad statistical tendencies, this does little to abate the sense of personal threat many people experience in relation to such conclusions. Not surprisingly then, this particular line of research is not widely popular, and the small amount of published research makes an appraisal difficult.

On the other hand, there does seem to be sufficient evidence, and a sufficient number of different studies, to discern the scientific consensus regarding somatotyping studies more broadly conceived. Sheldon's work, though generally regarded as overstating the degree of correlation between bodily characteristics and temperament, has been replicated in many successive studies and, though the correlations are universally lower, the proposed connections remain quite apparent. Many methodological and statistical reasons have been used to account for this but, in the end, the trend is very repeatable and explanations are required for what seems to be a fact – that body and temperament are, in some way, and to some degree, connected.

Evaluating Sheldon in their compendious *Theories of Personality*, Hall and Lindzey find themselves having to agree with the often-held view that his work really only amounts to the demonstration of an association between physique and behaviour, and to the creation of some very ingenious measuring techniques. They accept this regretfully as their overall opinion is that the research findings are very important, in spite of the fact that, as critics point out, it is virtually impossible to deduce any further propositions from the theory. In a strict sense, this is a reasonable criticism but not everyone reading Sheldon's work has come to the conclusion that its implications go so little beyond a psycho-biological demonstration.

Very few psychologists would want, or dare, to go so far as to say that knowledge of one's own somatotype, or that of others, can be a valuable aid to self-knowledge and the understanding of other people. However, in his book *The Master Game*, the American scientist Robert de Ropp has taken Sheldon's categories and explored the whole question of how far awareness of one's own somatotype, and the disposition which seems to be associated with it, might be valuable in optimizing one's personal development. In his view, people must be aware of their type in order to pursue appropriate lines of action and avoid the sort of problems often associated with the more pronounced types of physical constitution.

For example, he argues that the large digestive machinery of the endomorph is not only unusually large, it is also likely to be particularly efficient. Lack of dietary care will soon result in the individual becoming fat and, having done so, is likely to lead on to increasing appetite and sedentary habits. Going with this indulgent life style tend to be all the mental characteristics of the viscerotonic outlined by Sheldon and, if one is to escape the psychological destiny which physique can impose, the individual must persevere with diet, self-control and exercise. Even the excessive tolerance and amiability which endomorphy brings may be seen as a vice as it reduces an individual's ability to act objectively and decisively.

De Ropp continues his analysis of the likely problems awaiting other types: muscular mesomorphs tend towards insensitivity, extremism and their desire either to dominate or to give their unreflective obedience to a strong leader. In such cases, people looking for growth and self-improvement will need to compensate for their unconscious tendencies. In the same way the thin, linear, ectomorph must also be prepared to compensate for his tendency of being too absorbed in his own inner life to live harmoniously with other people. Neglecting to make appropriate compensations is, it is argued, often the cause of apparently inexplicable failure and dissatisfaction. In the case of the extremely cerebrotonic ectomorph, their relatively poor interpersonal skills, coupled with particularly strong fantasies, are much more likely to create a dominating and distorted sexuality, and can easily bring a life to ruin. Consequently, each individual is urged to identify his physical and mental type and to follow certain prescriptions which will offset the potentially destructive effects of approximating to one or other of Sheldon's more extreme physical types.

Interestingly enough, de Ropp draws attention to the problems which may arise from being of a fairly average or mixed type. The problem here is that the individual is compounded of opposing and self-cancelling tendencies which would be very difficult to integrate into a unity. Lack of any particular disposition may result in an indecisive, and so unsatisfactory and unsuccessful, life style.

De Ropp's case is based pretty firmly upon his acceptance of Sheldon's research. As a development and extension of this, it is obviously worthy of attention: however, the first issue to decide is whether the basic research is sturdy enough to support these ramifications. In the event, it is not yet possible to decide this with any certainty for, as we have seen, many investigators disagree about the number and nature of the underlying factors and, even when there is no great discrepancy on this particular issue, there is generally a considerable divergence of results relating to the degree of association between the mental and physical characteristics.

However, though the literature is full of disagreement, my overall impression is that a good provisional case has been made for some such body-mind connections, particularly where the more extreme cases are being considered. De Ropp is undeniably jumping the gun by applying Sheldon's results in just the way he has, yet speculations of this kind can have the effect of stimulating interest and suggesting further hypotheses. And, who knows, this particular example might also be pointing the way to future approaches in psychological counselling and self-analysis. On the other hand, the inevitable subjectivity of such applications will not be to all tastes and, in fact, the same deep-rooted distrust of judgement, as opposed to measurement commonly manifested in psychology, has already led to an uneven development of Sheldon's own work.

In addition to endo, meso and ectomorphy, Sheldon also drew attention to some rather more subjectively-assessed physical characteristics. One of these, *gynandromorphy*, refers to the extent to which an individual physically resembles a member of the opposite sex. To some extent, this feature can be quantified – in such terms as relative pelvic and shoulder measurements – but many other indicators are distinctly subjective. For example, most of us will have seen very feminine-looking men, and know just how obvious their apparent femininity may be: but to specify reasons for our judgement is a very subjective matter indeed. It might, for example, relate to the delicacy of facial features, the length and tilt of eyelashes, the size of hands, a swanlike neck, or the softness and roundness of flesh. So, Sheldon came to feel that, in addition to what might be apparent in the photographic data, a great deal more could be usefully coded through direct inspection – including an appraisal of voice, movement and gestures. Whether or not this material is predominantly subjectively or objectively determined, it is clear that such characteristics are likely to be of great psychological significance and Sheldon was not so methodologically rigid as to reject direct assessments, nor flinch at the need, on occasions, to make personal judgements.

Another important secondary component was what Sheldon termed the *textural aspect*. Again, though photographs may give a good deal of information, live inspection of the individual is the only realistic way to make a comprehensive assessment. What is involved is an appraisal of quality, as opposed to mere structure and shape, and this is again something which can only depend upon subjective evaluation. Such characteristics as fineness of skin, hair, or eyes, might influence an individual's total presence: subtle qualities of conformation and attractiveness which are nevertheless capable of substantially modifying our response to people of an otherwise identical somatotype. However, ageing must have a great effect on the stability of this particular variable and as Sheldon pointed out, these sorts of distinctions cannot be measured in the same way as can fat, muscle and skeletal construction; instead, they must depend upon the judgement of people of 'average aesthetic perception or of average appreciation of beauty of form and of proportion'.

As a matter of experience, few of us would doubt that we could make such distinctions but, as scientists, the demand for criteria and quantification is paramount and this has all but eradicated serious research on the significance of the gynandromorphy and textural aspects. Sadly, it is usually the case in psychology that precision in measurement is only attained at the cost of reduction of relevant information. Sometimes, as in the present instance, it seems as though the information abandoned might be of very great importance in modifying the primary sources. Common sense suggests that the life experiences of, say, a man who appears very feminine, or a woman who is either very beautiful or coarsely ugly, will be very different from those of someone else of the opposite aspect who just happens to share the same dimensions. As Schopenhauer remarked 'The fate of innumerable girls has been determined by the slight upward or downward curve of the nose.' And, despite all kinds of recent polemic on the subject of women as sex objects, the same is probably still as true now as it was in the past; just as a male's social, sexual and occupational prospects are probably not independent of factors of appearance and grace either.

Nevertheless, even Sheldon never felt secure enough to develop much research along these subjective lines and in view of the problems such material presents when it comes to publication, or even when defending one's scientific purity and integrity, it is not at all surprising that research along these lines is sparse and has remained at a fairly rudimentary stage.

Few people would argue against the desirability of quantification and experimental rigour, but a love of pattern and system which makes naturalistic observations unacceptable, is surely to be regretted. The ideal state of affairs is, of course, a combination of both and, fortunately, though somatotyping remains stuck where it is, great advances are now being made by a new wave of researchers interested in appearance and the physical self. Curiously enough though, these are, in some respects, appropriately seen as the ultimate heirs of the physiognomists who believed that temperament and character were to be read on the body's surface, and specifically in the face.

Physiognomy, like the gross morphology theories we have been discussing, also has an ancient lineage: sometimes a branch of folk-wisdom, sometimes a front for quackery, while at others the subject of ponderous pseudo-scientific treatises. In other words, its background has much in common with those other discredited theories of mind and body – phrenology and palmistry. Phrenology, a Victorian craze, was based on the mistaken rationale that localized brain development, causing mental biases, could be 'read' through bumps on the surface of the skull. Such ideas have long since been shown to be erroneous and, having no ingrained folk tradition, readily quitted the stage. But the deep roots of palmistry have made it entirely more durable, though mainly as a prop for fortune-telling. Yet there have also been fairly respectable attempts to relate the physical characteristics of the hand to behaviour, and to some forms of mental and physical disorder.

In her book *The Human Hand*, Charlotte Wolff, a one-time assistant director of the Institute of Experimental Psychology in Oxford, has made such a case. As a psychologist and physician herself, she attempted to combine the same approach which motivated Kretschmer and Sheldon with the statistical and clinical analysis of a large amount of her own empirical data. Her starting point was that 'the hand is a visible part of the brain', and a peculiarly sensitive extension of our nervous system: one that is both a major sense organ and an unusually subtle expressive, exploratory and executive extension of our mental activities.

The argument runs that, just as the hand's functions have significant representations in the brain, so too are certain very stable mental states reflected in its shape, colour, creases, fleshiness, nails and sweatiness. Material is presented to show how signs of such endocrine disorders as hypothydroidism and hypopituitrism may be read in the hand, and how the advance of rheumatism, the effects of stress, and current energy states, are also to be seen there.

But when Wolff begins to read personality and create psychological portraits in a way a palmist does, one might easily form an impression that the scientific and medically-based aspects of her case are there to make the pseudo-science more palatable. However, the book is a very interesting example of its type and does present a very comprehensive rationale for this particular method of exploring one of the possible interconnections between mind and body.

Physiognomists have also tried to codify, and make more respectable, their own ancient belief that the face reveals an individual's temperament, character, and personality. As with bodily constitution, the first known treatise on this subject also goes back to Greece of the 4th century BC, to a book *Physiognomica*, by Aristotle. Besides drawing up a comprehensive list of physiognomic signs by which personality might be assessed, with characteristic good sense Aristotle also made it plain that the only reliable basis for drawing conclusions was when there was agreement between the widest possible range of indicators. The face alone, though a major source of psychological information, was not regarded as a separate, or a sufficient, source of data: the body had to be considered as a whole.

In due course, physiognomy also became an instrument of quackery, degenerating into a branch and adjunct of fortune-telling. But there also occurred systematizers of a more or less scientific kind. Though by modern standards they would be judged as naive and gullible, and frequently as opportunistic, the work was sometimes a quite intriguing mixture of insight, ignorance and speculation.

One of these codifiers, Johann Lavater, created a series of stereotypes which were so clear and vivid that they are probably still responsible for many modern beliefs about appearance and personality. His four volume book *Essays on Physiognomy*, published in 1775, still has few equals as a guide to popular beliefs held about the psychological significance of particular facial features. Lavater's source material was drawn from stereotypes already venerable in his own day, but he refined them and added some of his own pet beliefs and observations too. To his new 'science' he added a crude methodology whereby the proportions of the face could be measured and profiles categorized. Given some of the trappings of science, physiognomy soon gained a new strength, and a new respectability.

Unfortunately, Lavater omitted the cardinal requirement of true science: he made no attempt to validate his claims against anything other than his own impressions. Nevertheless, his assertions evidently matched the impressions or opinions of a sufficient number of other people to prove widely acceptable. But, of course, given that his original source was the commonly held stereotype, it is only to be expected that the ideas presented should enjoy a good deal of popularity and seem to reflect 'common sense'.

The scientific achievement was minimal, if present at all, but what Lavater probably did achieve with his catalogue of relationships was to fix certain ideas – for example, that thick lips denote sensuality whereas thin ones indicate coldness or cruelty, or that chins, noses and eyes can be associated with strength, weakness, stupidity, or whatever – thereby ensuring their future survival. It may well be that no help was needed to sustain such notions but it clearly contributed to the crystallization of the stereotypes with which we are all still all too familiar.

What, if anything, there is in the claims made by Lavater and his successors is another matter, but it is quite certain that many of the stereotypes presented do have real psychological significance in so far as they influence the ways in which we perceive, judge and treat one another. So, it is reasonable to suppose that low brows, receding chins, eyes close together, and so on, are psychologically significant stimuli and should not be dismissed summarily however strongly we reject the evidence for any sort of pre-determined body – mind connection. If people believe these things to be true, then they do in fact have some sort of psychological reality. For this reason, modern social psychologists are often very interested in the personal and social consequences of holding these stereotypes.

Many more systems appeared over the following century, creating a host of variations on the Lavater theme which, in due course, became counterparts to other, somewhat associated, ideas. For example, Franz Gall and others attempted to prove that the conformations on the head itself – the bumps, ridges and masses of the skull – were the outward signs of the mind and character within.

Starting in prisons and mental institutions, and then moving on to distinguished individuals, Gall claimed to have discovered typical physical characteristics of degeneracy, high intellect and personality. Despite its improbable rationale, practitioners sprang up everywhere and the phrenologists' bust was soon to be seen in institutions and homes alike. But a day of scientific reckoning had to come, and once the ludicrous anatomical and physiological assumptions were laid bare for all to see, the fad soon withered away. But, as one bogus theory expires there is usually another waiting to take its place.

One of the last flowerings of these proto- or pseudo-sciences which treated the structures of head and face as psychological indicators was, remarkably enough, promoted by Francis Galton, a cousin of Charles Darwin.

Galton's achievements as a major pioneer of scientific psychology, meteorology and the development of the correlational calculus are great by any standards. Yet he too was caught up by the still prevalent belief that faces might be read as though they were maps of the psyche, and he set about making a series of composite photographs of prisoners to examine the characteristics of the typical 'criminal face'. Needless to say, Galton's positive conclusions have long since been more carefully scrutinized, and rejected. It was one of the very few wrong turnings made in the course of a long and distinguished scientific career.

That all these approaches came to so little is, in some ways, surprising for the key to success was quite well known to many writers from Aristotle to Lavater. But, despite a theoretical understanding, they always fell short of the ideal. The problem was always that too great an emphasis tended to be given to the static, or structural, aspects of appearance and too little to the dynamic qualities of the face and body in action. Like Aristotle, Lavater had made it quite clear that the expression of any psychological characteristic, whether it be timidity or a generous nature, is revealed not only in the essentially genetic aspects of form, but also in the creases which the habitual use of certain muscles and expressions imprint on the face. And to this should be added the colour and condition of the skin, the use and inflexions of the voice, and the postures, gestures and looks which people adopt.

However, a reasonable balance was never struck: the attractions of vivid stereotypes always seemed to prevail in the end. But, though such crude and primitive ideas can have no place in modern thinking, it is very doubtful if most of us would go so far as to say that personality, or important personal characteristics, are *never* apparent in appearances: indeed, research shows that this is not so. For example, an experimental study by Mary Sissons at Oxford in 1970 showed that people's social class could be quite accurately judged from a photograph of their face.

Having discussed the matter with a great many people, I have the strong impression that most are quite unsurprised by Sissons' finding and feel we can often identify at least those agreeable or disagreeable to us on the basis of quite brief contacts where little, if anything, of any significance has been said. It seems to be a widespread experience that, though one is sometimes misled, first impressions of strangers often turn out to be a reasonable clue to their subsequently revealed personality. The gentle people, the passive or domineering ones, the friendly and the taciturn, are often recognized from the first time we encounter them; or so it is claimed. But if this is so, what is the explanation?

It might be that the structures of the faces themselves – thin lips, high foreheads, hooked noses, receding chins, close-set eyes or wide mouths, are part of some genetic package which mediates both facial appearance and temperament. If so, there is no evidence that this is the case. Or it might be that such things as ruddy complexions, dingy and bad teeth, blackheads, clean and well-kept hair, clipped moustaches, bags under the eyes, all give important clues to an individual's habits, life style, and self–image. This again is difficult to determine in a strictly scientific sense, though it does appear to be a reasonable working hypothesis.

Rather more fully researched have been some of the dynamic characteristics of faces and the ways they are perceived. The residual creases left by much frowning or laughter, or their lack in the smooth, open face are hard to specify and quantify, hence they have received much less experimental attention than have the expressions themselves. Modern scientists who interest themselves in the relationship between particular facial features and individual personalities are all too likely to be ridiculed as dabbling in the murky ditches of pseudo-science. And there are very real methodological difficulties to be encountered in such research: for example, acceptable correlational criteria are few because faces do not lend themselves to being quantified or assigned to discrete categories. The work that has been completed is not only sparse in amount, but is often very subjective in its treatment: the impact is therefore minimal.

On the other hand, a more generalized interest in the language of expressions has made a great deal of headway since 1872 and the publication of Darwin's Book *The Expressions of Emotion in Man and Animals*. Always a widely fascinating subject, the book sold 5,267 copies on the day it was published and, as the first thoroughgoing study of innate determination of this type of behaviour, ultimately it became a cornerstone for the modern discipline of ethology.

Many of Darwin's original assertions have withered or been much modified by the new wave of naturalistic researchers and many sections, like those referring to the expressive repertoire of his dog Bob, may seem quaint to the stern scientist, though they may seem wise and nicely observed to those of us who share our lives with dogs. Essentially, the book is a work of natural history written by a biologist and it is perhaps the case that the material relating to human subjects is amongst the weakest. Even so, Darwin's study of children is an excellent first approximation, and material deriving from his questionnaire to missionaries and others living in widely separated parts of the world was also a very innovatory approach to the question of how far the expression of emotion is learned and how far it is of an evolutionary, and therefore genetic, origin.

His conclusion, which still enjoys a wide measure of acceptance by biologists, anthropologists and psychologists, was that some of the simpler emotional states, such as happiness, sorrow, fear or rage, are universally expressed in a similar fashion, and can easily be 'read' whether one comes from the remote rain forests of Guatemala or the suburbs of Glasgow. These appear to be part of a universal language of our species: one which has emerged through evolution and is sustained through heredity. But he also concluded that much of mankind's psychological subtlety and complexity is due to his social and cultural evolution, and it is through learning that a great deal of this bodily language is developed or compounded from simpler expressive elements.

Darwin was personally more interested in showing how similarities in the expressions of peoples ranging from sophisticated Europeans to the most isolated and primitive aboriginals indicated their common biological ancestry. The fact that we all recognize the significance of both smiles and tears, blushes and sneers, seemed to be excellent corroborative evidence. This is in sharp contrast to linguistic forms which, being entirely dependent upon cultural learning, may be quite incomprehensible to peoples separated from one another by even the most notional physical or political barriers. Obviously, a basic ability to interpret the emotional state of another person from their expression is something which can have practical, not to say survival, value.

More recent cross-cultural studies have contributed further to our understanding of the universality of expression and, between them, they have gone a long way to substantiating the data provided by the original 36 informants upon whom Darwin relied. But, additionally, they have also made us more aware of just how great is the amount, and significance, of the non-verbal signalling which is culturally determined and learned. In fact, this line of research is at last bringing to fruition the ideal of some of the old students of physiognomy and form as it involves not only the statics of face and physique but their *mobile* and dynamic attributes as well.

As a respectable branch of study, non-verbal communication (NVC) is still in its infancy: it was virtually unknown just a few years ago, though it is now an important growth area in ethology and social psychology. No doubt what intrigues many people is one of the things which appealed about psychoanalysis – it seems to offer its adepts a special insight into the normally protected unconscious of others, or ourselves. As we shall see, there is some justification for this view: one which was anticipated by Freud in his analysis of 'mistakes' and 'accidents'; by Wilhelm Reich in his claims that muscular tensions, leading to characteristic postures, are only the outward and visible representations of repressed sexual anxieties; and was most sweepingly promoted by Sheldon in his theory based on the proposition that the body *is* the unconscious.

Sheldon's assertion was seen by many as a great challenge, and it was certainly stated in the plainest possible terms . . . 'By the unconscious I *think* psychoanalysts mean the body, however shocking the thought may be to psychoanalysts. The body is really an objectivication, a tangible record of the most long-standing and deeply established habits that have been laid down during a succession of generations.'

However, Sheldon's claim is actually not as iconoclastic as it may seem: it is simply another expression of the old materialistic tradition which was fundamental to Freud's own claims. Such theories, regarding mind as a consequence of physical existence, generally lead on to accounts of motivation which draw for their most fundamental sources upon both the metabolic activities and needs of the individual and the innate, or instinctive, needs of the species. Psychoanalysis is actually the best-known product of this view, though this type of materialism is often a prominent component in more recent eclectic theories dealing with the many ways in which personality may be determined as a result of physical characteristics: or, of course, vice versa.

In either case, the physical self is increasingly coming to be regarded as a useful reflection of states of mind. More than being just an indication of man's evolutionary adaptations, and thus a clue to our general nature, each individual body is also a living record of many of the particular genetic, social and psychological events which have shaped that particular person's past development – and which will, in turn, effect their future interactions and adjustments.

Even so, with the exception of such work as Sheldon's, most theories which have proposed a link between qualities of mind or personality and static or structural features of the body have failed to carry much scientific conviction: and this in spite of a widely held private conviction that we can learn a lot about other people from their physical presence. The reason for this state of affairs now seems to be that, even though it may be conceptually or experimentally convenient to do so, approaches based on viewing people, or their features, as passive or inert objects tend to distort the way in which we customarily form our judgements. In real life, the social impact made by another person is largely a result of their *total* self-presentation; their actions, and their reactions towards others, or ourselves. So, researchers in fields as diverse as anthropology, sociology, psychiatry, zoology and psychology have, since the early 1950s, increasingly been undertaking studies of people in social action – mainly through naturalistic observations of social or cultural differences, or through carefully recorded interactions arranged by experimentalists. The results leave no doubt about the considerable degree to which our states of mind and intentions are apparent through our body's non-verbal communications.

This fact is accepted as a commonplace in relation to animals who obviously do a great deal of their communicating by means of their expressive gestures and postures. It is clearly a well understood language form, but for modern man, dependent upon high-technology syntactical language, the full meaning of our own more primitive modes of communication must be learned anew. Appropriate forms of interpersonal observation are only now being developed in detail as aids to increasing sensitivity to our own physical cueing, and that of other people.

Of course, one would not wish to imply that mankind has almost completely ceased to recognize the importance of non-verbal communications. Some of them, such as theatrical mime, ceremonial and sacerdotal gestures, sign languages of the deaf or of the racecourse, and actions like shaking hands, kissing, patting on the back, salutations, or making rude signs are culturally-defined conventions and present relatively few problems of interpretation: so long, that is, as these interpretations are made by someone who fully understands local usages.

In the same way, non-verbal communications may often be recognized in the choice of clothing, jewellery, or cosmetics. Certain conventions may, for example, be adopted by an individual to indicate that he is an orthodox Jew, a homosexual, a motorcycle gang member, a priest, a 'punk', or a member of any of the other innumerable sub-groups of society.

All these sources of probabilistically-based information about other people are likely to be a part, maybe too big a part, of our perception of them. But these easily encoded and decoded signals are mixed up with a great many subtle, and sometimes contradictory nuances of posture, gesture and gaze. Yet, despite the formidable problems this presents, the subject is now beginning to attract the experimental attention of a whole host of researchers – including such notable contributors as Argyle, Birdwhistell and Fisher.

Of these, most prominent has been the work of Ray Birdwhistell who, in the early 1950s really launched empirical research into the structural aspects of body motion communication, later codifying his system in such influential works as *Kinesics and Context*. Since that time, the flow of research in this area has become a flood: the technologies of videotape recording and slow motion cinefilm analysis have allowed scientists to make observations of the most fleeting and subtle movements, and to record their data in a form other than very subjective notes. One particularly important consequence of this has been that it allows the undertaking of scientifically mandatory reliability studies, and it also forms a growing information resource which can be used in the training of others.

The use of video recorders or cine cameras allows for unobtrusive observations of social interactions. One-way mirrors and film have now largely given way to closed-circuit television but, costs and questions of flexibility aside, both produce permanent records which can be repeatedly replayed and analysed in the finest detail. The difficulty arises when it comes to giving an adequate description of bodily movements. Common language is not well adapted to this task and some other form of data transcription was required. So, using a pictographic form of representation in the way that choreographers notate ballet steps, Birdwhistell developed his 'kinesic vocabulary' to describe expressions, and changes in expression.

There are now several systems available for categorizing facial, and whole-body movements, whether taken individually or as part of a social interaction, but all concerned would probably agree with Birdwhistell that any 'vocabulary' so compiled should not be supposed to have specific meanings, as words have. One cannot arrange expressions into some sort of 'dictionary' such that each element can be given a particular meaning. On the contrary, the same gestures or movements can have many different meanings, depending on their cultural or social context. Moreover, bodily movements and communications share with many areas of psychological functioning a likelihood that a person's age, sex, or social class are likely to modify the significance of particular actions: source and context are always fundamental in any interpretation.

Of course, any extended observation of interpersonal conduct is sure to contain many, apparently straightforward, formalized components – like greeting handshakes. But the study of expressive behaviour, even that from the repertoire of conventional gestures of politeness and etiquette, may reveal many possible meanings. After all, gestures involve inflexions of the body, just as spoken language is inflected. In either case, a slight variation in form can denote a vast change in meaning: *how* one does or says something is quite as important as *what* one does or says. This fact alone implies what practitioners are often quick to deny, that there is an essential subjectivity to most analyses of behaviour, however impressive the research equipment, the encoding of data, or the statistical treatments.

To take another example, we all know that bodily postures have conventional representation: few would have any difficulty in distinguishing the pattern for relaxation from that of anxiety and tension. Yet most of us will have faked it at some time: we may have sat back, smiled and put our hands in our pockets, whilst all the time our hearts were galloping, our hands were sticky, and we were strained and suffering all the miseries of apprehension. Sometimes, the deception may have been so convincing that others have commented on our remarkable coolness and ease though, in other cases, or on different occasions, a lack of feedback has left us unsure about our performance. In any case though, this sort of personal experience also makes it plain that, where one is looking for meaning, the process cannot be divorced from judgement and interpretation – however detached or mechanically recorded the original observations may have been.

Social life is, of course, very much a matter of controlling our own presentation, and trying to control the response of others to us. Because it is such a basic social skill, we have all spent much of our lifetimes learning behaviours appropriate to our sex, age group, social class and occupations. We all have many available patterns; different ones being called into play depending upon the context and whether our current role is that of parent, employee, lover, friend, wife, or any of the many other interpersonal relationships we may be called upon to adopt during the course of even one day. These many different 'selves' are not necessarily indicative of insincerity: they may be, but they are also likely to be reflections of our attempts to behave appropriately, as we see it, and to fulfil the expectations of others.

So, in many cases our smiles, gestures, postures and manner are quite consciously assumed, and we recognize the adopted nature of comparable actions in others: for example, putting on the face of wrath at one's children's, sometimes quite amusing, misdemeanours or gravely listening to outrageous nonsense from a superior. We quite consciously try to shape our bodily movements and words into an overall pattern of intentional action yet often, whether we ourselves are aware of it or not, there is a quite apparent mismatch between our verbal and our non-verbal communications, revealing our dissimulation or else our unconscious feelings. Freud, in his *Psychopathology of Everyday Life* described behaviour which, though unconsciously motivated, led to the sort of 'mistakes' or 'careless' actions which could turn an apparently loving wife into a widow. There are innumerable other examples to be found throughout the vast literature of psychoanalysis which are claimed to reveal the great extent to which unconscious feelings and attitudes can become physically manifested during interpersonal contacts. However, one should always look very carefully at these case histories, at the nature of the evidence and the arguments being offered, before accepting the interpretations offered. Ingenious as they may be, the problem with almost any psychoanalytic explanation is that it is based on the unchecked impressions of a single individual.

Whether the underlying motivation is conscious or unconscious, things are not always as they seem. A bowed head or a deferential stoop in the presence of a superior or a customer do not, as we must all have learned, necessarily indicate an attitude of respect. The extended hand and the smiling mouth are sometimes quite obviously at variance with their owner's 'cold' eyes of dislike or disdain. Softly spoken words are also sometimes markedly at variance with the tight fists, belligerent stance, or the white pallor of rage which accompany them.

Taken individually, none of these elements – eyes, words, gestures, postures or somatic changes are diagnostic. Hands which sweat, tremble, or shake *may* indicate an emotional state, but which state, and whether environmental causes or somatic disorders are involved may be hard to determine. However plausibly accounted for, there may always be more than one explanation for any particular observation. It may be that folding one's arms indicates withdrawal or resistance to social contact, but it may be no more significant than the fact that, for some people, it is a comfortable way of standing. When women, particularly adolescent ones, fold their arms across the chest, it is often taken as a sign of embarrassment or defensiveness about their breasts. On the other hand, the fact that women more frequently lack convenient trouser pockets to put their hands into may not be entirely irrelevant.

However, the greatest problem in understanding the meaning of bodily movements generally lies in assessing the degree to which an individual is consciously controlling his movements. Actors are only one small group amongst those whose living depends upon making a good job of directing their demeanour and expressions: they may or may not be the most accomplished, but they certainly have some competition from people in a great many other walks of life – including those making their living in sales, teaching, the professions, politics, and undertaking. But even if the job itself does not make particularly heavy demands on interpersonal skills, one can still be reasonably sure that private social life will. We are all actors to some extent, and though some people still have difficulty in reconciling the kaleidoscope of physical expression with their ideas about personality, the fact is that the very term itself was derived from the Latin word 'persona', meaning an actor's mask.

Despite an often encountered tendency to downgrade the external self in favour of a supposed underlying 'essence' or 'real self', the truth is that our reality has to be expressed before it can be known. And, except in unusual circumstances and some cases of sensory or psychiatric impairment, whenever and wherever interpersonal contacts occur, one can usually be sure that facial expression will play a crucial part in determining the projection and interpretation of whatever feelings, opinions, intentions and emotions are involved. It may not be desirable to rely on any one form of bodily expression when assessing non-verbal communications but the face is without doubt the most flexible, lively and revealing source of such information. If we were forced to choose only one focus of bodily expression, there can be few who would not select facial expression.

Fortunately, times have changed: when I was an undergraduate, textbooks and one's tutors seemed to be at great pains to discredit any common-sensical sources of information. Introductory texts typically contained several posed photographs of faces and the reader was invited to identify the appropriate emotion. A rather gleeful writer would then point to the 'correct' answers and conclude that, as a source of information, the face was an undesirable guide.

One of the most dramatic demonstrations of this view was given by a faculty member who presented us with face-only photographs of a Chinese woman: we were again asked to guess what her feelings were, and we again failed miserably. Then the scientific paper from which the photographs had been taken was produced. It showed a naked woman, impaled on a stake, being dismembered bit by bit.

The events in the photographs had taken place in a remote Chinese village earlier this century. The woman had been found guilty of adultery and the price was being exacted in the village square before her neighbours and, of course, the anthropologist with a camera. Such facial expressions as had been selected for reproduction were certainly not what might have been depicted by an actor, so stereotypes were of no use. But, in any case, judgements made on the basis of a two-dimensional black and white photograph of a split second of time are not only distortions but abstractions.

In real life, interpretation would be based on changes and movement of the face over time, and in a *total context*. In the cases mentioned fragmentation of the data source makes no sense at all, despite claims that this is in keeping with the scientific principal of reducing stimulus complexities in order to assess the affect of particular variables. This may be acceptable in many cases, but the significance of most social events can only be judged in their social settings. And when the context is unimaginable, whatever expressive behaviour is available is insufficient to form the basis for an interpretation. To ask for one in these circumstances is absurd.

As a shock tactic or piece of propaganda, the Chinese material served its purpose well: it was certainly a memorable illustration of the prejudgement that facial expressions make useless psychological data. But that was in the 1950s: since then a great deal of experimental work has totally upturned this view, and most people would now accept that the face can be a very rich source of information about ongoing psychological processes – though not in the sense envisaged by either the old physiognomists nor the correlators of photographs with questionnaires.

That it should take so long to come to this conclusion may be regrettable, but it is not altogether surprising. Psychology, being a science, can only progress at the speed of its experimental findings, and this is a particularly difficult area – presenting so many unique problems of interpretation and interaction, as well as those connected with the need to record relatively long periods of observation. However, with the arrival of sophisticated cine and video equipment and computers capable of handling massive amounts of data and their interactions, it has become much more practicable to undertake naturalistic studies.

But also priming the new thrust forward has been the great influence of ideas, strategies and methodologies drawn from ethology – that rapidly growing branch of the biological sciences concerned with studying animals in action, and in natural settings. So, a fortunate convergence of sciences and new technologies, combinating with the more established procedures of linguistic and experimental psychology, has created a renewed interest in bodily communication generally, and facial behaviour in particular.

Kinesics, the study of bodily communication is, as Birdwhistell has said, the study of a code: it focuses on the language used, not the bodily structures involved. To this extent, it is about learned behaviour and is more properly seen as a branch of social psychology than of an enquiry into the effects of morphological characteristics. Nevertheless, it is important to know that our own bodies, and those of other people, are phenomenologically very significant, and that their properties, whether learned or innate, conscious or unconscious, are important elements in our social and psychological transactions.

Research conducted into the language of facial expressions is particularly full of intriguing, and well-established, findings. For example, workers in this field are now well on the way towards providing us with a wide-ranging normative account of the use, and usages, of gaze. They have, in innumerable circumstances, recorded the length of glances, the proportion of mutual gaze and the amount of looking, and looking away, involved while people are talking to one another.

One could cite many different findings but, for example, it appears that males and females tend to differ in their patterns; that schizophrenics are more likely than most of us to avoid direct eye contact; and that there are characteristic dissimilarities in the patterns of looking when dominant individuals confront less dominant ones.

But the most extensively investigated area concerns the way in which eye contacts are used to synchronize conversations – to invite communications, to sustain them and to cut them off. The effect of this can hardly be overestimated as it allows for the smooth regulation of spoken language, and thus of social intercourse.

Anyone interested in the impact of the physical self should be aware of this work but, alas, much of it is beyond our present concerns. There are, however, a number of movement characteristics of the face which are much more physically based, and which are interactive with the final expressive effect. For example, pupil dilation and contraction is a piece of non-verbal communication well known not only to poker players, but to the more shrewd merchants of most cultures and times.

Middle Eastern rug dealers and Chinese jade merchants have traditionally watched the eyes of their, apparently uninterested, browsing customers to find out what it was that *really* interested them. The expansion of pupils must have ruined many a profitable deal for the buyers, and improved just as many for the sellers. This is only one way in which the autonomic nervous system overrules social learning and facial control to hint at the state of mind within. In the same way, sexual and social interest, or the lack of it, may also be revealed by the pupils' activities. Other autonomic effects – flushes, sweating, pallor and tremor – suggest something of people's emotional states too, and these may be telling clues for those equipped to see and interpret them.

Negotiators, doctors, teachers, business men and therapists can all gain immeasurably from such observations, as indeed can anyone who regards them as a source of hypothesis, not of proof. Taken by themselves, each physical sign can be misleading: sweating is a very variable human characteristic and it depends upon metabolism, distribution of sweat glands, fat and clothing, as well as present and antecedent environmental circumstances. Flushes, pallor or tremor are also best considered against at least a modest knowledge of the individual as, here too, constitutional differences or physical disorders can lead to very misleading conclusions.

But difficult as it may be to make unequivocal translations, the body has a language. Through it are expressed conscious intentions, a more or less unconscious reflection of the individual's emotional state, energy and interest, and perhaps too some of his fundamental personality characteristics. Finger tapping in anger or impatience may be performed with or without the awareness of the person encoding their feelings, but a message is being transmitted none the less and, however imperfectly rendered, is sure to be decoded by others.

Sly and shifty looks, blushes or rapid blinking are, like the clenched hand, the waving finger, or the face thrust forward, all a part of our perception of the psychological state of others. Our glances may reveal our seriousness, sadness, or our good humour: and the set of our mouths turning up or down, adopting smiles, sneers, or more neutral lines can just as easily complement or contradict other aspects of our communication.

Within our own culture at least, most of us can readily simulate a fairly recognizable physical expression of such attitudes and emotions as insolence and concern, tenderness or aggression. What is much more difficult is to know just when we are, and when we are not, transmitting unintended non-verbal communications. The expressive capacity of eyes is well known, so to hide the disapproval or concern we might wish to conceal, we generally avert them, and avoid access to these most expressive and revealing parts of our body. But our postures and gestures, anxious fidgeting or rapid, shallow breathing, are only some of the ways in which our attempts to conceal our true feelings are revealed.

Communication is not only a matter of opening verbal channels with others: it also has a gestalt property – being the sum, and more than the sum, of the apparent parts. Some ingredients, like odours, may be quite subliminal, passing undetected at a conscious level by both the person emitting them and the person responding to them.

Nonetheless, there is accumulating evidence to show that these too may be important factors influencing relationships. As research proceeds, more and more ways are identified by which our bodies conduct their own conversations, and so compound or confound our conscious intentions.

Of course, much of our communicating is done at the conscious, verbal, level but it is now apparent that there is also a remarkable amount beside which takes place without this type of language. Whether we will it or not, we transmit physically encoded messages to others about our states of mind, and they do the same. Clearly, this fact alone is of some practical importance in so far as there may be substantial room for us to improve our performance as efficient transmitters and receivers of these communications.

Chapter two

BODY IMAGE AND SELF-ESTEEM

Having already discussed some of the ways in which an individual's behaviour may be influenced and even substantially determined by physical appearance and physique, we can now begin to explore additional ways in which physical characteristics give rise to self-evaluations, and how these self-evaluations are, in turn, also influential in the shaping of personality.

We all have ideas about the nature of our own body: its general attractiveness or ugliness; its impressiveness or otherwise; its grace or clumsiness; and the important features which make it what we believe it to be. Needless to say, our own assessments do not necessarily accord very closely with the more objective facts, or with the opinions of others.

Even so, these subjectively held beliefs are of great psychological importance to the individual as his reactions to them are likely to shape strategies of social adjustment and supply clues – accurate or misleading – to others concerning his feelings and personality. These clues, or cues, are then the basis for interactions which may have many of the qualities of the self-fulfilling prophesy. Consequently reactions to, and outward projections of, our body image are some of the major factors affecting the development of self-esteem and personal relationships.

However, we all begin the same way: with the trauma of birth, the separation of bodies which marks the emergence of a new individual. From then on, each must set off on a personal odyssey to discover the nature of that individuality. All being well, we shall achieve a more or less satisfactory working idea of who and what we are within just a few years, but the early differentations are not easy, and we must first of all come to terms with our physical selves.

There is no shorter or simpler word than *I*, but neither is there a longer nor more enigmatic route to meaning. The beginnings of self-knowledge, discovering our own body boundaries, may or may not be fairly routine: we have no way of knowing because it mostly takes place before any of us can remember. However, we can observe the process in others, and the effort and frustration encountered by the very young is obvious enough. Clearly, correlating bodily sensations with movements, and finding what is, and what is not, part of oneself takes a lot of time and exertion.

For parents, it can be very amusing watching infants biting, scratching, scrutinizing, moving and sometimes shedding bitter tears of frustration and vexation in their attempts to discover the limits of their own persons, and the nature of things which move and react quite independently of their own wishes, sensations or efforts. But, however gradually, each infant develops his own body schema and acquires ever more complex skills of co-ordination and, with it, a growing ability to conceptualize his own boundaries in relation to other people and objects.

So, the first step on the way towards developing a self-concept is mainly concerned with building up the body-image, or integrated conception of how the parts of our body look and move, and how they relate to one another, and to the outside environment. But developmental sequences are not separate from one another: while awareness of the meanings of sensory feedback increases and knowledge of the boundaries grows, there also begins the lifelong process of evaluating this mental representation. And it is these evaluations which are ultimately of so much significance in determining our self-esteem.

Of course, self-esteem is the result of very much more than our physical attributes: as the years pass it comes to depend more and more upon our social and psychological resources. Nevertheless, the appraisal of our bodily features will still, to a considerable degree, continue to interact with psychological evaluations made by ourselves and others. In Chapter one, we discussed a few of the ways in which physical appearance might affect the development of personality. The size, muscularity, fatness, and other qualities of the body are, like the configurations and more subtle qualities of the face, all too likely to trigger social stereotypes in others. As a result, it is not only our social and occupational prospects which might be affected; also arising from the appraisals and degrees of approval and acceptance shown by others comes much of the material upon which we tend to depend for developing our sense of personal worth and esteem.

One's body image is very much dependent on feedback: initially, this will be mainly physiological but, increasingly, the reactions of others will become more salient. Their remarks, praise or criticisms, will become crucial data for constructing a picture of ourselves, but, unfortunately, the mirrors we must use are often distorted. The similarity between several such reflections may *seem* to suggest a good degree of objectivity, but the fact that a number of people of our acquaintance agree on something is not a guarantee of truth, only that they share certain values and beliefs in common. And, as our 'mirrors' will, for the most part, be drawn from a very limited circle of people who share much of their social and cultural background in common, the criterion of agreement is of less actual than developmental significance.

Evaluations of us made by others will always be to some extent stereotypical – that is, reflecting preconceived opinions which are held to apply to identifiable categories of objects, groups, or individuals. These stereotypes may be predominantly positive or negative in their intent or effect, depending upon the social norms or values of the people applying them. For example, those approximating to the 'scholarly' stereotype – tall, bespectacled, slim, and with a prominant Adam's apple – tend to be much more positively evaluated in some circles than in others. The same principle applies to most characteristics so that the favourableness of our emerging self-concept is likely to depend not only upon the givens of our physical appearance, but also upon our fortunes as being part of that section of society in which our physical attributes are accepted or esteemed.

The impact of other people's reactions to us will also be of greater or lesser significance depending upon who they are, and how old we are. Parental approval is, of course, most influential during the first few years of our lives and, thereafter, the opinions of our peers, and members of the opposite sex, are likely to become more potent. However, parents – as they are generally more than a little partial when it comes to attributing desirable qualities to their children – are especially important in helping lay the foundations of a positive self-concept, though they often have fierce competition and opposition from the beginning.

Even quite small children are remarkably acute in their perception of unusual features in others, and often quite as remarkably cruel in the ridicule, harassment, or rejection they can heap upon those so singled out. The cruelty may be more or less unconscious or unreflective in many cases, though the fear of persecution apparent in the persecutors often tends to make one suspicious of such generously-intended excuses. But whatever the intentions behind them, rejections or calling others 'four-eyes', 'fatso', 'pig-face', 'big-ears', or whatever, can be psychologically very damaging as they are an important part of the feedback data from which self-concept must be generated. And such disparaging caricatures cannot just be ignored as adults will advise: the arrows break off in time, but their barbs are often sunk deep.

Ethologists note that the persecution of individuals who differ from the norm is common enough in animal societies, and that it is probably an innate reaction which ultimately serves the purposes of evolution. Whether this principle has any relevance to the human case is impossible to say, but it is interesting to note how few positive appellations are generated in the school yard and how intolerant the young may be of unfortunate deviations from the norm or cultural ideal.

Whatever the source of children's evaluations of themselves and others, stereotypes begin early. Research into attitudes relating to body build has shown that even very young children tend to associate positive social and personal attributes with some physiques, and negative ones with others. Of course, findings vary somewhat depending upon the social and cultural background of the respondent but it is possible to make some generalizations which seem to hold more often than not. For example, endomorphy commonly suggests amiability, but studies have shown that often even preschool children also associate it with many of the more negative connotations. Fat people are typically judged as unattractive, and often comic; and, though the slim ectomorphic build is more highly regarded, it is the strong mesomorphic frame which is most universally admired.

Alas, we cannot all be modelled on the heroic scale and, in any case, we must all pass through the undignified changes associated with adolescence. Even the finest adult swans of the future must face the prospect of feeling themselves the ugliest of ducklings. For example, growth spurts can create very sorry creatures for a while – moreover, awkward and clumsy ones whose long arms and legs, poking through outgrown clothes, make it very difficult for their possessor to hold on to their earlier feelings of wellbeing and self-assurance. 'Puppy fat', pimples, fuzzy faces, breaking voices, menstruation and breasts or genitals which appear unexpectedly early or late, or else just do not seem right or normal, all lead to self-doubts and vulnerability. Like a soft crab, having shed one armour and waiting for another, the plight of the adolescent is not enviable: his condition may not be mortally dangerous as is the crab's, but the psychological hazards make it serious enough.

The inner turmoil brought about by the changes of puberty, coupled with the need to abandon childish ways for adult patterns, lead to the characteristic mood swings of this period. Phases of great energy and euphoria, feelings of near-omniscience and omnipotence alternate with ones of marked lethargy, depression and a sense of ignorance and worthlessness. Like the crab, small attacks launched at these most vulnerable times can have remarkably damaging effects. Any blemish, real or imagined, can be magnified to great proportions and any confirmatory disparagements coming at this time are likely to be similarly exaggerated.

One might think that, in view of the adolescent's own relative defensiveness, they might maintain a low social profile and be particularly sensitive and sympathetic to others in the same state. Not a bit of it: the peak of most people's aggressiveness, destructiveness and spite usually comes at the period around adolescence. Dog owners will know that an animal on a lead or tied up is very prone to snap at other dogs: it seems as though the personal sense of vulnerability readily gives rise to the feeling that the best form of defence is attack. Also, to victimize others is to draw attention away from oneself, so it appears that some children are destined to fulfil the role of scapegoat for the troubles of others.

Physical characteristics are only some of the personal attributes which may cause a child to receive more than its share of abuse at this time but, the body being the most visible aspect of the individual, it is not likely to be overlooked. Having to wear thick glasses, being unusually small, weak, or fat; having a speech impediment, sticking-out ears, a squint, or being unusually clumsy or unco-ordinated, all increase the chances that a minor physical problem can become a major psychological one through the rejection, ridicule and physical abuse of the pack. In such cases, the hammer blows to self-esteem may fall very hard indeed, and help shape fundamental attitudes and a personality which may endure throughout an entire lifetime.

Depth psychologists have always stressed the great formative influence of early experience on the growth of the self-concept and, consequently, upon mental health, self-acceptance and self-assurance. These early events can have very considerable ramifications in that they also affect trust in others, inhibitedness in various circumstances, ability to integrate socially, and the likelihood of setting, and following, realistic life goals.

Naturally, positive experiences are just as formative too, and a sense of worth imparted within the circle of family and friends can make a great deal of difference to the psychological impact of experiences occurring in other contexts. But, all else being equal, the child with an average appearance – or one with superior looks, strength, physique, or co-ordination – will undoubtedly have a head start in developing positive self-esteem.

As Adler pointed out, we are not all created equal, nor are we treated equally, but a bad start is not necessarily a misfortune: there may even be considerable disadvantages to being one of nature's golden girls or boys. The approval of others, beyond a certain point, can lead to complacency and lack of motivation to prove oneself. Unless the will has been completely broken by ill-treatment and negative attributions, a sense of inferiority might very well prove to be one's greatest asset. At least it was Adler's contention that it *could* be.

Adler himself had been a very frail and sickly child. In fact, one of his earliest recollections dates from the age of about two when he was sitting on a bench, his limbs bandaged because of rickets, watching his elder brother jumping and running about. The sense of deprivation and inferiority created at that time was sufficient to drive him along a road of aggressive physical competitiveness and was, in all probability, to colour much of his personal and professional life thereafter. So, the starting point of Alderian *Individual Psychology* was very much connected with the sense of physical inferiority.

After a period as an ophthalmologist (perhaps a significant choice of specialization for the short-sighted Adler) he was to join forces with his fellow citizen, Freud, and develop most of his subsequent ideas from an elaboration of compensatory behaviour. Freud had already drawn attention to the way in which the psychological distress resulting from organic deficiencies or deviations might be off-set through positive actions. For example, anxiety about one's sexual characteristics, at least in some cases, seemed to result in an unusual emphasis on sensual pleasures; and stature markedly above or below average sometimes seemed to cause quite anomalous compensations – like the sturdy six-foot woman whose 'little-girl-in-need-of help' style is hard to reconcile with its physical opposite. However, whereas Freud noted this sort of tendency as an unusual aberration, Adler came to regard it as the most fundamental characteristic of human adjustment – normal as well as abnormal.

Adler's development of this idea began with the completely physical analogy of organic compensation – whereby undamaged parts of the system are commonly recruited to offset some of the disability which would otherwise occur as a result of damage or disorder. But not only can a kidney, a cerebral hemisphere, or an eye take over much of the load when half a system is destroyed, the blind person's finger can be used to read Braille and the deaf person's eyes can be used to lip-read spoken language, and so on. More or less dramatic examples of compensation are familiar enough to us all, my own favourite concerning the most unusual blacksmith I ever knew. He was an ex-jockey apprentice who, due to an appalling fall in which his horse crushed him, stood only about 4′6″ high on his twisted and stunted legs. But his powerfully developed arms and chest made him a match for almost anyone at his forge.

Fortunately, very few of us have such severe and persistent organic problems to overcome in our lives. But whatever additional burdens we encounter, none of us can avoid the extremes of incapacity which are inherent in infancy and childhood. A sense of inferiority is inescapable at this time for we *are* inferior – in strength, endurance, stature, autonomy, skills and just about everything else – mental and physical.

For Adler, the infantile sense of helplessness marked the real psychological beginnings of the individual: the problem with which we begin, overcoming our inferiority feelings by adapting ourselves and manipulating our environment, is a never-ending one for most, if not for all, human beings. Even if we can fully achieve these objectives for a while, circumstances, other people, and we ourselves – perhaps as a result of our illness or ageing – are always changing and creating new situations of relative inferiority.

Furthermore, the process of compensating for our inferiority feelings is also made an unending one because we persist in measuring ourselves against ever-receding goals. As infants, our ambitions will include a very large proportion of compensatory wishes and activities related to our physical appearance and capacities. As we grow older and achieve many of these aims as a result of our activities and the processes of maturation, the pattern changes and our goals become more concerned with social and occupational matters. But body-related feelings of inferiority may be unusually deeply-seated in some people – whether or not they are due to objectively-based inferiorities – and in any case, are likely to re-emerge in all of us as our health, appearance and vigour decline.

Adler spoke of us as *striving for superiority* in all aspects of our lives but he did not mean that the most basic motivation is always to be better than the next person. On the contrary, this is regarded as a primitive or neurotic impulse: in adults, there should be more basic motivations towards positive growth, both personal and social. The latter, *social interest*, is expressed most fully in the psychologically healthy and well-adjusted individual, and reflects a fundamental desire to help others overcome their own problems of inferiority and assist them towards achieving their goals of superiority. In other words, our deepest underlying goal is twofold: to get rid of these sources of distress which cause inferiority feelings and to replace them with a sense of harmony and positive regard in ourselves and in others.

While admiring Adler's picture of ideal mental health and social adjustment, it is hard to deny that altruistic social sentiments are more difficult to detect in real life than the compensatory drives by which each individual tries to get ahead of others to overcome his own feelings of inferiority and inadequacy. Of course, though he was undeniably an idealist and social propagandist as well as a practical psychologist, Adler was in no doubt as to where the springs of most actions lay – in the competitive spirit created by comparing ourselves unfavourably with others, and with the ever-expanding goals we set for ourselves, and are set for us by society in general and, nowadays, advertisers and media people in particular.

As has been mentioned, Adler's Individual Psychology was not only a psychiatric formulation, though it is that too. At least as importantly, it is about the adjustive problems of ordinary people seeking a sense of independence, personal regard and dignity in the complex social structures of industrial society. Of course, much of his work goes far beyond our present interest in body-related issues affecting psychological adjustment, but he was certainly also one of the most perceptive and focused investigators of the relationship between normal and abnormal physical development and the growth and unfolding of psychological attitudes and feelings.

Moreover, the theory deals with a much broader spectrum of physical events than is examined from any other single point of view. The psychological parallels of the whole developmental trajectory – from the physical limitations of infancy to those of old age, including such high points along this route as puberty, pregnancy and menopause, can all be considered in relation to the coping or compensatory strivings generated. Inevitably, serious cases of a pathological kind – deformity, disfigurement and disease – provide some of the more dramatic examples, but though the effects may be much less obvious, the principles involved in understanding their consequences are precisely the same as those which apply in everyday life.

Naturally, Adler did not suppose that any particular defect would lead to similar outcomes in all, or even most, cases. In fact, one can identify at least three main categories of compensation, the one most likely to occur being a matter of an individual's temperament, previous experiences, personal resources, social and interpersonal support and all the many other environmental and particular circumstances and opportunities pertaining. These very notional categories which, only for the sake of conceptual tidiness, may be grouped as *direct*, *indirect* and *miscellaneous*, contain strategies of quite opposite types yet they all serve the same purpose – superiority strivings.

Different as they may seem, inferiority and superiority complexes are actually complementary for, as Adler points out, we should not strive if we did not feel inferior. As he wrote in his book *The Science of Living*, 'Whenever we see a person constantly in motion, with strong tempers and passions, we can always conclude that they are persons with great feelings of inferiority. A person who knows he can overcome his difficulties will not be impatient. On the other hand, he may not accomplish what is necessary.' So again, Adler stresses the possible advantages of inferiority feelings – but only if they are effectively guided.

The first category of adjustive strategies is, by definition, appropriately directed – though there is no guarantee that the strategy will be effective. This is the *direct* approach whereby the individual specifically attempts to overcome the actual source of his inferiority feelings. Famous historical and public figures tend to be taken as the best examplars of this approach: the ancient Greeks being, as always, in the van here too. For example, Demosthenes, reputedly the greatest orator of his time, had a speech defect which, by dint of great practice, often with a stone in his mouth to make the process more challenging, ultimately turned inferiority into a great superiority.

One of America's most flamboyant Presidents, Teddy Roosevelt, also had a poor start in life. Physically frail and underdeveloped, with poor eyesight, he was also to become a notable figure not only through his rather self-conscious lion hunting escapades but, more substantially through leading his 'Roughriders' in their remarkable South American adventures, and becoming a Head of State. In Britain, the late Sir Douglas Bader, despite losing his legs, successfully fought his own personal battle against the sense of inferiority waiting to claim him, becoming a virtuoso of artificial limbs, and once again a formidable World War II fighter pilot.

Clearly, direct compensatory activities can work very well in some circumstances. The 'seven stone weakling', whose widely illustrated woes in advertisements included the anguish of having sand kicked in his face by male bullies and ridicule heaped on his head by female bathers has been a familiar figure for many years. The sequel, after he had followed a particular body-building course, was the complete opposite: predictably, inferiority was turned to superiority, with all the accompanying social admiration and sense of self-esteem. Still, though the strategy undoubtedly works for some people in real life as well as in advertisements, one can only deplore the fact that the portrayal of such stereotypes continues to perpetuate these unfortunate social attitudes concerning those less physically well endowed.

Many cases of inferiority feeling begin with negative social attitudes, and not a few relate to a trifling difference rather than an actual imperfection. For example, left-handed people have often been made to feel inferior for no other reason than that they are different from the majority. The reaction in some cases seems to be by means of direct compensation: the superiority strivings thus triggered motivating the left-handed person in such a way that they may become unusually skilful in painting, calligraphy, tennis, or in some other area of high dexterity. But for some, the consequences are very unfortunate, often involving a marked sense of inferiority and clumsiness, particularly where the 'fault' has been corrected.

Of course, not all physical differences or disabilities could be overcome in a direct and conscious fashion. However hard they try, some 'plain Janes', undersized men, or handicapped people will not be able to offset the source of their inferiority feelings in this way: there is a limit to what can be achieved through will alone. In such cases, there are the options of a second category of compensation – *indirect* strategies.

Where direct compensations are impracticable, self-esteem and the esteem of others may often be more appropriately achieved by counterbalancing feelings of inferiority in one area with those of superiority in another. Success in business, academic, or artistic activities are just some of the routes by which the physically disadvantaged can compensate for any sense of inferiority they may feel. Of course, by the same token, those with intellectual or other psychological disadvantages might equally find their solution in the pursuit of excellence in sporting or other physical activities. However, before developing this argument any further, it should be made quite plain that there is absolutely no implication that superior achievements in one area are necessarily the result of inferiorities in others. It is merely that this is so in some cases.

And when the nature of a particular superior achievement does not relate in any obvious sense to some supposed source of inferiority, it becomes a matter of considerable background knowledge and judgement to discern whether compensation for inferiority feelings is involved. One wonders, for example, about such people as Henri de Toulouse-Lautrec. If he had not been crippled and stunted in a youthful riding accident, would he have simply gone on to be a well-adjusted member of his class, hunting three times a week and attending to the duties of running an estate? It is impossible to say, and he might just as easily have become a distinguished painter of the French country scene.

In the event, his father's rejection and the painful sense of inferiority created within his milieu, drove him to Paris and the company of others flawed in one way or another. Whether or not he would have become a painter whatever had happened, the remarkable power of his work seems largely attributable to the great sense of compassion and identification which his own personal sense of rejection and alienation brought. So, in this sense, the actual paintings created by Toulouse-Lautrec might be said to have their origin in his feelings of inferiority.

Another often quoted example of an indirect compensation developing into a pathological overcompensation, is the case of Adolf Hitler. It has often been argued that much, if not all, of his burning ambition to become architect of a 'Thousand Year Reich' can be seen as the result of efforts to handle the rejection of earlier, more prosaic, attempts to gain admission to the local art school in order to become a real, bricks-and-mortar architect.

There can be no doubt that this rebuff actually did have the effect of spurring rather than deterring Hitler's desire to re-build German towns in the grand style, but a close look at his biography suggests that many strands of explanation are needed for understanding the complex motivations of this, psychologically speaking, fascinating man. Compensation was undoubtedly one though, as

August Kubizek, his only youthful friend and biographer of his early days noted, he was already thoroughly enmeshed in the grandiose ideas of Wagner and Nietzsche, and showing many of the signs of paranoia which were to characterize his later life.

However, Adler's unbounded enthusiasm for his 'explain-all' principle was such that whenever he encountered a highly motivated achiever he was always apt to suppose that . . . 'If we enquire into a superiority complex and study its continuity, we can always find a more or less hidden inferiority complex'. Inevitably, such ideas were as unpalatable as the psychologist's ethnic background to a man like Hitler, and Adler was to die in exile – well out of reach of, arguably, the world's most extreme example of inferiority compensation.

As a matter of fact, there are many interesting parallels between Nietzsche and Adler himself: not the least being that physical frailty was a marked source of inferiority feelings for both, and that both developed systems of ideas dominated by the 'will to power'. Not that Adler's ideas led in the same egocentric or political and militaristic directions which resulted in German Fascism, but both men were acutely aware not only of the anguish, but also of the potentially enormous motivating characteristics, created by the feelings of helplessness and inferiority due to physical inadequacies.

Again, it is all too easy to light upon the dramatic example, although most adjustment problems are far from remarkable. No doubt there are 'captains of industry' whose great energy and success is based upon their feelings of physical unattractiveness or inferiority, and no doubt there are champion runners or boxers whose driving power depends upon a real or assumed sense of social or intellectual inadequacy. But, though many of us may be compensating, or overcompensating, in our attempts to achieve a counterbalancing force, it is in the nature of things that outstanding achievement in any area is beyond all but a minority. For the rest, if the strength of our inferiority feelings is not too great, more modest superiority goals must be set, otherwise we must accept either the emptiness of fantasy fulfilments, or the pain of actually accepting inferiority and failure.

Developing skills, even becoming a 'specialist' in some area – whether it be pigeon breeding, stamp collecting, cave diving, gardening, or whatever – can be one indirect way of heading off an incipient sense of inferiority. So too can becoming an indispensable committee or club member, or an active community worker. Such adjustments are often as unconscious as they are oblique but all degrees of self-awareness are likely to occur with indirect compensations. Some will recognize that they are making the best of difficult circumstances and will accept their strategies for what they are. Others, often apparently less aware of their motives, may be more inclined to reject or ridicule activities or situations about which they unconsciously continue to have feelings of anxiety and inferiority. Most of us, though, are probably at least dimly aware of the compensatory nature of our activities or feelings.

We termed the third category of compensatory response *miscellaneous* for want of a better word to encompass the remaining types of reaction to marked feelings of inferiority. However, if one was pressed to identify a central characteristic in this grouping, it would probably be a one-sided manipulation or a moral blackmail of others to achieve a feeling of superiority. As Adler pointed out, such strategies are commonly neurotic in nature; allowing the 'patient' to dominate their families and friends because they are 'ill'. Next to, and sometimes even more than babies, the domination of parents and others is often most strikingly achieved through the symptoms of mental disorder. Adler summarized this by saying 'Depressed and insane persons are always the centre of attention in the family. In them we see the power wielded by the inferiority complex.'

Hysterical paralyses, amnesias, depressions, phobias, and the like may all, it seems, be regarded as a failure to make responsible social contributions: instead, the unconscious mind adopts infantile dependency tactics in order to gain the attention and importance which the individual demands but cannot achieve because of inhibitions generated by the inferiority feelings. So, holding these views, Adler finally rejected the protracted and expensive Freudian form of analysis, which he had come to believe represented a collusion with the neurotic person. It seemed to him that such a therapy provided the ideal means by which families could be financially punished for not acceding to unreasonable superiority demands while, at the same time, providing the perpetrator with a protected patient status.

As was mentioned earlier, Adler's response to his own childhood physical disability had been through direct compensation – taking a personal responsibility for, and overcoming, the primary source of his inferiority feelings. He therefore had little sympathy for those he saw as, albeit unconsciously, acting in bad faith towards their friends, families, and society. Nietzsche too had earlier referred to such people as 'pale felons'; taking from others by subterfuge and giving nothing in return. So, Adler's treatment was geared to disarming those who would use psychological extortion: though caring, his therapeutic style was to be much more direct and challenging than any of the other 'depth' approaches. The cause of inferiority feelings, and the inability to participate maturely in social life, were relentlessly explored and exposed, and alternative adjustment strategies worked out with the patient.

Of course, most neurotic disorders do not have their causes in physical deficiencies, nor is there any reason to believe that most organic or other somatic defects result in any sort of neurotic compensation, but Adler's theory does illuminate a surprisingly wide range of interesting matters relevant to our explorations of the interaction between mind and body.

Unfortunately, many of these are difficult, or virtually impossible, to appraise in a rigorous scientific fashion. For example, he also asserted that each of us had one particular bodily system which is relatively less robust than the rest and this will tend, when we are under severe psychological stress, to malfunction and become the physical focus of our underlying psychological disorder: the skin, joints, respiratory or digestive systems are only a few of the more obvious loci. But though rashes, rheumatic conditions, asthma and stomach ulcers are certainly commonly associated with emotional disorders, the idea that we each have a quite specific 'Achilles heel', vulnerable to mental attack, is more difficult to establish, except as a *post-hoc* explanation or near tautology.

However, whether Adler was right or wrong in this particular instance, there is no doubt that psychological distress is often just as significant a cause of physical illness and disability as the latter is of psychological suffering. This, though, is a matter which can be developed more fully when dealing with hysterical and psychosomatic conditions in Chapter five. Yet it cannot be too emphatically stressed that many physical conditions which may lead to psychological anguish may not be at all realistically judged by the individual concerned: distorted body images can, and frequently do cause untold psychological harm to those with even quite normal bodies.

Psychological anguish arising from feelings about one's body is not only, or even mainly, a minority problem concerned with pathological cases of disablement or disfigurement. There are great individual differences but, to a greater or lesser extent, it is the probable fate of us all as we grow older. So, maintaining self-esteem in relation to the ageing process is a perennial human problem: one which may be met with many different strategies – often with very different payoffs. But, in addition to the powerfully, culturally reinforced need to by young and beautiful – which is, of course, an impossible aim over the lifespan – there is an amazing range of, objectively speaking, more or less trivial hang-ups which also affect us all at sometime or another. At any stage in our existence worries about teeth, nose, complexion, breasts, etc., can make life absolutely miserable, or else they can much restrict the scope of our activities.

Inevitably, then, psychologists and psychiatrists have long been interested in obtaining more precise insights into people's perception and conception of themselves in order to understand more fully the processes, normal or abnormal, affecting mental wellbeing and socialization. Much of the focus of this interest is upon behaviours which lead to unhappiness or maladjustment and, of these, being severely over- or underweight as a result of diet comprises a major category.

Yet, whether conditions like obesity are 'problems' at all is largely a matter of opinion for the person concerned. We may run a finger down the actuarial tables of life expectancy and disease prevalences for various height/weight combinations and marvel at the apparent indifference shown by some people, clearly at substantially increased risk, but whether this should be regarded as a medical or psychological problem we must leave for them to judge. After all, skydivers, stressed businessmen, and motorcyclists also balance the satisfactions of their lifestyle and pleasures against health and safety considerations. In fact though, obesity is acknowledged by a vast number of people to be their greatest and most intractable problem.

Quite obviously, eating is a pleasurable activity and it requires no explanation as to why people should eat up to the point of satiation. But, for some, the quite consciously acting compulsion to go beyond this point, despite feelings of guilt, self-disgust, and the accumulation of unwanted fat, proves too strong for them to resist. As with smoking, gambling, drinking and many other activities, the addictive and appetitive aspects are evidently sufficient to offset the far greater, and much more distant, likely punishing consequences. Nevertheless, the person concerned has to find some way of handling their body image and maintaining their self-esteem.

Despite objective evidence from ever increasing clothes size, some very stout people will continue to insist that they are not obese and do not have a problem. By contrast, others will greatly exaggerate their bulk and demand treatment as addicts. In between are the majority of those overweight people who are concerned about their size, and their apparent inability to reduce it substantially, but who do not regard it as an immediately serious problem.

However, at all weight levels there are, in addition to those who are realistic about their bulk, a good many others who, objectively speaking, seem to have a very mistaken image of their bodies. Though no precise figures can be obtained, family doctors and specialists alike are emphatic about the vagaries of subjective judgements of appearance. Patients asked to draw their outline or match it with a series of pre-prepared outlines or photographs are extremely likely to make, what may seem to an observer, remarkable mis-matches. Not only may the grossly fat see themselves as much less so, the painfully thin may judge themselves as quite the opposite. Naturally, this is not always, or even generally, the case but it is clear that people's self-perceptions may be strikingly at variance with reality: sometimes quite dangerously so, as with obesity or anorexia nervosa. In such cases, clinicians usually have the very difficult job of trying to uncover something of their patient's body image and related sense of self-esteem: this being of supreme importance in guiding the course of therapy.

Obesity has many causes, and, though overeating is a basic one, underlying psychological states are more basic still. Of course, obesity is closely connected with many forms of distress, mental and physical – both as a cause and as an effect. But it is generally not the medical aspects which figure most prominently in the minds of people seeking treatment: rather, it is the mental pain that their fat bodies inflict on their sense of self-esteem. Because obesity is so often associated in people's minds with weakness, greed and laziness, the very plump are often deeply shamed by their bodies, and what they seem to tell other people about them.

So, far from being jolly, fat people are often quite the opposite. The eating which originally led to their obesity was often, in itself, a misguided way of counteracting stress, depression, or boredom due to some other cause, and the additional burdens imposed by obesity add to this. The pleasures of eating may make life superficially more agreeable but the only alternatives apparent to some people, of either remaining fat and ashamed or else seriously dieting and giving up the gratifications which kept the original worries and tensions at bay, may both prove unacceptable. Serious depression and even suicide is, sadly, all too often a consequence of this terrible dilemma.

Happily though, one bright ray of hope has recently penetrated the gloom of the hyper-obese: it is now possible, through a surgical bypass procedure known as jejeuno-ileostomy, to remove part of the small intestine and so drastically reduce a person's weight by decreasing the calorific intake from a given amount of food. This means that, in suitable cases, people may continue to enjoy what are often compensatory gratifications while not, at the same time, having their troubles exacerbated by the physical or social consequences of being overweight, or suffering the additional blows to self-esteem caused by a distressing body image.

Unfortunately, there is no comparably direct solution to the problems of the gravely underweight; the compulsive self-starvers. *Anorexia nervosa* is a particularly dangerous condition for, without skilled intervention, it would lead to even more deaths from starvation than it does at present. Unlike obesity, which is likely to occur at all stages in life, and particularly in middle age, anorexia is typically a disorder of the young. Middle-class girls in their teens and early twenties are the main victims: males are seldom affected, and the condition is virtually unknown in cases where the individual concerned has ever suffered from unavoidable deprivation or starvation.

The cause, or causes, of anorexia are fairly obscure – despite the several, confidently held, theories. One account emphasizes the girl's strivings for independence: a way of rejecting her mother's controlling influence over her life in general, and her body in particular – with the added zest of punishing her mother and gaining a neurotic control over the family and others. Another account also works backwards from the consequences of starvation: particularly the fact that it wastes away breasts and causes menstruation to cease. In other words, the girl can avoid becoming a woman, with all the responsibilities that physical and psychological maturity bring, yet achieve her neurotic superiority strivings by playing on the concern and anxiety of others.

On any account, anorexics are very maladjusted people, but whether the control they undoubtedly tend to exert over others is a primary aim is another matter. It is also possible that the anorexic is someone who is suffering from a powerfully conditioned sense that flesh is intensely disgusting; perhaps in part due to her observations of the censure and ridicule heaped on the overweight by others. Certainly fat can become a cause of great anxiety if excess flesh is contrary to an already established set of goals and ideals. For example, ballet students are particularly prone to becoming anorexic: careful and even stringent dieting to maintain an unusually slender frame becomes a way of life for many, with the underlying anxiety that failure may mean the end of all their hopes. Inevitably, a proportion go too far and some become so fixated in the process that they become anorexic – sometimes with fatal results.

This kind of obsessional behaviour undoubtedly has many of the characteristics of other neurotic maladjustments, but there is another, perhaps additional, possibility also: anorexics may suffer from some unusual distortions of their body image. To most people, one of the most remarkable features of anorexics is that, despite their emaciated appearance, they insist they are too fat. Standing them in front of a mirror or presenting them with a photography of their naked body is of little use – even when direct comparisons are made with other undeniably slim, but not anorexic, figures. However, that this intractably wrong image of their own body is shaped by abnormal perceptual characteristics is actually highly improbable as there appears to be no detectable impairment in judging the proportions, shapes or distances involved in neutral objects.

Transsexualism, where a perfectly well-formed individual of one sex seeks radical surgical or cosmetic remodelling to change their appearance to that of the other, is not without some parallels with anorexia. This is particularly so in so far as both highlight the extent to which a person's self-image and self-esteem can be geared to quite extraordinary misjudgements concerning their physical characteristics. In each case, neurosis and the rejection of normal sexual functioning is almost universally involved – though transsexuals do retain powerful, if misdirected, sex drives and, again unlike anorexics, their neurotic motives do not seem to include the aim of gaining control over their families – at least, judging from the usual course of events.

Such great departures from the norm are, of course, by definition, very rare indeed. For most of us, our problems only involve coming to terms with the inevitable minor imperfections of our bodies. But, as we have seen in numerous examples, one's body image, though referring to palpable physical structures, may be related only tenuously to what others would consider objective reality. The image we create of ourselves is a unique psychological, and therefore largely subjective, amalgam of actual mirror reflections and photographic likenesses, perceived in terms of our understanding of the ideals and norms of our particular social and cultural niche. This is further modified by feedback from others concerning ourselves in particular and, in a more general sense, by what we think the influential figures in our lives find especially attractive or repellent.

Naturally, the content of this feedback is likely to vary considerably from era to era and from place to place. The current notion that truly desirable women must have straight teeth, firm breasts, small bottoms and a generally boyish figure and appearance, is largely a product of saturation level commercialism deriving from the cinema and advertising. By constantly casting the good, the successful, the desirable and the attractive in terms of stereotypes, those who do not fit this bogus norm must needs accept a more negative body image. Men too, are presented with their own versions of the stereotypically most attractive and acceptable pattern for their sex. Unless one is tall, lean, youthful and handsome, it becomes progressively more difficult to look into the mirror and feel satisfied with the image one sees reflected back.

If a positively regarded body image is important for one's self-esteem, then modern commercialism makes it very difficult for most of us to achieve it. The financial and entertainment motives which underlie promotion of generally unattainable stereotype ideals may sell more toothpaste or girdles by creating yearnings as well as anxieties, but their real cost must be counted in human as well as monetary terms. The insidious images created by advertisers and film makers, mindless as they may be, are nevertheless all too readily absorbed into the ideal against which we shall come to judge ourselves and others.

Yet, in addition to the bald patches, large ears, moles, receding chins, long noses, or whatever – which are unfortunately as common in ordinary folk as they are rare in the idealized figures of the media, there is the fact that most people will assuredly deviate from the flawless utopians in at least one major way – whether it be height, weight, symmetry, or complexion. But, even supposing one conformed completely to the nonpareil pattern, there is still no possible way of permanently avoiding circumstances where one's physical characteristics will be a negative weight in the balance of self-esteem.

Pregnancy is, for some women, a time when their self-regard swells with their body, though this is becoming ever-rarer in industrialized societies. No doubt the falling status of motherhood relative to 'career' (even if this is the simplest routine work) helps to make pregnant women feel as though they are more pitied than envied or admired by others. 'An accident, was it?' must be one of the most common first questions put to the prospective mother. Now that fecundity is regarded more as a potential personal and social disaster, to be fought off as long as possible with the aid of contraceptive technologies, it is not surprising that the pregnant woman should often regard herself as a 'loser' and her physical condition, the evidence of her defeat, something to feel ashamed about.

Of course, this is only one of the many scenarios which might have been outlined and one can only guess how general it is, but the fact remains that pregnancy is very often a time of negative self-esteem when, as husbands know, a good deal more reassurance and loving concern is desirable. Swollen ankles and stomach, changing breasts, sickness and constipation, varicose veins and breathlessness, coupled with the flat heels and formless clothes which are demanded, all make it hard to hang on to an attractive self-image. On the other hand, those who value the processes and fact of motherhood highly, and are surrounded by others who share their view, are particularly fortunate as they are much more likely to avoid negative self-feelings and, on the contrary, are much more likely to experience their bodies as a source of very positive self-regard.

Unfortunately, the small glimmer of hope in pregnancy is much more dim when it comes to that inevitability of all lives, sickness and old age. In both cases, the body becomes a liability: often it and its functions become objects of embarrassment: more certainly, it is the distressing cause of our return to a state of helplessness and dependency. These are issues we shall treat more fully in due course but, for the present, it is sufficient just to make the point that no one, except those whose lives are abruptly terminated, can reasonably expect to escape the experience of disfigurement and disablement.

Yet many people, no doubt quite rightly, do their very best to avoid, or minimize, the consequences of ageing: something which is becoming increasingly more practicable. For, in addition to the more conventional palliatives – exercise, dress, make-up, and sustained concern with affairs – there is now the additional possibility of plastic surgery to remove wrinkles, re-shape sagging features, and generally reduce the external signs of decline.

Not being seen as an old person, nor seeing oneself that way, certainly should help free people from the shackles of restricting social stereotypes, and allow a more prolonged period of relative youthfulness. Though whether the underlying anxieties about changes in appearance become any the less is another issue, and one about which there is remarkably little research to guide us. In fact, research into the psychological effects of most aspects of disablement and disfigurement is more sparse than the scale of the problem might lead one to expect.

Serious malformations, acquired or congenital, are likely to have far-reaching consequences in all aspects of an individual's career and life style – occupational, economic, and social status not excepted. But it is often during the fairly early stages of personality development that some of the more painful and intractable psychological problems are created. Whether they fully realize it or not, before occupational considerations become so important in setting the limitations and presenting the frustrations which must be met later, the circle of family and friends is mainly responsible for the evaluative feedback which sets a pattern of self-esteem, or the lack of it, which can persist for many years to come.

Of course, severe physical problems in offspring can be a great shock to parents, but if they experience and communicate their negative feelings about the child, its burden will be increased immeasurably. By the same token, the problems for parents and child alike may be very much increased in those cases where the child blames its parents for their presumed part in creating, or allowing, the deformity.

Though unconscious of its origin, a great deal of anger may well be generated in the families of disabled or disfigured people, making it very difficult to achieve the sort of mutual respect which is often the foundation of self-esteem. On the other hand, a remarkable degree of mutual love, caring and regard may equally well result from all concerned being drawn more tightly together in response to their shared difficulties. But, whichever way families react, they are likely to be under a considerable amount of pressure, and in need of whatever outside support may be available.

The additional problems created by schooldays need no further elaboration and have led, in the case of the most obviously incapacitated – such as those who are blind, deaf, paralysed, or otherwise gravely physically incapacitated – to a good deal of special concern, both theoretical and practical. Their difficulties, educational and occupational, are quite rightly the subject of considerable interest, yet we sometimes forget that the magnitude of psychological problems is not necessarily in direct proportion to the degree of incapacity or malformation.

Until fairly recently, in even the most socially and industrially advanced societies, children would have to cope as best they could with the less physically disabling somatic obstacles to their social and self-acceptance. Club foot, strabismus (cross-eyes), cleft palate, a hump on the back and all manner of lesser deformities had to be borne and overcome.

Achieving a satisfactory social and personal adjustment in such cases appears often to have been very difficult indeed for, though people may pity the paralysed or those in pain, they seem much more likely to be repelled by obvious impediments and deformities. Partly as a result of this, developing and sustaining a positive image of themselves proved impossible for many, and the cause of an uncounted number of sad and unfulfilled lives.

Nowadays, medical advances and facilities make it much rarer to encounter anyone very obviously suffering from these correctable physical conditions. Reparative surgery – repairing defects, restoring functions, and improving appearance – has done a great deal to ameliorate the lot of all those persons whom Irving Goffman described in his book *Stigma* as being disqualified from full social acceptance, and pressured towards accepting a second-rate social role.

Goffman, being a sociologist, is naturally particularly interested in the interactions which developed between stigmatized individuals and their social milieu. But these interactions, and the analyses of how social roles develop, and how the stigmata affect educational, marital and occupational opportunities, cannot also fail to be about the problems of individual personality development. It could hardly be otherwise: there being an almost universal tendency to take any abnormal attribute of others as the basis for stereotyping them.

The cripple, it seems, is expected to play the cripple's role; to accept a demeaning view of himself and not, on pain of society's displeasure, to act like an ordinary human being who just happens to have some equipment difficulties. Pressured into an inferior social status, and not really accepted by normal people, the physically impaired often drift into patterns of self-mockery, resentfulness, or withdrawal, which can only exacerbate their problems.

Sometimes their bitterness, frustration, or the ambivalences created out of their fragile and unstable sense of self may upset others and deprive them of the support they so desperately need. By adopting the 'sick role' or through using their disabilities to excuse all failures, laziness and inadequacies, they may run an additional risk to their self-esteem of provoking contempt and finally the withdrawal of others. Alienation may then lead on to actual loneliness and further depression, and thence to the despair which being unwanted and abandoned so readily creates.

Of course, this gloomy picture is not the inevitable consequence of physical deformities: many, if not most, people so affected make excellent adjustments, but there is no doubt that such misfortunes place people at far greater social and psychological risk. In a sense though, it is perhaps those suffering from handicaps of an intermediate degree of severity who have some of the greatest difficulties to overcome.

Depending on the age of onset, people with quite severe conditions may have many compensatory advantages as a result of special schools and facilities, and through the clearer and more realistic sense of self which clubs and societies for the disabled may help produce. By contrast, marginally impaired individuals are likely to have relatively greater difficulty in developing satisfying self-images, not only because they lack many of the supportive facilities, but also because they cannot so easily locate appropriate or desirable models to imitate.

This important developmental process of identifying with others and adopting some of their attributes can be made so very much harder if one feels somewhere between a clearly disabled person and someone for whom all things seem possible. As a result, an unrealistic denial of any handicap, or an adoption of a severely handicapped role can equally lead the individual into developing unreasonable expectations, or into aiming for failure. In either case, the confusions which are likely to be experienced, unless wise guidance is available, are likely to cause much frustration and aggression.

Even if we escape serious hereditary or congenital defects, burns, injuries, and strokes may yet bring us into the ranks of the severely physically impaired with the need to revise our self-image and maintain, as best we can, our own positive self-esteem. As has already been mentioned, disablement is not just about a special category of people; it is about all people, presently or potentially, and therefore represents a major sphere of psychological concern.

By definition, most of us are, for most of the time, 'normal'. But behind this rather banal statistical conclusion lies considerable individual variation. Those whose disabilities are marked enough to involve them in some form of special social or medical treatment are, so to speak, only the tip of the iceberg; the small but visible part of a very much larger whole. Naturally, they merit special attention in so far as the severely disabled do tend to have certain special problems of their own, but they are also appropriately seen as occupying the extreme on a continuum of distressing physical variation which extends well into the 'normal' population.

Yet, though the idea of a continuum is reasonable enough, and may help establish a broad perspective for considering disability or disfigurement, it can nevertheless be very misleading if it is taken to suggest the possibility of ranking psychological and physical distress in some way. Such a procedure would be impracticable for many reasons, though this is most obvious in respect of the criterion problem. How one could develop criteria for precisely ranking or scaling the severity of even somewhat similar disfigurements – for example, facial birthmarks, misshapen ears or crooked teeth, on a single continuum is very difficult to imagine.

But even if this were possible, such a scaling of physical disabilities would still lack any practical value as it is quite clear that the psychological effects of physical deviations are not necessarily closely related to the type or magnitude of the deviation. In practice, the effect of any physical deviation is always likely to be very much dependent upon the combined and interactive character of the individual and his social milieu: the former being particularly susceptible to the type of positive reactions or rejections previously encountered.

For example, a sense of self-esteem developed in one set of circumstances can be expected to carry over into another: early experiences of acceptance or rejection may colour not only present and future expectations, but may affect manner and bearing in such a way as to influence the actual responses of others. A sense of self-assurance is just as likely to elicit acceptance as the expectation of being treated as an inferior is liable to provoke rejection or, at best, patronization.

Unfortunately, though many countries now arrange treatment for the more disabling conditions, there are a number of other defects of appearance which are not routinely rectified. For example, a beaked, bulbous, or otherwise misshapen nose, though perfectly functional, may be the source of untold misery and of very poor self-esteem. A nasal hump, in addition to its unpleasing appearance, may also result in equally unattractive mouth breathing, speech, or eating, adding to self-consciousness, and also making social relationships much less successful than might otherwise have been the case.

In many instances, rhinoplasty – reconstructive surgery of the nose – could easily prevent such problems. The plastic surgeon's ability to do such things as reshape protruding ears, receding jaws, protruding or pendulous lips – as well as being able to remove or reduce what may be gross imperfections due to birthmarks, growths and the effects of severe burning – is often a remarkable psychological as well as medical achievement. In fact, the plastic surgeon Adolph Apton has presented a very reasonable and well-supported case in support of his claim that 'plastic surgery is a surgical method of psychotherapy'.

He argues that, if physical abnormality is really an important causal factor underlying marked inferiority feelings or neurosis, then reparative surgery can often remove, or substantially relieve, the mental and emotional symptoms. Of course, Apton fully realized that defects may simply be used symptomatically for the expression of mental disorders of quite different origin but his examples of personality change, drawn from a range of circumstances from clinic to prison, do suggest that 'psychoplastic surgery' can be a very powerful therapeutic tool in many cases.

The mouth, being a major focal point of the face – many believe it to be a more important expressive area than the eyes – is also one in which defects and deformities can have a considerable influence on how we are judged by others, and hence by ourselves. However, though teeth are one of the most important features of the mouth, it is quite apparent that not everyone with unsightly teeth necessarily feels flawed, or seeks treatment. It may be that fear of the dentist or of having to wear dentures is part of their conscious or unconscious decision but, whether or not their body image and self-esteem is much affected, it may still be that their relationships with others are.

In our culture at least, broken, discoloured, and crooked teeth are not considered attractive, and may even prove repulsive to potential lovers because of the mouth's close connection with sexual behaviours. However that may be, it seems that those who are indifferent to their own teeth, or the teeth of others with whom they come into close contact, are in a minority. Unsolicited feedback is often hard to avoid and, as always, it is likely to be children who are the least inhibited when it comes to drawing painful public attention to the defects of others. Being called 'Fang' or 'Dracula' is hardly likely to enhance one's body image or self-esteem. Yet, for a variety of reasons, quite a number of children grow to adulthood with very unsightly features.

Corrective orthodontic treatment of misshapen teeth and mouths is by no means always practicable or available: and, if it is, the often considerable amount of time or expense necessary to achieve something approximating to the ideal may not be acceptable. Consequently, many people present themselves at dentists asking for their unattractive but perfectly healthy teeth to be removed and replaced with dentures. Unless the patient seeks private treatment from a dental surgeon who is sympathetic to cosmetic considerations, it seems that such requests are usually denied on rather puritanical grounds, though justified on medical or functional ones.

However, though not necessarily promoting any specific policy, organizations like the British Dental Association are now becoming progressively more concerned about the psychologically damaging aspects of bad teeth and oral deformation. Within the last few years, it has become increasingly accepted that the embarrassment which unsightly teeth can bring may be much more than a minor misfortune. The avoidance of smiling, and indeed the complete avoidance of many social situations themselves, may do a great deal to reduce the actual quality of people's lives. Recognizing this, many dental surgeons are now beginning to treat appearance considerations as matters of much more serious clinical moment.

Then there are the myriad other aspects of appearance for which direct professional intervention can be of little help. We may not be able to define ugliness to everyone's satisfaction, or even achieve unanimous agreement as to whether a particular individual is ugly or not; yet beauty and ugliness are not completely subjective, and the social and psychological consequences of tending towards one or the other are not insignificant. For example, a woman with coarse square features, a bad complexion, poor hair and small mottled eyes will have a lot of problems to overcome. And, by the same token, a man with a pinched face, prominent ears and a receding chin may fare no better. Unless they have other compensatory advantages, both are likely to find the pursuit of happiness and fulfilment an uphill struggle. But it would be misleading to suppose that a person's attractiveness or otherwise lies only, or even mainly, in their most superficial or genetically inherited features. Zest, humour, consideration and kindness may all stamp their mark on actual appearance, just as petulance, hostility and bitterness can. Anaesthetists have often commented on how, when the facial muscles are completely relaxed, an apparently very attractive or unattractive person can come to look the opposite. Nevertheless, though personality can modify a person's unattractive appearance, it seems more than likely that most would gladly be rid of their physical blemishes and able to engage in life on equal terms.

Yet there are many more minor, and more common, flaws than the ones so far discussed – though these are sometimes even more difficult to rectify, and may be of a surprisingly far-reaching significance in shaping the course of our lives. For example, unusually sweaty hands may not only create very unfavourable impressions in others, but they can easily cause their possessor to become shy and tense in company, or even avoid completely social situations in which holding or shaking hands is involved. Scars, spots, wrinkles and varicose veins may also have considerable psycho-social implications, but these too only amount to a fraction of the many trifling things which can isolate people from others when it comes to such activities as sunbathing, swimming, or sports.

The list of physical features, from baldness to amputations, which can negatively affect our body image and self-esteem may, by now, seem almost endless – despite the fact that only a minority of these factors are, objectively speaking, in the slightest degree physically disabling. But this heterogeneity is further compounded by the great variability of psychological responses towards them: a factor which depends not only upon the bodily aspects, but quite as importantly on such things as age of onset, environmental resources and the individual's intellectual and emotional development and control. The range of possible coping strategies which this number of interacting variables could give rise to suggests, on mathematical grounds alone, innumerable possibilities.

Adler may well be correct in his declaration that perceived sources of inferiority always lead to compensatory behaviours but, if so, this must clearly be interpreted to embrace a very unpredictable range of activities, including gaining relief through fantasy and withdrawal, or adopting a rational and stoical attitude towards one's afflictions. But when theoretical constructs become so diffuse and stretched by their heterogeneous content, it is difficult not to question their utility, or wonder whether further attempts at redefinition are not overdue.

Of course, a person may not even be aware of his imperfections, despite the efforts of others to acquaint him with them. But, if he is aware, and feels that his reduced sense of self-esteem is having an adverse affect upon his life, then entering some sort of therapy seems to be the appropriate thing to do. Coming to terms with our bodies, perhaps discovering that we are not alone in our anxieties, or that we are not so unusual after all, is not only to bolster self-confidence but may also counter tension and anxiety, paving the way to greater spontaneity and zest.

An *Encounter Group* is perhaps the most natural choice for those with bodily anxieties as their problems, generally being well rooted in beliefs about how others see them, may often best be dealt with in this type of social situation. The composition of such groups tends to be somewhat indeterminate but, characteristically, comprises a professional leader – usually a psychologist or psychiatrist in the broadly 'humanistic' tradition – and up to a score of individuals variously intent on release from tensions or 'hang-ups', or simply seeking heightened awareness of themselves or others. A common opening gambit is to ask the members to say what they like about their appearance and what they dislike or find upsetting. At a later stage, some encounters may be held in the nude – where all structures and properties of the body, with any attendant feelings of anxiety or inferiority, can be considered in a social setting. Of course, it places a great responsibility on both the leader and the group to avoid adding to the difficulties or pain of others and, instead, through discussion and acceptance, to find the best ways of conveying esteem and reassurance to each of the members. How well this is achieved will, of course, always be a function not only of the procedure, but also the particular mixture of people comprising the group.

In principle, the counter-conditioning implicit when a person's source of anxiety comes to be associated with the warmth, acceptance and support of a social group, ought to be an effective way of changing their self-regard. So too, should the catharsis which it might be hoped would follow a discharge of the negative emotions connected with repressed or suppressed painful images of oneself. However, whether these experiences carry over into ordinary life, with its far greater degree of competitiveness and censoriousness, is not known.

Unfortunately, humanistic psychologists seldom have much interest in classification or quantification so it is especially difficult to come to definite conclusions about the effects of encounter groups on body image and self-esteem. But the prima facie relevance of this approach to body-related problems does suggest it may be particularly helpful in many instances. It is, though, a risk that not every socially anxious person might care, or dare, to take.

At the other end of the scale there are, of course, many people whose body image is extremely positive. There are even those whose beautiful appearance is so widely admired that one might suppose their greatest problem to be avoiding a narcissistic, and therefore immature and almost equally maladaptive, mode of adjustment. But such people are rare: many more will simply have average or above average well-formed bodies which, during the course of their development, have always proved an asset and source of positive self-regard.

For such people, their physique and appearance may have added so greatly to their self-assurance that disablement later in life, or the typical human destiny of glasses, false teeth, thinning hair, and all the other signs of decrepitude, will find them particularly able to make the necessary adjustments. On the other hand, it may be that just the opposite is the case. Once again, we are left to surmise as this is yet another aspect of the mind-body connection which still awaits thorough empirical investigation.

But though more research is urgently needed in this area, there is an even greater need for compassionate understanding. The problems outlined in this chapter are, in many respects, avoidable: being judgemental and adopting the stereotypes which exclude so many people, and making them feel second-rate or tainted, is not an inevitable process.

If we can continuously bear in mind that those who suffer from a sense of inferiority, whether due to an apparently major or minor source of physical imperfection, are desperately in need of acceptance from the rest of us, we can begin to help them develop and maintain a greater sense of positive self-esteem. And, if we can do this, it might just be possible to add something to the sum of human happiness and to the quality of civilized life. If we cannot, we shall all share the consequences.

Chapter three

SEX AND SEXUALITY: GENERAL

At one time, it was thought to be completely self-evident that one of the most, if not the most, powerful influence on psychological development and functioning was the physical fact of a person's sex. The majority of people would probably still not demur too strongly from this view although, nowadays, they are more inclined to moderate the emphasis; bringing further into the foreground the effects of individual differences in temperament, aptitudes and capacities, regardless of sex.

This line of thinking obviously has a great deal to commend it: there can be no doubt that it makes a good deal of sense to deal in cases rather than vast and heterogeneous sexual categories. Nevertheless, however many exceptions one could list, the mental worlds of men and women are still very distinctive. And, though the fact of being born physically male or female may not absolutely and universally determine any particular psychological characteristic, probability is clearly at work – whether the underlying moulding forces are primarily cultural or biological. Either way though, social and psychological effects may be said to have their origins, at least partly, in bodily causes.

The whole issue of the existence and genesis of male-female differences is, of course, not only an extremely complex area of scientific study but also one of fierce polemic. Unfortunately, the two are often confused or conjoined and then it becomes difficult either to unravel or to judge cases.

However, where a straightforward claim is presented to the effect that equal respect and the same educational, political and economic opportunities are the due of all human beings, there is no problem. This is clearly the expression of a perfectly proper and admirable social aim. But if, as often happens, the argument is advanced along lines which insist that all differences between men and women are the consequence of discriminatory treatment and conditioning, then purely ideological assumptions are being introduced and, moreover, ones which run quite contrary to the empirical evidence.

Physical dimorphism – the fact that men and women and physically very different from one another in many ways other than their reproductive apparatus – has always led to questions and far too many doctrinaire answers, as to whether there are equivalent mental differences. A number of reviews of our present knowledge have achieved considerable objectivity but few have surpassed Corinne Hutt's *Males and Females* for its broadly based sources of psychological and biological data, and the high degree of scientific detachment which it maintains throughout. Her treatment of the subject includes much that lies well beyond the scope of our present concern with sexuality but, in addition to material concerning such traditional psychological preoccupations as intelligence, creativity and temperament, there is a great deal of relevance to gender and sex role determination in relation to hormonal and nervous system differences.

Needless to say, the very idea that male and female brains may be programmed quite differently from birth is repugnant to many people's beliefs. Nevertheless, a great range of evidence from both human and animal sources is marshalled to show that distinctive hormonal activity in the foetus results in a whole range of sex-typical differences, and that these are extremely resistant to change. Even though levels of circulating hormones may be drastically altered or modified later in life, perhaps as a result of injections or even castration, once virilized in the womb by the appropriate male hormones, the behaviour of either genetic males or genetic females exposed to the hormones will assume a very stable male pattern of activity, aggressiveness and sexual drive. Yet, though male and female patterns can undoubtedly be tampered with by scientific means, or affected by accidents, there are clearly different underlying norms in nature.

Such findings, however, are given very little prominence by most of those who see a 'political' need to minimize differences between the sexes. But some, like Mary Sherfey, a well-known specialist on female sexuality, take the opposite line, emphasizing 'embryonic female primacy' or the way in which male sexual characteristics are differentiations from what would otherwise yield female forms. In other words, making the case that females are the basic human design, and that males are functionally useful variations produced only for reproductive purposes. The sexist implications of such arguments are obvious enough, particularly when set beside other assertions to the effect that the problems of female sexuality are largely due to the ways in which men have repressed and undermined women in pursuit of their own selfish preoccupation with inheritance and property economics.

Whatever interpretation one puts on this sort of embryological data and reconstruction of history, it is very hard to avoid becoming aligned with one faction or another. Inevitably, one is drawn deeply into those ideas about the basic nature of males and females which have taxed the human intellect, and patience, for a good many years. And now that individual freedom from any pre-formed system of behaviour has become so important a contemporary goal, it is quite natural that the whole area of gender role, sexuality, marriage and parenthood should be critically reconsidered.

Many of the current questions are about who should, or should not, do what. Such questions of what is *fair* and what people *ought* to do cannot, of course, be answered in scientific terms: they are matters for social and ethical decisions. Research will therefore not settle questions concerning the most desirable division of domestic duties where one or both have outside jobs: these are practical matters for individual couples and their solution depends upon the attitudes and temperament of each. But though such arrangements, or lack of them, are likely to affect the mutual and self-regard of the couple, and thus influence their love and sex lives, the varied possibilities so created must remain somewhat beyond the range of this present discussion.

However, determining whether or not males and females have different biologically grounded dispositions liable to affect their sexual behaviour is absolutely central to any discussion of body-mind issues. Even if it can be shown that any disposition which might be revealed could be modified, or even eliminated by appropriate social conditioning, the tendency itself would be of no less scientific and practical significance. An evolutionary perspective is helpful in this sort of investigation: sociobiology, which draws together the findings of evolution with those of experimental science and natural history, being the most comprehensive in its treatment of sex and sexuality.

Moreover, sociobiology is not the brash newcomer it is often thought to be. The name has only recently become familiar, but it rests on an idea which was most elegantly expressed by Freud some 60 years ago when he referred to the individual as only 'a transitory and perishable appendage to the quasi-immortal germ-plasm bequeathed to him by the race'. This same idea, generally more prosaically put nowadays as a variant of 'a chicken is just the egg's way of making more eggs' or, 'a human is just the genes' way of making more genes', still carried the same implication that sex must be the major preoccupation of all species. And, always more important than the individual's survival, is successful rearing of the next generation.

Such a view is not always well received: being, perhaps, only slightly less controversial than the characteristic attitude of sociobiologists towards sex differences. One of the implications generally accepted is that, in a species such as our own, where the young are so few and take so long to become self-reliant, survival must have depended upon stable pair-bonding and a division of parental responsibilities, such that females would remain with their children while the males were engaged in hunting and protecting the band. Certainly this pattern is universal in hunter-gatherer groups: the question is, though, whether this arrangement is instinctively ingrained or whether it simply represents the rational solution to the practical problems of a distant lifestyle.

Of course, the answer to this question is of more than scholarly interest: it also has quite definite psychological relevance when it comes to cases. If, as the sociobiologists argue, motherhood imposes certain instinctive duties on the female which have always meant she must select, and hold on to, a dependable mate in order to ensure the survival of her children, then her apparently much stronger tendency towards monogamy may not be something which can be easily sloughed off; however sound, reasonable, or attractive the reasons for doing so.

By contrast, sociobiologists tend to see the male's sexual imperative as quite the opposite. For, whereas the female has only a few eggs to carry her genes, and must devote a great amount of her life to any that are fertilized, the male has a virtually unlimited supply of gene-carrying sperm, and this encourages him to mate as often as he can in order to increase his own chances of genetic survival. So, it seems that males and females may have basically opposite, and incompatible, sexual and therefore psychological tendencies: certainly their typical behaviour is very different when it comes to what used to be called 'fidelity'.

It is also true that males usually enforce monogamy on females rather vigorously, regardless of their own disposition or wishes. After all, a women's genetic success is always assured so long as she mates with virile males and can find the necessary support to rear her babies. Who the father is matters much more to the male – whose genetic immortality is at stake, and whose whole life may become subservient to the genetic success of another if the children he supports have been fathered by someone else. So the 'double standard' of males becomes more explicable on this theory. They are driven to scatter their seed as widely as possible, yet must enforce behaviour which would discourage both the mates with whom they raise children, and potential rivals, from doing the same.

In case the above should be interpreted as merely a charter for male promiscuity and female restraint – the ultimate biological justification for male chauvinism – it must also be said that the case advanced would be regarded as very convincing if it did not refer to human beings, and to their present aspirations for social change.

The better known exponents of the sociobiological position, Edward Wilson, Robert Ardrey and Desmond Morris, have all been severely pilloried for the ideas they expressed as to the significance of such incontrovertible facts as human physical dimorphism and the unparalleled sexual receptivity of the females of our species. Understandably, they were as unable to *prove* their cases as were their opponents to *disprove* them, and they drew the sort of fire which is entirely to be expected when dealing with such widely taboo subjects as sex differences, sexuality and the animal origins and aspects of human beings. Worse still, they wove these elements together, giving prominence to breast and penis, pelt and physique, to construct an evolutionary account of human nature.

Social scientists were outraged: humanists and ideologists of many persuasions were equally incensed, and abuse did not stop short at words. Meetings were broken up and the sort of disagreeable behaviour which befell the early proponents of evolution was not uncommon for a while. Yet, regardless of how far one accepts either the premises or conclusions of this work, fascinating and intricate cases have been proposed to account for some of the underlying factors involved in relation to even the individual sexual encounter. Only a bigoted mind can reject ideas without considering them, or because they conflict with more acceptable preconceptions, though similarities between the hostility directed at evolution and sociobiology should not be seen as evidence of the latter being similarly well-founded. That must lie in the realms of further research and more detailed analysis.

For the time being, however, we can only consider the various arguments being advanced in relation to sex and sexuality, then form our own conclusions. We may seem to be faced with mutually exclusive alternatives, necessitating a choice between cultural and biological explanations of sex differences and sexual customs but this is, of course, not the case. We are demonstrably as much evolved animals as we are sentient, and perhaps spiritual, human beings: this much is not at serious issue. What is, is the relative contribution of each, and whether this balance is necessary, or sustained by particular circumstances.

Quite obviously motivations and dispositions must, like any other psychological process, emerge from a mixture of personal and social learning to yield outcomes which are unique in their expressions. Yet, in spite of these sources of individual variability, and the great diversity of economic and cultural circumstances operating worldwide, so uniform is the historical and anthropological record that it is difficult to accept explanations of sex-typical behaviours which are based only upon the principles of social learning or post hoc analyses of the structure of particular societies.

This is by no means intended to minimize the great influence that social and psychological factors have on all aspects of sexual behaviour: it is simply to present the case that their function may have more to do with creating the cultural forms by which nature's aims are expressed than with determining them. Form follows function very closely in nature and, given the great differences in the male and female form, it would be very strange if this did not imply some equally marked differences in function, and therefore in typical psychological aims and dispositions.

So, sexual encounters between individual men and women may involve many unconscious motivations, as well as those of which we are conscious. If this is so, misunderstandings are likely; members of each sex may seem unreasonable or baffling to the other, and their disagreements related to sexual matters may be far less amenable to counselling than a purely rational view of human beings might suggest. Even at the intra-personal level, as Freud pointed out, conflict between one's unconscious needs and wishes and conscious attitudes and motives can result in situations which create anxiety however one responds or acts. And, as has frequently been suggested, female promiscuity may be just such a case – where, irrespective of the conscious desirability of the goal, such behaviour is likely to bring more mental pain than pleasure.

Yet another way in which female sexuality often proves to be more limited and less satisfactory than that of males is with respect to orgasm. Women experience it far less often than men, and are nowadays inclined to blame this almost entirely on the incompetence or selfishness of men for reaching orgasm, and therefore terminating intercourse, before they themselves are sufficiently aroused or satisfied. There is perhaps some justice in this, at least in many instances, but it is also quite certainly a misleading and mischievous oversimplification.

The anthropological record shows that the relatively low incidence of female orgasm is a universal phenomenon, suggesting that the cause, or causes, are not to be found in particular social, cultural, or interpersonal factors alone so, once again, biological evidence has been invoked to provide an explanation. It seems that, compared with the male climax, the female equivalent is of a more recent and therefore probably unstable, evolutionary origin. In fact, so rare is it that, besides our own species, it only occurs in other primates; and then far less commonly than in our own case.

The explanation advanced for the marked difference between male and female orgasmic behaviour is that it is of relatively less survival significance in females, and therefore has not been so strongly selected for. In the case of males, a combination of the female's ever-receptive state and the powerfully reinforcing effects of orgasmic pleasure, were evolved to ensure that the male would always return to his mate, and progeny, however distant the hunting.

Whatever the cause, or combination of causes involved, the keenly felt sense of injustice and inequality created by a public discussion of women's lesser orgasmic satisfactions has led to a widespread feeling that something should be done about it. And, judging from the enormous literature on this subject, it appears that men are now proving much more willing to explore ways of controlling their own responses so as to help improve women's chances of attaining orgasm during intercourse.

Understanding, learning, and technique are apparently quite effective antidotes and, whatever biological factors may be operative in retarding women's orgasm, it seems that they can often be offset by restraint on the part of the male, together with a greater attention to foreplay stimulation and the fuller use of non-genital erogenous zones during copulation. Nevertheless, even though we may successfully compensate, biological differences between the sexes remain – in women's superior capacity for multiple orgasms no less than their generally slower speed in coming to climax – and all this too must be grist for the scientific mill.

However much we may bring to our partners in terms of love, tenderness, or technique, the act of mating is fundamentally an expression of our biological nature. The very bodies with which males and females confront one another contain, and reflect, the processes of evolution itself and, when we engage in sexual intercourse, we are essentially fulfilling the same reproductive urges as any other animal. So, despite the marked reluctance to accept it, a bio-evolutionary context is an appropriate starting place for most discussions of sexuality, and an indispensable one where the significance of physical form and constitution are central.

Between instinct and intelligence there is no necessary conflict: the one is concerned with final goals, the other with attaining them – then consolidating the solutions through learning and teaching. But, though those who emphasize biological findings never doubt the vast importance of learning they are far less likely to encounter the reciprocal view among either behaviourists or sociologists. Yet, emphatic as the rejections of biological data and hypotheses may be, the underlying reasons for disregarding them are frequently remarkably weak.

Counterarguments which depend more upon alternative speculations couched in terms like 'conceivably', 'it may be', 'quite possibly', 'probably' than upon contradictory empirical evidence are seldom convincing, and to claim a rebuttal on the grounds that 'there is no conclusive proof' is absurd in relation to an inductive science like psychology. There can only ever be relatively more confirmatory evidence for one proposition than another. The 'all is learned' theory cannot itself be 'proved' nor, it must be said, does the balance of evidence favour such an exclusive theory.

Still, no one is likely to disagree that, except in some very rare instances, the form and expression of human sexual behaviour is very dependent upon social and cultural learning. Custom and laws regulate all sexual encounters to some degree; this control being variously justified on grounds as diverse as religious, philosophical and political beliefs as well as the practical need for society to deal effectively with rape and other sexual outrages.

Societies vary in the scope and emphasis of their control but there can hardly be a single piece of sex-related behaviour that has not been subject to strict rules, often enforced with astonishingly harsh penalties. That rape should be treated severely is to be expected, in view of the violation and humiliation of the victim, and the very precarious future created for any child which might be so conceived. But control and punishment do not stop at situations where the safety of individuals is concerned; they are also very apparent wherever it is thought, rightly or wrongly, that the individual's soul, or society itself, is imperilled.

In the Western world particularly, the rules of society have tended to develop from those of organized religion. The Bible itself, beginning with the 'Garden of Eden' and continuing through Sodom and Gomorrah to the New Testament, has identified innumerable varieties of sexual behaviour to be condemned. Sex and sin have been associated ideas for so long now that it is still difficult to disentangle them. But worse, such was the political power of the church that sins also became civil offences and their perpetrators had to contend with gaolers and executioners as well as an avenging god. Small wonder then that sexual anxieties and neuroses ultimately came to occupy the place they did in the minds of Inquisitors and Victorian ladies alike.

Unfortunately, once a law relating to moral behaviour is enacted, it becomes extremely difficult to discard. One reason for this is that change necessitates people speaking in favour of something others still regard as an offence or sin, and this can be a dangerous business. History shows that the reformer is always likely to be accused of special pleading on behalf of his own inclinations and charged and punished for either committing the offence himself, or else for seditiously supporting it. That one does not have to be, say, a homosexual or a fellow-traveller to argue that homosexuals should not be sent to prison may seem obvious enough nowadays but this was far from the case when people began to argue for a reform of that particular law.

So, though the power of religion has greatly diminished in recent years, a wide variety of *sins* which became legal offences still remain as such. Even now, we are far from free to do what we choose with our own bodies, and much less free in some places than others.

No doubt as a result of its very diverse cultural and religious origins, and the extensive possibilities for variety in law-making created by its state legislatures, the United States still has some of the most surprising laws governing sexual behaviour. For example, in some states pre-marital petting is a criminal offence and other heterosexual non-coital activities, such as anal intercourse or oral-genital contacts, are also criminal – even within marriage. Fornication – sexual intercourse by an unmarried person – is also an offence in some areas and mutual masturbation, whether within or between sexes, is also a criminal act in some places.

It has often been remarked that the laws of any society, in

addition to their function of protecting the individual from violence, fraud and exploitation, are also strongly indicative of the special interests and ideology of its ruling classes; mirroring their fears and revealing their methods of controlling the ruled. If this is so, then it is quite apparent that the body in general, and its sexual aspects in particular, were among the major preoccupations of our predecessors: a not entirely surprising fact in view of the social, economic and religious significance of reproduction, particularly when one considers the peculiar mixture of cultural origins and experiences from which Western society developed.

We usually think of our cultural roots as going back to Greece and Rome; and indeed they do, particularly in relation to the way society has developed since the Renaissance. But it was Jewish culture, and the Christian church that grew from it, which proved most influential in shaping our moral outlook. In his book, *Love Locked Out*, James Cleugh has recorded the stages and many of the episodes through which sexuality was first institutionalized, then debased, and finally corrupted in the name of a 'higher' love. In it, he traces the people and events most responsible for the condemnation of physical pleasure, and shows how far extremist spiritual aims brought ruin rather than redemption to great numbers of people, not only throughout the Western world, but wherever else its representatives exerted an influence. It makes fascinating reading, but it is much more than an engrossing, if grizzly, account of past events; it also illuminates and explains much of the present.

Jews of the later pre-Christian period were already highly repressive of even the most normal sexual behaviour – nudity itself being sinful and masturbation a major crime. Then the early Jewish Christians encountered an additional set of circumstances which were to interact with their already established attitudes and beliefs, leading to an even more inhibited attitude towards the body as a source of pleasure and gratification. From the first century onwards, they had to contend with the appalling Roman carnality and sadism of that period, often with themselves as its object. Perversions, sexual 'games', immolations, castrations, and other mutilations were commonplace: the Circus Maximus provided spectacles of death and agony, and local prostitutes were in great demand to quench the passions fired by these public degradations of the human body.

As prime targets of perverts such as Caligula or Nero, these early Christians naturally became even more inclined to condemn the cult of physically-based pleasures. Gladiatorial display, 'games', orgies, and sexual delights all became the natural enemy of this increasingly influential people – whose own code of sexual modesty and restraint proved strong enough to survive not only the pressures of this corrupt empire but the chaos created by its final collapse. All of which is admirable but, unfortunately, the sexual attitudes inherent in the Judaeo-Christian teachings came to be interpreted with an ever-increasing zeal and harshness by the early Church Fathers.

Masturbation continued as a major sin, and complex penitential codes were drawn up to punish and regulate any and all forms of sexual pleasure. Even married sex was discouraged by the introduction of days of the week – Monday, Wednesday and Friday – during which copulation was forbidden, and additional prohibitions were also attached to certain religious festivals and duties. Anything other than basic procreation, preferably as unpleasurable as possible, became an anathema.

Sex from the rear was prohibited, not because it is the almost universal pattern by which animals copulate, but on the grounds that it offered greater pleasures than face-to-face coitus. It might, for example, have allowed the man to use his penis and hands to arouse his partner more effectively: stimulating her clitoris or breasts more fully might very well have led to much greater satisfaction and a desire to repeat the experience more often. That was, of course, entirely to be avoided.

In spite of its deep cultural roots, scientists of a more biological cast of mind are, it seems, all too likely to underestimate the significance of such powerful social moulding when discussing contemporary sexual behaviour in general, and the relative prevalence of female orgasm in particular. Deeply ingrained customs, habits and taboos are not discarded easily, and though sexual statistics may be based on samples drawn from all over the world, it should be remembered that the ubiquitous missionaries carried with them, in addition to trousers, dresses and the church's more general rules and dogma, the 'missionary position' – often with a confessional through which acquiesence to the required sexual patterns could be monitored and enforced.

In every possible way, the Church Fathers attempted to devalue physical, and particularly sexual, pleasures. The female body became a special focus of their attention, both as a deplorable source of earthly delight and as the origin of mortal, anti-spiritual, flesh itself. St Augustine summed up the church's distaste for the whole process in his observation 'We are all born between urine and faeces.' This sort of deprecation of women's maternal functions, and the even more offensive propaganda against the female body, describing it as unclean and disgusting, found expression over and over again – as in Tertullian's portrayal of women as 'a temple built over a sewer'. The crushing effect on women's self-image can easily be imagined: that their self-respect and confidence should be deeply undermined, and that their sexual behaviour and feelings should become profoundly subdued, is hardly to be wondered at.

The fact that women were singled out for special disparagement although male arrangements are hardly very different is, presumably, due to the church inheriting an ancient Old Testament tradition in which women were always regarded as inferior. However, it also reflects the power of female attractions to deflect men from their spiritual aims – for which celibacy was thought virtually mandatory. Some of the Church Fathers obviously felt this threat to their resolve very keenly. St Paul often wrote of his own passions, and the need of all Christians to suppress them if they were to avoid lasciviousness and uncleanliness.

Origen or Alexandria had earlier castrated himself to quell temptation, but even this extraordinary course of action was scarcely more drastic than the unnatural and repressive policies demanded in the church's interminable rhetoric on behalf of sexual curtailment. Anatole France once commented, 'Of all sexual aberrations, chastity is the strangest.' Whether one agrees with this or not, the celibacy and hatred of flesh fostered as a central aim of Christian policy undoubtedly had some very strange and paradoxical consequences – many of which would, no doubt, have been to the great delight and amusement of the pagan Romans.

Sexual abstinence, with its consequent build-up of tensions, brings with it dreams and fantasies which, psychoanalysts say, represent repressed wishes and desires trying to find expression. For priests and nuns denied masturbation, and even punished for the involuntary nocturnal emissions they were obliged to confess, there was little chance of significant sexual release without accepting an intolerable amount of guilt. So, anxiety-ridden and caught in an impossible dilemma, the response of many was predictable – neurotic defence mechanisms.

Where *sublimation* failed, though every avenue from work and brotherly love to a passionate adoration of God and the Virgin might be tried, more disruptive mechanisms tended to flourish. For the most part, such disorders were probably only personally distressing but they sometimes seem to have followed a decidedly paranoid pattern, and one which proved widespread enough to have serious consequences for others.

Taking the defence mechanisms apparent in the paradigm case, *denial* of lust was followed by a *projection* of their own unconscious desires and fantasies onto others, as though that is where they originated. Then, as a *reaction formation*, their unconscious desires, now externalized as originating in others, led on to behaviour which was, in some respects, diametrically opposed to their own repressed desires. However, as we shall see, this paradoxical behaviour actually allowed the condemners a considerable and astonishing freedom to express a compound of both their repressed carnality and the pent-up aggressions which sexual guilt and frustrations had exacerbated. As a final step, they *rationalized* the behaviour which achieved their unconscious goals; justifying their actions in acceptable terms. In short, they unleashed the Inquisition and witch-hunting.

Heinrich Kramer and Jacob Sprenger, the two main architects of the Holy Inquisition, projected their own incredible fantasies and beliefs directly at womankind who, they claimed, are so sexually insatiable that they can easily fall prey to the devil. Satan, it was believed, had so great a libido, and so remarkable and gratifying a penis, that sex-hungry women might trade their immortal souls for congress with him. The guidelines set down in their book *Malleus Maleficarum* for interrogating suspected witches were, therefore, markedly concerned with sexuality: a fact with justified intensive examination of not only their victim's beliefs and behaviour, but their bodies as well. Indeed, witch-hunting proved to be the ideal vehicle for the repressed and sexually obsessed to shed the guilt of their own fantasies and desires, while proving their purity.

Men were by no means exempted from these examinations but it was women who were the main target, and who most commonly had to endure being stripped and inspected in the most minute detail. Signs of the devil's mark were sought in every crevice, including the vagina and anus, and needles pushed through tissues and organs to ascertain whether or not the devil had affected them. Then more severe tortures were applied until the wretched victim confirmed her tormentors' fantasies – and added a little more for good measure – plus the names of others said to belong to her coven. And so the cycle went on until tens of thousands had been 'inspected', degraded, tortured and killed. Perhaps, after all, the

Roman reaction would not have been so much one of amusement as of wonder and admiration that all this could be done, not only in good conscience, but as the sign of a higher idealism.

Of course, the Inquisition and witch-hunts were amongst the most spectacular manifestations of gross sexual repression but there were others, particularly amongst those individuals and groups subject to the more severe forms of sexual control. For example, the convents and monasteries of Europe witnessed many equally astonishing outbursts of sexually-motivated hysteria and neurosis. Some, like the sixteenth century Carmelite nun, Maria Magdelena of Pazzi, had herself tied up, and her naked buttocks whipped before the others, ostensibly as an act of penitence, though she vigorously deplored the state of ecstasy it also brought. This too was no doubt an excuse for further punishment!

Sometimes, whole communities were caught up in the acting out of their corporate sexual neurosis: hysterical outbursts, with the most lewd behaviour, were not uncommon and the mental strain of strict sexual control, in word, deed and thought, continued to take its toll on individuals as one of the most burdensome and wretched aspects of the cloistered or clerical life.

Had the problems remained with those who created them, the church's anti-sex attitudes would have been of no more than minor historical significance. But the influence of church teachings also permeated society, affecting relationships not only between individuals, but also between people and their own bodies. And though religious beliefs may have waned, the social customs and attitudes forged so long ago continue to exert their influence on the present. Indeed, for many people, morality is still a matter of sexual behaviour and, for the actual or would-be reformers and censors of film and television, the sight of a naked body is still widely regarded as much more obscene than spectacles of torture, violence and murder.

Things change more slowly than we might sometimes think, in the world of morals if not technology, and we are heirs to all that has gone before. In many respects, the past explains the present and will probably continue to shape the future – despite all attempts to modify its influence. We inherit not only a biological past, but also a cultural one, and it may be that the latter is even more resistant to change than the former.

A member of my own family attended a convent boarding school where, to her near disbelief, she discovered that regarding one's own body was still strictly prohibited. Even baths had to be taken with only the upper or lower half uncovered at any one time; special garments being provided for the purpose. It appears that just the sight of one's own naked body may lead to the sin of pride, or even to lustful and voluptuous behaviour which was far too sinful and shameful to be more than hinted at. Again, the example is unusual and the behaviour extreme, but the underlying attitude of unease and moral distrust of nakedness is still surprisingly prevalent, even in the liberated 1980s.

Avoiding seeing one's own naked body is almost certainly very rare, yet actively looking at it and examining the sexual organs is still taboo for many people. Similar reticence is also apparent in interpersonal relationships: many couples are far too deeply embarrassed to make love other than in the dark. Unfortunately, representative statistics for these behaviours, or lack of them, are hard to come by: estimates vary, but studies show that a not inconsiderable number of people have never seen the sexual organs of their partner.

This degree of modesty, at its most formalized once achieved by means of the *chemise cagoule* – a nightdress with a hole through which the penis could be inserted – may not survive too much longer in competition with the new sexual morality, but it is still perfectly normal to feel bashful when naked before the opposite sex. There is, of course, an understandable anxiety about the other's reaction, but the major cause of diffidence is probably that most of us have been taught from infancy onwards to conceal our vital areas from the opposite sex: breaches of this code bringing shame and punishment. So we are likely to experience severe conflicts: sexual behaviour requires the most intimate contact, and our curiosity and libido drive us forward but, even in the socially sanctioned institution of marriage, there is an almost inevitable contradiction between what we have learned and what we want and must do. For some, concealment within darkened rooms or in nightclothes which act as variations on the chemise cagoule may serve, but for most it is usual to seek some mutually satisfying balance between a total veiling of the body and its complete exposure in bright light. Other considerations aside, people often discover that, beyond a certain point, the erotic appeal of normally clothed parts is negatively correlated with their level of illumination, and that some sort of compromise arrangement is more attractive and arousing.

And compromise it seems likely to be for, though we have so far emphasized only the promulgation and learning of what may seem pathologically prudish attitudes and beliefs, there is another side to the matter. Without suggesting for a moment that the anti-sex, anti-flesh ideas discussed earlier were anything but socially and psychologically dangerous, as well as absurd, it is rare that such powerful movements entirely lack a broad public sympathy at some period in their development. Just as Fascism required public assent before it could reach a position of strength in which extremists were able to dictate policies which went far beyond anything envisaged by most people so, it seems, the church's excessive anti-nudity programme might also have been built on pre-existing inclinations.

Religion has undoubtedly been a major instrument for the enforcement and escalation of modesty but, it has been argued, the basic impulse was already present as a natural and innate characteristic of our species. In his book *The Expression of the Emotions in Man and Animals*, Darwin had noted that human beings are the only species that blushes: monkeys may flush with passion, but only humans have evolved a distinctive bodily reaction to a purely subjective state – shame. And though he was not particularly concerned with breaches in codes of sexual modesty, Darwin nevertheless did acknowledge that they were among the more common and world-wide causes of shame and blushing.

Explorations in the most remote corners of our planet have continued to confirm earlier anthropological observations – that there are very few societies which do not regulate sexual exposure very rigorously. Even in the most naked tribes, the vagina is usually concealed by a foot whilst women are sitting in company, though leaves or aprons are more common, and almost all men manifest a sense of shame at their nakedness in some situations. Moreover, the withdrawal of couples from the view of others to have intercourse is a universal phenomenon even among the most unclothed groups. In his book *The Evolution of Modesty*, Havelock Ellis summed the situation up by writing 'All such facts serve to show that, though the forms of modesty may change, it is yet a very radical constituent of human nature in all states of civilization, and that it is, to a large extent, maintained by the mechanism of blushing.'

How far blushing actually maintains or regulates modesty behaviour by simply signifying contraventions is another matter, but that some sort of connection occurs is beyond question. Yet, though blushing is commonly related to sexual display, this is only one of the many circumstances in which it can occur. It may just as easily be brought about by acts of greed, dishonesty, cowardice, meanness, and indeed any feelings or behaviour that run contrary to our moral sense. Generally though, the most ruddy appearance occurs only when we are caught *in flagrante*: the object of someone else's judgement.

However, there are many occasions when blushes have no obvious connection with moral infractions of any kind. For example, when we behave stupidly, clumsily, or find ourselves singled out before a gathering of other people, we may 'blush for shame' or say that we feel 'completely naked'. The expression itself is an interesting one, showing as it does the way in which nudity before others is often equated with feelings of shame and vulnerability, and with fear of ridicule, contempt or rejection by others.

So, sexuality involving exposure of the physical self can bring together two somewhat different sources of anxiety. In the first place, there may be moral conflict arising from the incompatibility of our desires, ego ideals and ethical codes. Secondly, there may be apprehension about our actual physical exposure. As Simone de Beauvoir notes in her book *Nature of the Second Sex*, shame is always a likely reaction when we find that we have become an object to another person.

We therefore stand doubly vulnerable and naked in the sexual encounter. Our behaviour, attractiveness and attributes of masculinity or femininity are all quite literally laid bare for appraisal and criticism: sensitive and normally well shielded aspects of ourselves, ones which have been invested with the most profound personal significance, must be disclosed. So some degree of anxiety and reticence is entirely to be expected though whether, as some scientists have suggested, sexual modesty also depends upon an innate impulse is another matter.

In the event, the argument that modesty and concealment of the genital and other physically attractive areas is an innately governed mental barrier against casual impersonal sex has often been made, and generally along the following lines. We are a species in which successful breeding has always, to the best of our knowledge, depended upon pair-bonding: that is, two people contracted to one another not only for sexual purposes but also for mutually responsible participation in child-rearing. Other primates have developed along different, less successful, lines but our own tendency to treat sex as part of a contract implying certain onerous duties has, as population figures show, already proved itself a survival advantage – though it may yet prove to be too effective in view of our other successes in technology and medicine. That, however, is another issue: the biological success of parents is measured in raising their young, not in terms of future global economics.

To achieve this pair-bonding, something more than an object-relationship is required and, in order that a free giving of the self should take place, evidence of caring, affecting and constancy might well be a prerequisite. An important part of this process, it has been argued, involves some degree of modesty and restraint, which may not only indicate the special psychological nature of the couple's activity, but act as a sexual attractant also. Dependent upon context, the blush may be part of this attraction: indeed, a female's blushes have long been the delight of males – so long, that is, as they are not accompanied by too much restraint or inhibitedness. But certainly, brash sexual advances by either sex are seldom regarded as stimulating: generally, it is just the opposite. So, most sexual encounters are marked by a gradual revelation of the physical self, often by means of petting, which becomes progressively more intimate as the couple begin to establish their relationship.

There are, of course, great cultural differences in sexual conventions, just as there are in every other aspect of interpersonal behaviour. Even the major areas for concealment from the other sex vary from culture to culture: as, for example, in the case of Egyptian women whose modesty was often a cause of shock or else delight to visitors who discovered that it depended much more upon covering their face than hiding the rest of their body. But whatever the main focus, some sort of physical concealment, breaches of which are connected with a sense of embarrassment, shame or guilt, is typically human. And this is particularly characteristic of the female who, until recently when effective contraceptives became available, was under far more pressure to limit her sexual invitations until she had received reassurances that the male was committed enough to share the consequences of their mating. Naturally, there have always been plenty of exceptions to the general rule but, for the majority, only then could disclosure taboos be completely suspended without guilt, though embarrassment due to being the object of someone else's gaze might take some time to overcome.

On such grounds as these, a case has been made out that, particularly in so far as females are concerned, reticence and physical concealment of parts of the body from the opposite sex is an innate as well as a learned impulse, and one based on the soundest possible survival and evolutionary grounds. But the universality of behaviour is no guarantee of its instinctive origin so, until a more conclusive case is advanced, many prefer to believe that such behaviours and dispositions are of an entirely social or practical, rather than an evolutionary, origin. Even if the behaviour which has characterized our species for so long has been evolved for survival purposes, there can still be no conclusive evidence that it is innate: it may only be part of the cultural evolution by which mankind has come to code behaviours in language and learning rather than genes and chromosomes.

But to return to the question of sexual modesty: to the feelings of bashfulness most of us experience when we arrive at the point of disrobing as part of the sexual encounter. Whether or not biological factors are involved, it is quite certain that personal as well as cultural ones are: for, in addition to the particular rules of modesty impressed on us, we are each subject to idiosyncratic anxieties arising from our body and self-images.

In the last chapter, we devoted a good deal of attention to the ways in which body-image can create anxieties and deeply affect our sense of self-esteem. The exposure of areas of specific sexual interest is particularly capable of creating some of the more acute disruptions and, though people may differ in this respect, there can be relatively few who have not suffered from disagreeable and unsettling anxieties about their sexual features at one time or another.

However, anxiety and distress do not only occur in relation to the opposite sex; either or both may just as easily take place as a reaction to the presence of anybody at all. Even a medical examination, where one believes the doctor or nurse to be quite detached, may be an occasion of acute embarrassment, depending upon the particular principles of modesty absorbed during our early development, and the way they have expanded since. But in addition to these broad attitudinal considerations, specific feelings about the superiority, acceptability, or inferiority of our appearance, may also be involved in our response to disrobing.

Again, research is difficult to undertake, and is still too sparse to be of much help when it comes to explaining why certain people bare their bodies with great casualness, or even delight, while others suffer miserably when they must do so. Among the many problems presented is the fact that people's attitudes to nakedness are not uniform in all circumstances and sex-mixtures. Moreover, the compound of cultural, social and personality variables working on formative experiences may be of such complexity as to deny simplifications. After all, the determining elements – the individual's accepted attitudes towards physical display and the negativeness or positiveness of his own body image, may vary quite independently of one another.

In the end, we can say little more than that though people with definite doubts about their sexual features are seldom eager to expose them, it does not follow that those who are without such feelings are any the less reluctant. A sense of physical inferiority may, in many instances, be a sufficient cause of inhibited behaviour, but it is not always a necessary one. However, too much attention to the effect of moral codes would carry this present inquiry far beyond its intended scope: instead, it will be more appropriate to consider the physical foci of negative or positive self-regard, and trace the origin and cause of some of these feelings.

But, before dealing with the most intimate sexual areas, it is as well to remember that physical attractiveness is complex; depending not only upon particular features but an overall impression, mental as well as physical. Tenderness, wit, intelligence, practical abilities and achievements, are all of incontrovertible importance in determining appeal and sexual interest. Once again, though, it will be necessary to limit our scope: simply noting that physical factors are never completely independent of the mental characteristics of either the possessor or the beholder.

Strikingly good looks seldom fail to attract some members of the opposite sex, even where the personality leaves much to be desired, and even the most unprepossessing looking individuals, may astonish members of their own sex by their apparent allure. So, one has to accept that the interaction of mental and physical characteristics with the widely different tastes of members of the opposite (or same) sex make it very difficult to identify anything which is, in itself, appealing or repulsive. All we can ever do is consider typical reactions, and prepare to be wrong in particular cases.

Nevertheless, we can begin by looking at those physical features which seem most attractive to members of the opposite sex. For the most part, though, these are the same attributes we have already discussed in the previous chapter as affecting even the most non-sexual appraisal of another – for example, face, eyes, hair, complexion and so on. But there are other features which, though they may often be of much less importance in determining allure, are characteristically and specifically related to sexual appeal. Of these, height and shape are two of the most important.

For a man to be below the average height of women, or a woman to be above the average height for men, is a very distinct disadvantage. Whether or not the body in question is perfectly proportioned for its height, the foreseeable problem is the same; women tend to prefer men taller than themselves, and men favour women who are smaller. On the other hand, beyond a certain point, a man's height or a woman's shortness may be equally disadvantageous. For a variety of more or less obvious reasons, extreme statures are likely to be most unacceptable to those members of the opposite sex whose own deviation from the norm is pronouncedly in the opposite direction. But so powerful is the sexual stereotype of attractive men being tall and desirable women petite that even fairly pronounced deviations in this direction tend to be much more acceptable than in the other.

There is seldom a great deal that can be done about height – except in the choice of footwear – but shape can be controlled to a considerable degree, and so made to conform to what is thought pleasing to the opposite sex. There is, however, a catch: what is attractive is not always correctly judged for, though women are fairly accurate in their assessment of what men find attractive about their sex, it seems that men are all too likely to assume women will share their own ideals of masculine good looks.

In their book *Love's Mysteries* Glenn Wilson and David Nias have drawn together a good deal of research concerning sexual appeal, including some interesting studies of what women actually find physically attractive in men. Not altogether surprisingly, when these findings are compared with men's beliefs about what women find sexy, considerable disparities become apparent. For example, a massive muscular frame and big penis are by no means as appealing to most women as is commonly believed by most men. Instead research shows that women's preferences are more likely to be along the lines of slenderness and attractive eyes, and that they are more likely to be repelled by the hairy, muscle-bound torso than admire it. For once, 'male chauvinism' seems an appropriate way to describe the causes of men's misperceptions and ignorance of women's sexual tastes.

In another collection of research sources, *Sexual Attraction* by Mark Cooke and Robert McHenry, the same general conclusions were presented, though they also cite findings which show that, whatever an overall consensus might be, it would be most unwise to underestimate not only individual differences but also social class differences in what is regarded as sexy. It appears that, though middle-class women do prefer tall slim and sensitive types, lower-class women are somewhat inclined towards more heavily muscled men.

However, experimental studies are quite liable to oversimplify matters if we suppose they have clear-cut behavioural implications. Their very structure is often such that they distort or parody the actual ways in which we regard other people and judge their physical attractions. For example, many studies demand preference choices in response to paired presentations of photographs or silhouettes showing alternative combinations of attributes – long or short legs and trunks, large or small buttocks or breasts, and so on. And, so long as experimental subjects are prepared to co-operate in this way, it is quite simple to produce percentage statistics for such choices; even, as has been done in some studies, making elaborate comparisons between age groups, social classes, those with sporting versus those with non-sporting interests, and groups who differ markedly in artistic, intellectual or social interests.

The trouble is though, it is virtually impossible to assess their real-life significance. The fact that a certain percentage of, say, young American, middle-class, college-educated women prefer the silhouettes of men with slender torsos and legs, whereas a quite differently constituted group have a greater tendency to opt for a heavier build is not very illuminating – in either theoretical or practical terms. Of course, one can identify the characteristic statistical distributions and stereotypical responses of different groups, but evaluating these findings is another matter entirely.

The empirical results are commonsensical enough; it seeming perfectly reasonable to expect that a particular bodily configuration might be more admired and sought-after among potential mates of one group than of another. And it is virtually self-evident that the possession of certain physical attributes is likely to give someone a head start with the opposite sex – all else being equal. But, 'all else' is seldom equal, and when a slender figure or handsome face is competing against a lively wit, a generous nature or the appeal of economic or professional success, who can tell what significance to attach to physical attributes?

An attractive physique may find favour, but without obtaining any sexual advantage: after all, we do not necessarily wish to marry, or even become involved with those we find most physically seductive. Physical attraction may facilitate encounters which are little more than impersonal discharges of sexual excitement, or it may be an important basis for a durable mate selection. The whole spectrum of possibilities occurs in every meeting where there is some attraction between a couple, but it seems that there is no simple and universal formula for determining the specific value of physical factors in the equation for sexual attraction.

Moreover, even the statistical norms and stereotypes of what constitutes physical attraction are far from immutable. For example, at a particular time and in a particular culture, fatness or thinness may be more desirable; just as filed teeth, tattooed bodies, and pierced lips may seem either to heighten or destroy good looks. Universal standards just do not exist and, if it seemed that they did, history and anthropology would provide abundant examples of their impermanence and relativity.

However, though judgements of beauty are as dependent upon the shifting ideals of culture as upon the particular person making them, conceptions of physical loveliness do seem to be variations played on a very definite theme. For, despite the great cultural differences which have marked some of the high points of Indian, Oriental and European development, their ideals of feminine comeliness have not been so very different. Conventional womanly beauty, whether represented in Tantric, Taoist or Greek art was remarkably similar, and would still be regarded as lovely by most modern men.

But, having said this, it is also quite apparent that there is now a stereotype for attractiveness in women which is widely current in advanced societies: a convergence of taste which closely parallels the development of modern forms of visual mass-communication. They may not have created these tastes, but the cinema, television and advertising media have certainly done a great deal to influence, exaggerate and shape them.

Though the process has been going on since Victorian times, the last few decades have witnessed a remarkably growing rejection of that ampleness of form so fondly celebrated by such painters as Rubens, Rembrandt and Renoir. Voluptuousness is apparently not compatible with women's new ideal image of themselves: a more athletic, rather boyish outline, is preferred – one which minimizes hips yet highlights breasts as tight, firm, forward-thrusting affirmations of sexuality rather than maternity.

The complex sociological events leading to these changes in taste and behaviour are far from clear but it does seem that, though their momentum may be sustained and accelerated by professional image-makers, their origin owes much more to women's aspiration to fill a more vigorous and assertive role in society. Consequently, standards of feminine beauty have tended to become manifestations of this new womanly ideal: soft, delicate and yielding characteristics giving way to a more trim and sporty standard.

The torso seems to have become the main object of conformity pressures: to be judged beautiful by the most recent criteria, a woman's trunk must not only by firm and slender but, ideally, her hips should be smaller than her breasts. The problem is, though, the ideal is at variance with nature: women are just not built this way. There are variations from country to country but, based on norms compiled by clothing manufacturers, and these just have to be accurate, it would seem that most younger women's hips average between two and three inches more than the bust measurement.

Moreover, the process of ageing and 'middle-aged spread' tends to make this ratio of bust-to-waist-to-hip even less close to the ideal. Those who do conform to the 'pin-up' standards of 37–24–35 – large bust, narrow waist, small hips and buttocks – are great rarities; particularly so if their figures are not dependent upon severe regimes of diet and exercise. Under normal circumstances, most women tend towards the opposite configuration: that is, hips bigger than bust.

So, the model-girls used in fashion, advertising, 'centre-fold' and men's magazines; and the actresses chosen, and moulded for their approximation to the new pattern of desirability, are demonstrably quite atypical. Yet, through the distorting impact of the media, they have managed to suggest a norm against which ordinary people are now judging and being judged. As a result, most women find themselves confronted with an unattainable pattern which, even if it is approachable through dieting and exercise or the use of girdles and padded bras, must remain a receding goal over the life span.

Irrespective of how it came into being, or how forces combined to form the current model of feminine beauty, a definite new standard has emerged: one which places great emphases on slimness and breast development. And women, in so far as they do or do not approximate to this often incompatible requirement, are likely to experience enhancement of diminution in the quality of their body-image and self-esteem.

Of course, men are by no means exempt from the desirable stereotypes so assiduously promoted by the media. The ideal of a tall, firm-chinned, rangy figure with broad shoulders and narrow hips haunts them in just the same way. But, though men are no more likely to approximate to the idealized form of their sex than are women, the consequences of this are not just the same in each case.

Rightly or wrongly, women are specially likely to feel that their physical appearance will have a much greater effect on their sexual and marriage opportunities than it does in the case of men. It may not be an acceptable principle nowadays but, however one reacts to it, it is probably quite realistic: men have always tended to place a greater emphasis on the looks of women than women have on the externals of men, and there is still little evidence of this changing to any great degree. For all sorts of practical reasons, women have *had* to take a broader view of their spouses' attributes when confronted with the facts of marriage and having a family. They have always been more inclined to look beyond appearances for, by placing their happiness, status, aspirations and potential to explore the wider world of people and places in the hands of another individual, they have had to be more circumspect. A poor choice of mate may be a misfortune for a man, but it is more likely to be a disaster for a woman.

Social arrangements are now changing rapidly and, with it, women's attitudes to everything – including sex and marriage. Just the same is true of men for, though their risks and restrictions might not have been so great, they too appear ever less inclined to relinquish personal and economic freedom. Consequently, unless there is a desire to have children, or individuals find themselves wanting in close companionship, the major problem becomes making satisfactory sexual arrangements.

So, as the traditional links between sex, marriage and raising a family weaken, and sexual encounters become briefer and more casual, it seems entirely likely that the bases upon which people are attracted towards one another may shift such that physical attributes become progressively more salient as determinants than they have been in the past. One consequence of this may be greater sensitivity and anxiety about our appearance: another is that we may set ourselves unrealistic standards or allow others to do so.

Of course idealized goals can serve useful ends if they are attainable but, if they are not, and if they are held or promoted too vigorously, they are all too likely to create distressing feelings of inadequacy and failure. This is particularly the case when the subject of these promotions concerns people's sexual attractiveness for, on this, depends so many hopes of love, family and security.

Unfortunately though, sex and sexual attractiveness have become prime areas for the creation of unrealistic standards. The cinema has been particularly responsible for establishing the desirable image of men and women, while television reinforces these notions and advertising, employing every known artifice of the persuasive and graphic arts, has achieved a dizzying new height of illusions and fantasy. Reality, with its wrinkles, warts and all, can hardly be expected to seem anything other than flawed when compared against these completely artificial standards of physical excellence.

Love scenes on the media are almost invariably played out between handsome or beautiful men and women: bald, flat-chested, or chubby people are seldom represented – except as objects of humour or malice. To be any of these things is, at the very least, to suspect one is unattractive. And this is where the mischief lies – in the way it undermines people's self-concept and self-esteem. Cosmetics, hairdressing and dress can do a great deal to help but they may prove sadly inadequate devices, particularly when it comes to the final stages of sexual encounter.

At this point, with props and many defences inoperative, a sense of inferiority and shame in the face of prevailing stereotypes and ideals becomes entirely likely for even the most normal individual. And, for those more susceptible to the media's influence, bogus and romantic images of what constitutes attractiveness in their own and the opposite sex may be so firmly fixed that self-denigration, disappointment or, in the most extreme cases, disgust for themselves or their partner is an altogether quite possible outcome.

No doubt most people have a sufficient degree of realism, and enough robust sensuality, to overcome the worst effects created by the glamorized illusions of professional image makers. Yet, though romantic notions about what is attractive and appropriate may be exaggerated by the media, they are not invented by them. All advanced civilizations have created standards and customs specifically intended to enhance the charm or mystery of one sex for the other.

Social arrangements of lavatories, changing rooms, dress and other customs are all aimed at preventing the sexes from developing too great an objectivity or candour in physical matters. Fancy is encouraged and down-to-earth frankness is definitely discouraged in the intuitive belief that reality is not the friend of lovers: that the body is essentially unattractive, and that restraint, modesty and embellishment result in a more tender, respectful and satisfying relationship than could be achieved otherwise.

So, most modern people find themselves beset by opposing pressures: on the one side are those urging an increasing degree of openness; on the other are those which act to preserve traditionally valued conventions governing bodily exposure. At present, the forces supporting frank display seem to be in the ascendant: nude bathing beaches and the commonplace presentation of nudity in magazines, films and television seem to suggest that concealment is on the way out.

Yet the inroads made are still less deep than they may sometimes appear: genital display, though permitted on nudist beaches, continues to be widely resisted as being crude, offensive and disgusting and is still likely to be punished when it occurs outside of certain authorized places. Even exposure of the breasts remains a rare and generally strongly discouraged act. The body, it seems, is as equivocal a subject as it has ever been.

As we have already discussed, the power of custom, habit and ethical-religious beliefs is of immense importance in maintaining these public attitudes, despite the countervailing attractions of newer ideologies of openness. However, as we shall see in the next chapter, our ambivalence is far from being due only to conflicting ideas or usages. Much may indeed be due to such clashes, but it has also become clear that a good deal of reticence is of a far more earthy origin: the result of fears and anxieties about the nature and acceptability of our bodies, and particularly the genitals.

Nevertheless, physically-based explanations of sexual behaviour are by no means limited to such obvious considerations. Patterns of sexual behaviour involve the whole personality so, by examining the underlying physical basis of certain mental characterisitcs, sexuality can be seen as but one aspect of a much wider body-mind whole. Some of these ideas are no less controversial than those of Freud, though their material is more frequently culled from genetics or neurology than from detailed analysis of case histories. But, because they shed light on a number of otherwise puzzling occurrences and correlations, they too will receive extensive discussion in the chapter which follows.

Chapter four
SEX AND SEXUALITY: SPECIFICS

Nowhere is the association between self-esteem and body-image more severely and directly tested than in relation to sexual feelings and behaviour. In such circumstances, our nakedness is laid open to others for their judgement, and their reactions cannot but be of the greatest importance to how secure and self-assured we feel.

Sexual encounters are often described as confrontations: no doubt because this kind of face-to-face meeting is inherently challenging to our self-concept, making us more than usually likely to behave in a tense or even hostile and defiant way, at least until we have managed to reassure one another. In due course, wide experience or familiarity with a particular partner will diminish the acute anxiety that was experienced at first, but these feelings are easily re-evoked. Changes in our body-image, whether objectively justified or not; a feeling that we are being unfavourably compared with someone else; or any of an almost infinite number of other reasons can, with surprising ease, transform the most familiar relationship back into a painful physical confrontation.

Ambivalence, swings from pleasure to pain, and sometimes a puzzling and paradoxical fusion of feelings seem to be the hallmark of everything connected with love and sex. In this, the body is never likely to be considered an exception even though, publicly at least, we only tend to stress its pleasurable aspects. And, of course, just because we lay so great an emphasis on delights and gratification, we are likely to create more pain and dissatisfaction than need be.

An egocentric quest after sexual pleasure is perhaps no different from any other form of selfishness for, in so far as personal advantage and satisfaction is the main criterion, other people are likely to be exploited and even hurt. However, sexual exploitation is particularly unfortunate as our very sense of dignity and humanity is often tied up with our sexuality and sex role.

One gets some indication of this from responses to sexual indignities and humiliations, like being raped or stripped, where the experience is often thought far more excruciating than the pain inflicted by other forms of physical aggression.

Naturally, attacks involving the genitals can lead to a good deal of ordinary physical pain: the vagina may be made sore or even lacerated and the testicles are notoriously sensitive to rough handling. But a more keenly felt and lasting part of the distress may be due to the fact of laying the person bare as it degrades them, opening them to abuse and ridicule, and turns them into an object for others. In some cases there may be real fears as to what damage may be done to the body, but it seems that most anguish derives from the unusually deep sense of violation and defilement created by such assaults.

The experience of rape has been widely reported and is nowadays widely discussed, particularly as part of the feminist movement's concern with finding ways to prevent it happening. However, when it does, they are equally concerned to make sure that appropriate psychological support and counselling is given, and that one set of criminal humiliations is not followed by an almost equally insensitive series of legal ones.

Sadism and other forms of sexual perversion directed at the unwilling are less well publicly understood, though books like Colin Wilson's *Origins of the Sexual Impulse* have made a very good job of simplifying the somewhat daunting technical literature which has been accumulating at an accelerating rate since the time of Freud and Havelock Ellis. This chapter is not concerned with gross abnormalities of this kind; nevertheless it is as well to bear in mind that, such is the potential for harm of everything connected with sex, that even apparently quite mild affronts or insults to its bodily structures may be quite traumatic, have wide ramifications, and remarkably long-term consequences.

For the male, the penis is one of his major sources of ambivalence. If it is large and well-formed or, more importantly, thought by its possessor to be so, then it may be a great source of pride and self-confidence. If, on the other hand, it is felt to be undersized or unusual in any way, then it may cause a great deal of anxiety and negative self-esteem. In such cases, the individual may become shy and bashful in the presence of his own or the other sex; careful to conceal his penis, and fearful of situations which may lead to its exposure. For the more nervous sort of person, genital anxieties may become quite serious, limiting and inhibiting behaviour in even the most ordinary circumstances.

As in most cases involving self-perception, it transpires that here too objective reality and subjective response to it are far from perfectly correlated. Studies in which men were asked to rate the relative size of their penis showed that more thought them below average than average or above. Statistically, this cannot be so, but it does reveal that a good deal of potentially troublesome doubt exists. Of course, because a supposed inadequacy is felt as a social stigma, there is very little serious discussion of personal feelings related to the penis, but scarcity alone should not be interpreted as any lack of interest or concern. With so many codes of modesty and conduct also involved, it is hardly surprising that the subject should be so widely avoided.

Notwithstanding phallic worship in some parts of the world, the penis is widely thought to be both an obscene and a ridiculous object. In its non-erect state particularly, its shrivelled and drooping appearance could hardly be judged attractive or impressive by any aesthetic standard. Yet despite the fact that this is its normal appearance, it must serve as a badge of gender and, supposedly, as a unique feature with which to lure and excite the female. Small wonder that there are doubts and anxieties about its appearance, particularly when these take the form that it might not metamorphose into its more impressive form in the presence of the other sex.

Impotence, the inability to achieve or sustain an erection through intercourse, undoubtedly has many different origins but anxiety about the woman's reaction to his penis, coupled with the stress of being expected to produce an erection and be able to perform in a certain way, is certainly a major cause of many men's problems. Under such circumstances, some men become so tense and self-conscious that either the erection fails to materialize, or else it does so to some degree that then flags and disappears before ejaculation. Naturally, this is likely to create even greater pressure for the next occasion; often leading to a series of failures in which not only self-esteem suffers badly, perhaps for both sexes, but the relationship itself may founder under the weight of guilt and embarrassment thus created.

Women too may be afflicted in a comparable way. Frigidity,

leading to difficulty in lubricating, vaginal spasms and other tensions which make copulation difficult or impracticable, can also result from serious self-doubts. Fear of being psychologically overwhelmed, or anxiety about being the object of shameful and unwished acts are certainly among the possible causes, as are previous experiences which involved failure, pain or humiliation. But then, sexuality has many more implications for women than for men: it involves not only the actual, if temporary, invasion of her body by someone else but the certainty that a pregnancy will lead to a much more permanent invasion, to pain and service, and to radical transformations of her appearance. Life-style considerations aside, the likely physical consequences of the sex act are obviously much more daunting than men often realize.

Nevertheless, when women encounter practical problems relating to their ability to engage in coitus, they are more readily amenable to treatment than in the case of men. Artificial lubricants make copulation at least possible whereas there is no comparable prosthetic for the penis which will not erect. As a result, it is more difficult for a man with erectile problems to behave normally than it is for a woman with inadequate sexual responses. It is also impossible for the man to overcome his inhibiting anxieties by engaging in intercourse until it becomes a more familiar and reassuring event.

In response to such disruptive problems, and where there is no physiological impediment to hinder progress, sex therapists have recently been applying the principles of conditioning and behaviour modification to their solution. A typical approach would be to teach or advise on relaxation methods and then provide programmes which couples can follow in the privacy of their own homes; moving ever closer towards full copulation by way of gently graded affectionate and erotic behaviours. The object of these programmes being nothing more than to associate each step forward with positive feelings, freed from all pressures to perform.

Extreme examples of this kind of sexual dysfunction, leading people to seek professional treatment, are relatively uncommon but milder manifestations of similar anxieties and incompetencies are not. Clinical impotence and frigidity are only the more obvious tip of a problem which affects great numbers of people, to some degree, during at least some part of their lives.

The precise causes of sexual inadequacy are as varied as the people concerned. Age, boredom, physical debility and body-related anxieties being only some among many. However, one reason why people develop these problems certainly concerns a mismatch or poor synchronization of the couple's activities.

Women have a much greater potential for regular and sustained sexual activity than men and, though this is often an unrealized ability, or is not matched by an equally powerful drive, some women are quite capable of overwhelming their partners with their demands. When this happens, pleasurable lovemaking may be transformed into a challenge to respond, resulting in ever-decreasing enjoyment and an ever-increasing sense of performance stress and resentment. By the same token, incompatible demands made on women may also produce discomfort and provoke irritation, perhaps coupled with excuses and claimed indispositions which, being suspect, a source of frustration, or both, may make all subsequent relations more difficult still.

Sex manuals, following the pattern of Alex Comfort's *The Joy of Sex*, have gone a long way towards educating people on the desirability of using foreplay as a way of extending the sexual encounter such that the slowest reacting member of a couple can almost be assured of an orgasm – before, during, or even after intercourse. Such works have also made people much more aware of the variable physical eroticism of individuals for, though that of women was known to be generally more diffuse than that of men, both sexes manifest wide individual differences.

Men may be able to achieve rapid and sufficient pleasure by means of genital stimulation alone, but this is far less true of women. In their case, such focalized attention may come before they are sufficiently erotically aroused and, even if this does not result in a negative reaction, it may prove inadequate by itself. As a result, where their partners underestimate a woman's needs, many are left frustrated at the end of intercourse.

Worse still many feel an additional pressure to signify their, all too absent, satisfaction and so simulate orgasm to please and reassure their partner. Such mental and physical tension and distress as is so often unwittingly caused need not occur if men understood more about women's bodies. Selfishness will always be a cause in some cases, but ignorance is something which can be corrected if the will is there. Natural as reproduction may be, human sexual behaviour and lovemaking has to be learned. As with anything involving interpersonal relationships, a good deal of knowledge and mutual understanding is required if the individuals concerned are to integrate and synchronize their behaviour so as to optimize their joint satisfaction.

No doubt the current boom in sex manuals has revealed a great deal more about body sensitivity than many people might otherwise have suspected. Individual differences are again quite marked but it seems that appropriate stimulation of quite unlikely areas can give rise to the most intense states of arousal, even release. The extent, and obscurity, of some of this pooled knowledge is such that any one person's ignorance of a good deal of it is not surprising. What is more remarkable is that so many people should, until so recently, have thought so little about the erotic potential of their own, and other people's, bodies.

The explanation is, as was discussed in the last chapter, largely cultural: our own traditions contrasting sharply with those, say, of India. In that country, Vatsyayana's *Kama Sutra* has long enjoyed respectability, and has been recognized as an aid for attaining both mental and physical joy, and then equilibrium. Indeed, as Philip Rawson richly illustrates in his book *Tantra: The Indian Cult of Ecstasy*, sophisticated sexual delights have even been made central to certain Hindu and Buddhist spiritual practices; the interactions of mind, body and spirit being most intricately explored.

But if Western man's ignorance of physical eroticism is not entirely to be wondered at, it is nevertheless still surprising to discover that the potential of even such obvious structures as the female breast should be so poorly understood. Of course, their appeal and effect on men is beyond question: what is extraordinary is that women's own experiences should have been given so little attention up to the present time.

In fact, many men have been surprised to discover that women may experience more pleasure from attention to their breasts than they do themselves: some women even achieve multiple orgasms (which may pass unnoticed by their partners) as a result of his stroking, touching or sucking. Moreover, not a few women use self-stimulation of the nipples as a major part of their masturbation technique.

This latter datum being just one more of the many pieces of information about erotic activity which are only just becoming widely recognized now that such matters are the subject of best selling books like Shere Hite's *The Hite Report*. The surveys upon which such documents are based may, scientifically speaking, leave a good deal to be desired, but they do at least suggest hypotheses for more controlled research and serve to open up delicate subjects for discussion. They would only be seriously misleading if one was unwise enough to extrapolate from such problematical samples to wider populations.

Curiously enough, normal male psycho-sexual behaviour seems to be receiving relatively less attention at the moment: perhaps because the variety and range of their sexual activity was more easily studied at an earlier time, or perhaps because the new interest in all aspects of women's behaviour is directing more attention in these areas. In the event, Shere Hite has again performed a useful service with her more recent book *The Hite Report on Male Sexuality* through drawing attention to, among other things, masturbation as an important facet of sexuality.

The mind-body implications of masturbation have, for the most part, been grossly underrated. It tends to be overlooked that self-stimulation generally involves a sexually arousing fantasy and that the strength of this fantasy is positively reinforced every time the content is associated with a pleasurable orgasm. In consequence, the fantasy will tend to be repeated in similar circumstances and will thus tend to become progressively more highly eroticized.

Violent, perverted, or exhibitionistic themes may well put the individual in serious jeopardy if they gain so powerful a grip on the imagination that they provoke, or sustain, acting out of the behaviour. Treatment too may be virtually impossible unless sex offenders or otherwise sexually disturbed patients can be persuaded to co-operate by modifying their fantasies. For example, the exhibitionist who continues to masturbate to his imaginary self-display scenarios is most unlikely to improve, whatever the therapy. The physical reinforcement of orgasm upon motivation and other mental processes is such that the individual may be drawn back again and again into actions which run contrary to the rest of his, less intensely focused, wishes and scheme of values.

In most cases though, masturbatory imaginings are harmless unless the individual becomes so fixated upon them that they replace normal interpersonal reactions of intercourse. Or worse, the fantasies may become so powerfully eroticized that they can lead to a more or less complete fixation on masturbation because it allows a less distracting concentration on the fantasy.

Alternatively, and much more likely, where masturbation is not comfortably absorbed into the individual's accepted activities, the content or the compulsive repetition of the act may be damaging to self-regard. If either the behaviour or the content are strongly at variance with someone's moral or religious standards, or run contrary to the otherwise established or desired self-image, then a certain amount of distress and even self-contempt is to be expected.

Unfortunately, avoiding such problems is often quite difficult. Where either males or females are lacking in other sexual outlets, or where intercourse outlets with their partners are insufficient in number or unsatisfying in quality, it may prove very hard to abstain from self-stimulation. And, when this happens, there will almost invariably be a favourite accompanying fantasy or scenario: the choice of which may ultimately prove to make the difference between normal adjustment and serious maladjustment.

The consequences of female masturbatory fantasies are more difficult to judge at present. Nancy Friday's book *My Secret Garden* is a recent attempt to illustrate their vast scope, demonstrating that women's fantasies also range from what would generally be regarded as perverted or violent to lascivious or romantic. Naturally, the acting out of female anti-social scenarios tends to be much more difficult than in the case with males, but then their imaginings tend to be far less vicious than those of men in whom anger and fear have been commingled with their sexual feelings. All that can be confidently said at present is that, contrary to most beliefs of a generation or so ago, masturbation and associated exotic fantasies are extremely prevalent among both males and females alike.

In normal face-to-face intercourse, a man's penis very often fails to make much contact with a woman's clitoris and, as this is the major site for her genital arousal, copulation can be very unsatisfying for her – particularly in view of men's much more rapid response, and the likelihood of their reaching climax before their partner has achieved it. Moreover, women are now under great pressure to have orgasms. Books, magazines and talk all make it clear that failure to do so is failure indeed; a great misfortune, even a question mark over their femininity and equality. Consequently, self- and alternative forms of stimulation have a particular attraction for women – even those who are married and having regular intercourse.

Of course, the moral and self-esteem problems often associated with masturbation may merely result in exchanging one type of strain for another. At present, whether such a dilemma exists, and to what extent, is an incompletely answered empirical question. On the basis of her own survey, Shere Hite is inclined to believe that such a predicament is far more apparent than real. The women whose sex lives she probed led her to conclude that masturbation was not only a generally effective method of reducing sexual tensions and appetites, but that it did so with minimal untoward consequences.

On the contrary, masturbation was heralded as a superior form of sexuality: one which great numbers of women may find more ecstatic and satisfying than intercourse. Sexist overtones are everywhere to be found in Shere Hite's pronouncements, and one might suspect special pleading as well as her sampling as contributory to her downgrading of the male role in female sexuality. But this again is an empirical question, and not to be dismissed out of hand just because the evidence yet available is weak, or the conclusion perhaps unwelcome.

Since Kinsey's famous scientific surveys of all aspects of sexual behaviour, and Masters and Johnson's detailed laboratory analyses of the physiological events involved in copulation and masturbation, there has been such a flow of new information that it is proving exceedingly difficult to evaluate and assimilate it. This new candour regarding sexual matters is currently being pursued with some enthusiasm.

Many women, sensing a real opportunity to shed the old restrictions and taboos have been glad to help destroy the pedestals upon which many have been so reluctantly placed by men. By bringing their sexuality out into the light, and by dealing with the fears, guilts and embarrassments which they feel have inhibited and oppressed them for too long, many women hope to exchange negative attitudes and actions for positive ones, creating more joyous and satisfying sexual experiences.

But by no means all women share this view, or the desire to publicize female sexuality. After all, the content of these revelations will be quite alien to many; and many more believe that, even if the disclosures made are absolutely true, it is unseemly to discuss them as they may undermine women's traditional sense of propriety and dignity: not to mention diminishing their sex's mystique and special place in society. Nevertheless, the welter of publications by and for women on the subject of maximizing physical pleasures in masturbation as well as sexual intercourse does indicate a growing tendency to welcome openness and the sharing of experiences which free women to enjoy their bodies without guilt, and without doing so through acting out a stereotyped role.

Each of the various major studies of sexuality has done something to demystify sex and make it a more or less acceptable topic for conversation. The body and its drives are therefore, to some extent at least, beginning to lose something of their old power to mortify and humiliate. Now that women's magazines contain articles and letters about the most intimate sexual matters among the recipes and fashion notes, and TV regularly brings nudity and fairly explicit sexuality into the family sitting room, one might suppose that the subject matter of normal sexual behaviour had virtually ceased to be a disturbing psychological issue.

No doubt this is so to a very large extent, but there remain vast individual differences in attitudes towards sexual behaviour: embarrassment, prudery and downright hostility to the whole subject are still remarkably common among young and old alike. Openness and discussion can do a great deal to overcome irrational beliefs, even bigoted points of view, and can often disarm unspoken fears and apprehensions, but conscious and rational approaches may still not be able to tackle all of the problems created by our sexual feelings and our attitudes to sexuality and our sexual structures.

Sad to say, in the Western world, all things connected with sex are still popularly classed as 'dirty': for example, we speak of a 'dirty mind', 'dirty talk', doing 'dirty things', and so on, when we are actually referring to things which are simply, and often quite wholesomely, sexual. Jokes and humour epitomize this characteristic conjunction and confusion of scatological and sexual themes: lavatory and sexual matters seem to twist and intertwine with one another in an apparently completely natural way.

The reasons underlying this unfortunate blending are, no doubt, too complex and obscure to do more than guess at. Cultural factors leading to the degradation of sex, like the attitudes behind St Augustine's hostile description of our origins 'Inter faeces et urinam nascimur', have clearly had their effect. But, whatever the causes, it is certainly the case that copulation and excretion are now often as closely associated in feeling as they are anatomically. And, as the genital and excretory equipment of both sexes are indeed set within a few inches of one another, both capable of giving great pleasure through the elevation and discharge of tension, it is not entirely surprising that some confusions should arise – though particularly so where cultural forces have prepared the ground.

Exposure as an immediate preliminary to copulation is so powerfully and positively eroticized that moral and aesthetic reservations, doubts about the unappealing appearance of the genitalia and associated organs, and much else, may be set aside. But some quite natural features, like bodily odour, may create especially acute embarrassment and lead to a considerable degree of inhibitedness where it is feared that the aroma may be pungent or offensive to others.

For many people, discussing or even acknowledging the effect of body smells may be extremely difficult: the very subject being treated with considerable distaste and unease. Nevertheless, olfaction is an important facet of sexuality, and deserves the same consideration as the more obvious tactile and visual aspects.

Both men and women produce characteristic odours in the genital region and, despite the fact that our species' sense of smell is only a vestige of that possessed by our predecessors, scent may still be an unexpectedly important component in sexual attraction and stimulation. So far as males are concerned, though the sebacious glands of the genital region are very strong-smelling, it seems likely that the principal source of odours attractive to the opposite sex is contained in sweat from other parts of the body: emanating principally from the profuse glands and hairs which serve to trap underarm aromas.

The armpits are, of course, particularly abundant producers of sweat – a fact which has caused some to comment on how significant it is that the sexual preliminaries generally involve the female burrowing her nose into the male's chest or putting her head under his raised arm. In mutual, face-to-face embraces the sexes may alternate in raising their arms, putting them around their partner's neck, and so bringing the armpits close to the other person's nose. Often the people concerned are unaware of the odours, unless they are so strong as to suggest the chronic lack of hygiene. Nevertheless, for both sexes the smell of the other may be a prominent part of sexual attraction.

However, the prime focus of a female's sexually attractive odours is the vaginal area, where secretions very similar to those of sweat are produced. But, because the scent produced may be confused with perspiration, and can be quite strong, and because it refers to a very private and personal part of the body, it is generally suppressed as far as possible. Even so, members of both sexes are seldom unaware of the qualities of allure inherent in some odours.

Oral sex is, no doubt, arousing in many ways and motivated by many impulses but, judging from the literature on the subject, the smell and taste of vaginal secretions is not an inconsiderable part of feminine attraction. Statistics show that oral sex seldom precedes coitus between couples: this, if it occurs at all, would normally take place at a stage when the pair had got to know one another well enough to be more confident in such physically bold activities.

Indeed, there seems to be a progression by which anxieties are allayed (or not) from the first encounter – in which there is little or no direct looking at the partner's genitalia – to procedures of much greater familiarity. At each stage, a positive response from the partner helps to remove reticence, reduce anxieties, and facilitates self-acceptance: that is, if unyielding moral taboos are not involved.

As animals ourselves, we share with other species certain basic characteristics and tendencies; not least those relating to sexual behaviour. Yet any such shared tendencies, though they may still be present, are likely to be as much attenuated and removed from normal human conduct as those relating to any other sphere of behaviour. That we may be sexually attracted, or repelled, by bodily smells is demonstrable but their importance is now very much reduced not only by our diminished olfactory capacity but also through bathing and the barrier created by wearing clothes.

Additionally, we apply aromatic perfumes, including aftershave lotions, to more exposed areas of the body. Or, in the case of those who are still at a technologically more simple stage of development, they can achieve the same effects by rubbing their skins with fragrant oils, or wearing sweet-smelling flowers in their hair or on their bodies. The purpose and effect is the same: an alternative form of sexual attraction, coupled with the masking of body odours which can cause anxiety or embarrassment if they are unusually strong.

So, direct and natural sexual attractants are frequently very much muted in favour of delightful, though more neutral, substitutes. One important effect of this is that it distances intimacy somewhat: allowing a respite for individuals to become acquainted with one another whilst they decide upon the mutual desirability of embarking on a sexual-reproductive union. Perhaps this is our species' intuitive way of ensuring a more rational and responsible pattern of mating; in contrast to other primates where genital odours signalling mating readiness are unconcealed and have an almost irresistible effect. Still, human motives and responses are never as straightforward and uncomplicated as those of other species, so such an interpretation is never likely to be more than a speculation.

In fact, there is a serious shortage of scientific studies and solidly based theories in this whole area. In part, this is due to the practical difficulties inherent in trying to create, objectify, and measure the smells themselves, but a not inconsiderable element is also due to an anticipation of the embarrassment such studies might be expected to cause. Data may be scarce, but anthropology and history are replete with examples of the great variety of ways in which people respond to the body's odours. Excellent anecdotes can be culled from history to illustrate the great variety of individual differences: some decidedly exotic. For example, it appears that, whereas Mme du Barry made herself attractive to Louis XV by placing tiny fragile sachets of sweet perfume in her vagina, it was said that Napoleon's delight depended upon Josephine not destroying her strong natural odours.

Whether or not the royal examples are literally accurate, the fact remains that responses to sex-related smells are variable and unpredictable. Aware of this, or assuming it to be so, people tend to be extremely cautious about their own odour, particularly in so far as they suspect that they might cause offence or adversely affect a budding relationship. Deodorants and perfumes are therefore important resources not only for dealing with other, decidedly unpleasant, body odours but also for eradicating or transforming those of sex into something more subtle and safely alluring.

Advertisements in sex magazines seem to cater for just about every imaginable, and many unimaginable, requirement of their readers, including perfumes and other aromatic substances. Somewhat predictably though, their readership's interest seems to be centred more upon the aphrodisiac possibilities of these products than upon their more general aesthetic or pleasing qualities. In the event, it seems recent scientific developments may actually be responsible for supplying such needs for, among the products now being offered for sale, is a new product – aerosol canisters of an artificially synthesized biochemical, androstenol. Androstenol is a substance which, in its natural form, occurs in the sweat and urine of both sexes. Nevertheless, it is present in far higher concentrations in the body fluids of males and is thought to serve as a sexual attractant: being most active in attracting women to men.

The refined product has none of the strong smells of its naturally occurring state so it can be sprayed on a jacket lapel and allowed to do its claimed aphrodisiac work unobtrusively. Clearly, if it really does have the effects on womankind which are being claimed, the consequences of using such an unfair and furtive weapon in the 'war of the sexes' might prove devastating, as well as extremely profitable for the manufacturers and suppliers.

A host of rather unsystematic experiments in which, it is claimed, women were unknowingly lured by the chemical are cited by its promoters as support for its effectiveness, but their methodology is far from being beyond reproach. In a number of cases, the procedures involved were extremely casual, simply involving spraying someone's suit and then comparing women's reactions to him with those directed at someone who had not been sprayed. But, where the men involved were aware that they had, or had not, been sprayed with the chemical, the potentially contaminating effects of suggestion and elevated confidence are so obviously involved as to make the results unworthy of serious consideration.

However, not all the research done on this subject is equally dubious: much of it is of the highest quality and suggests that androstenol probably is quite an important natural sex signal as it is demonstrably capable of triggering powerful mating responses in a number of mammals. In fact, animal research is beginning to show just how widespread and influential such *pheromones*, or chemical odour signals, are as a method of communication in the animal kingdom. We may find that human beings are exceptions to this as our evolution has undoubtedly led us away from instinctive control and emphatic dependence upon olfactory information; however the process is by no means complete.

Though we may exhibit far more cerebral control than any other animal, even over our rebellious sexual urges, full rational control is only possible where there is awareness of the forces operating. Sex pheromones, being imperceptible or at least unrecognized as such, are therefore excepted from rational processes. So, the argument runs, however controlled conscious decisions or actions might appear, they may nevertheless be highly susceptible to unconscious influences. And if chemical odours can operate subliminally, bypassing consciousness, it is entirely likely that they are able to modify moods and response thresholds, as well as people's consciously-held attitudes towards the source of the emanation.

Whether such effects actually occur is an empirical question, and one which is demanding an increasing amount of attention. Pheromones are one of the newer growth points in human sciences, though they have been the subject of a fair amount of work in biology in general, and entomology in particular, for some time. In her book, *Scent Signals: the Silent Language of Sex*, Janet Hopson has drawn together a good deal of the work relating to sex pheromones, including a number of studies which seem to show that body odours can indeed operate subliminally to influence the psychological and physical states of other people. As the evidence accumulates, it seems to confirm not only that mankind shares much more in common with even the insect world than he often cares to admit, but that much of the unsystematic folklore about the power of bodily smell in human love is essentially correct.

Even the menstrual cycle appears to be markedly susceptible to sex pheromones. Airborne odours emanating from the underarm sweat of women during their period have now been shown to influence the timing of other women's periods. As American psychologist Martha McClintock was able to demonstrate, there is a very strong tendency for close friends and roommates to come into phase with one another, in what she called 'menstrual synchrony'.

In a most ingenious study, another American researcher, Michael Russell, was able to confirm the source of these events. He did this by showing that when a donor's tincture of underarm perspiration is smeared just below the nose of other women, they come to synchronize their periods with this unknown female. A control group, treated in a similar way but without the perspiration component in the smears applied to them, were completely unaffected.

The exact purpose served by this synchronization must depend upon psychobiological speculations, not all of which are agreeable to those who stress our human uniqueness and rationality. However, the main point is that experimental work has now clearly demonstrated a wide range of physical and psychological effects due to vaginal and underarm secretions: generally, without their being the slightest suspicion on the part of subjects as to their origin. Pheromones, sexual or otherwise, are obviously something to be reckoned with for, aware of it or not, we all exude them and are all sensitive to the information they communicate about our physical and mental states.

Menstruation, and the odours as well as the pain, discomfort and general messiness which occur at this time, have long been referred to by women as 'the curse', or something equally adverse. So it might be supposed that this particular bodily function, because it has so many negative connotations and has so long been a source of embarrassment and disability, debilitation and distress, would be an aspect of the body which the mind would wholeheartedly reject, if it could. Certainly this would seem to be the commonsense conclusion in view of the very real misfortunes menstruation has brought down upon womankind.

In many cultures, and not only primitive ones, a woman's period makes her 'unclean', so that cleansing rituals are necessary before she may be allowed to touch food, sit down with men, or just get on with her life. Inevitably, through a prolonged process of indoctrination, women as well as men have come to accept some aspect or another of this kind of hocus pocus, and have come to share beliefs about the shamefulness, and even dangers, connected with the process. All sorts of nameless fears have been associated with the flow of menstrual blood but, whatever the nature of the beliefs, they have all tended to undermine the self-esteem of women, as well as depressing their social and spiritual status.

So it came as a considerable surprise when, in 1975, a study conducted in twelve countries by the World Health Organization revealed that women's own feelings about menstruation are by no means purely negative: that the prospect of suppressing the monthly period through a simple hormone intervention was not universally welcomed. And, correct as she may be on many issues regarding women's feelings, even Germaine Greer got it wrong when she wrote in her book *The Female Eunuch* 'The fact is that no woman would menstruate unless she had to.' Unless, that is, the implication is that no woman would be female if she had the choice.

In their response to the WHO study, many women actually expressed a quite positive desire to continue with menstruation, giving a variety of reasons in justification. Some were nonsensical and based upon a poor understanding of the process, as with those who believed a monthly period was necessary to discharge 'bad blood'. Other reasons were more practical, like having the welcome reassurance of not being pregnant. But there were also other, more deeply-seated psychological grounds given for wanting to continue menstruating. For example, it appeared that young girls welcome the menarche as a sign of their maturity and, though time removes the need for this concrete token, once women enter their thirties, and begin to fear the onset of the menopause, they again welcome their period as a sign of femininity. Reassurance about reproductive status remains something of the gravest psychological importance, and presumably will continue to do so wherever fertility continues as a deeply ingrained criterion of worth.

Germaine Greer's interpretation of what she believes are typical of men's and women's feelings about women and the female body undoubtedly represents a landmark in the discussion of body-mind issues in relation to sex and sexuality. It is not, though, a work which reflects a scientific, detached, or balanced picture. On the contrary, it is emotional and polemical; apparently more concerned with changing women's lot than with making a contribution to knowledge. However, despite some very pessimistic and subjectively-based generalizations, it has a sufficient amount of both qualities to make it an important and influential contribution to learning and social reform alike.

In the course of her book, Greer traces many of the ways in which aspects of the female body, particularly the period and apparently wound-like vagina, have aroused great antipathies in both sexes. Rightly or wrongly, she then lays the full responsibility for this on the male and, though one might feel a more equitable distribution of this guilt might also include women's own negative and irrational reactions towards menstruation, she does present a powerful and urgent case for change.

How far such arguments have been responsible for increasing women's valuation of themselves is difficult to say. But, whatever the agents of change, more and more women are dismissing, and causing to be abandoned, the censorious taboos connected with menstruation; instead, coming to look on it as emblematic of a more positive part of their nature. What was once 'the curse' is now in the process of being transformed into part of a new and assertive feminine mystique. Things change slowly, and not at all for some people, but wherever the pendulum settles, it seems that the bodily fact of menstruation will continue to maintain a deep significance in the psychology of women.

Great as the problems and pleasures connected with the vagina and penis may be, it has often been said that mankind's major sex organ is not the genitals at all, but the brain. By this is meant that, in contrast to the lower animals which simply respond to biological and instinctive motivations, the sexual behaviour of human beings is much more dependent upon cerebral factors. External sexual organs and their associated biochemistry may sensitize and eroticize our bodies, but it is the contents of our mind which channel and characterize the urges, fancies and anxieties which drive, and trouble us, most.

This is where weaknesses so often occur in matter-of-fact biological treatments of sex education, and sexual advice or counselling: the model used is too simple. The actual course of sexual development lies much deeper than conditioned social attitudes or the processes brought about by puberty: its final expression involving a far more complex interaction of body and mind than is generally recognized. And, though there is no accepted consensus as to the exact nature of these abstruse interactions, psychologists as fundamentally opposed as Eysenck and Freud are agreed that they occur.

Of course, Freud is widely unpopular nowadays: the premises

and subjectivity necessarily involved in his procedures having made it very difficult for anyone except psychoanalysts to confirm or properly evaluate his theories. Yet, a good deal of critical analysis has taken place, leading to many revisions of the original formulation. Some concepts, like the 'death instinct' have been almost universally rejected, though many more have proved to be entirely more durable, despite the many upheavals, reformulations and schisms which began almost as soon as psychoanalysis was founded.

Orthodox Freudians are a rarity nowadays, most analysts presently belonging to one or other of the 'schools' which split from the main body. Within these, an enormous amount has been discarded and emphases have been radically changed, but few of Freud's successors would doubt that the sexual drive should still be regarded as of enormous significance in shaping our lives, mental and physical. Even the least 'depth' orientated can hardly demur from this view as experience, if not scientific experiments, make it obvious in the lives of us all.

Freud's great discovery, that the sexual drive rules much of our lives, and often in ways we do not recognize, was one of the most fundamental claims ever made about the mind-body relationship. It implies that much of our motivation is rooted in the sexual needs of the body and the reproductive needs of the species, and that our conscious thoughts and activities, as well as the unconscious processes affecting our dispositions, though mediated by the mind, are not of it.

Psychologists committed to the doctrine that virtually all behaviour, including mental events, depends almost exclusively on the outcome of people's previous behaviour often suppose that they are more fundamentally at variance with psychoanalysts than they really are. Freudians insist on an instinctive source to account for the origin of sexual drives, but no one, least of all Freud himself, was unaware of the other modifying effects of behavioural conditioning. Indeed, inhibitions, repression and many of the other mechanisms of psychic defence outlined in psychoanalysis, were presented as the outcome of conflict between basic drives and behavioural conditioning.

Yet, despite great sensitivity to the modulating consequences of social learning, Freud's theory is more concerned with chronicling the biologically inevitable stages through which the sex instinct unfolds, creating personality almost as a by-product. In a nutshell, the theory states that as we develop, so too does our sexuality; it being centred upon different parts of the body as we pass, by stages, from infancy to maturity.

During the *oral stage* of the first year of life, feeding and oral contacts with the mother provide the greatest potential for libidinal development. Through sucking and biting, the baby learns how to use its mouth, not only for simple gratification, but also as a means of controlling its love object. In the second year, there occurs a shift of emphasis such that the greatest pleasures are experienced as deriving from the anus rather than the mouth: this marks the beginning of the *anal stage*. Toilet training involves the pleasures associated with evacuation, maternal handling and praise, as well as the power aspects inherent in the child's choice of when and where to discharge.

In due course, the anal stage is superseded by the *phallic stage*, marking another shift in erotic emphasis. During this period, which normally extends from about three until five years of age, the child is said to become mainly preoccupied with erotic pleasures deriving from handling its penis or clitoris. Primitive forms of masturbation begin at this time and sexual fantasies about parents occur, inevitably giving rise to the mass of conflicts which Freud quaintly, and somewhat misleadingly, termed the Oedipus Complex.

Not surprisingly, proclaiming the inevitability of such disagreeable elements in all children's development proved by far the most repugnant aspect of Freud's theorizing, involving as it does libidinous yearnings for the opposite-sex parent and a mixture of jealousy, fear and hatred for the other – albeit tempered by a certain ambivalence, and even affection. Still, it should be remembered that, however outrageous this account of the child's mental world might seem, psychoanalytic therapy is invariably and principally concerned with unveiling the events which took place up to, and including, the Oedipus Complex.

The developmental stages which follow the phallic/oedipal period are regarded as being of relatively little significance in determining personality. The *latency stage*, following the phallic, was considered as mainly a time of sexual quiescence; a hiatus before the onset of puberty, when the genital organs become not only much more sensitive, but functional, and commanding of their deeper purpose, reproduction.

The last epoch of our sexual development, the adult *genital stage*, was, for Freud, not the most important psychologically. The driving force of our hormonal state becomes obvious enough: we spend a vast amount of our time and energies discharging these tensions, pursuing and securing sex objects through courtship, marriage and affairs. Yet psychological determination of what we actually do, and how we feel about it, is largely a consequence of the events which took place during the pre-genital stages of our lives. Unresolved and repressed oedipal conflicts are held to be of prime importance because they not only influence the choice of sex objects – mother or father figures, and even homosexual tendencies – but because fears and anxieties about violation of one's physical self are generated at this stage, many persisting at an unconscious level over a lifetime.

During the earlier phallic stage, girls are supposed to fantasize that they too once had a penis and that the vaginal 'wound' is evidence that they must have been castrated – either by accident or as a result of the mother's envy or rivalry with her child. According to Freud, this *castration complex*, closely associated with envy for those with a penis, may become a source of inferiority or of hostility – leading to the, metaphorically speaking, castrating personality whose jealousy provokes the individual towards belittling or undermining the self-confidence of men.

The male counterpart, *castration anxiety*, derives from the boy's oedipal conflicts. At this time, he fears that his sexual lust for the mother will be punished by his rival: in other words, father, the potential castrator. Though most of either sex pass through their oedipal conflicts by temporarily renouncing the opposite-sex parent and identifying with the same-sex one, repressed yearnings and fears retain their psychological energy and may have serious later consequences for personality development. Unconscious castration anxieties may later re-emerge in forms as diverse as self-abasement, overassertiveness and exhibitionism. Psychoanalysis is about backtracking to the source of these and other conflicts in order to expose them to the light of adult reason, there to strip them of the terrible emotional power generated in the mind of a child.

Freud's theories are, of course, far too complex to fully elaborate here and, in any case, this would take us far beyond the simpler mind-body connections presently being explored. But it is important to note that, whatever reservations one might have about much of Freud's work, this is one of the most thoroughgoing theories dealing with interactions between mental and physical development. Each stage from early infancy is about the psychological significance of one part of the body or another and, though people are often inclined to be even more dismissive of the sexual nature of infantile oral and anal experiences than they are of those connected with the genitals, there is no doubt that the mouth and anus are capable of playing a considerable sexual role.

Oral sex and sodomy are, perhaps, the most extreme expressions of non-genital sexuality, and it may be that psychoanalytic or other psychological theories can illuminate the reasons why some people prefer these foci more than others for the most intense expression of their sexuality. Perhaps, as Freud argues, vast tracts of people's non-sexual mental lives have also been shaped by the way parents dealt with such matters as weaning, toilet training, genital play, childish self-stimulation, passionate behaviour towards the parents, and so on. Certainly Freud thought so: for him, meanness, generosity, authoritarianism, dependency, creativity, much guilt and many unconscious fears, all have their origin in the events accompanying the development of our bodies and the shifting, or fixated, focus of our principal erogenous zone.

Few nowadays accept Freud's overwhelming emphasis on sexuality as the key to psychological development. However, the point was well made that, in the course of socializing unruly sexual and other physically-based drives, far-reaching consequences for the formation of normal and neurotic personalities occur. Compromises, sublimations and repression are certainly a part of the process, just as are conscious and unconscious anxieties. Moreover, like the appetite for food, the sexual appetite cannot be satisfied once and for all; being similarly recurrent, there is no question but that it holds us in a state of dynamic tension for the greater part of our lives.

Naturally, such a combination is likely to present formidable problems of control. The body's sexual demands can, unless we are fortunate, easily drag us into conflicts and absurdities; behaviour so infantile, embarrassing or irrational, we can only blush for it – and then, perhaps, repeat the whole performance over and over again. But despite the fact that this is by no means an uncommon experience, modern books on the subject have a remarkable tendency to assume that sex is a rational business, and that it can be regulated in a logical or mechanical fashion. Sex education texts and how-to-do-it manuals are particularly prone to this: they seem to assume that if only a broad-minded attitude is adopted, and the techniques for optimizing pleasures learned, then the psychological problems which they associate with a repressive Victorian society will simply become a thing of the past.

They may well be right but, in the actual world of the present, and the only one that can be examined by empirical science, this degree of openness, wisdom and clinical detachment is still very rare. Conscious attitudes are undoubtedly changing from what they were in Freud's day, and this is bound to have considerable implications for our patterns of child-rearing and for psychosexual development. But, if Freud is right, much of this formative development takes place so early in life, and depends so heavily on the relative eroticization of different parts of the body, and the infant's characteristic response to this, that psychological dispositions may be firmly set long before it is practicable to communicate more liberal and rational views. If so, the same processes of conflict and repression; fixation at oral, anal, or genital stages of development; regression, and the whole range of defence mechanisms necessary to handle incestuous impulses, fantasies and memories, may still occur – even in a world proclaiming liberation and freedom from the past.

Psychoanalysts have no doubt that such changes in sexual behaviour as have recently occurred are of a much more superficial nature than is generally supposed. Public attitudes, changing moral and social standards, and a tolerance regarding once-suppressed books, magazines and programmes, though by no means unimportant to the conduct of our lives, do not imply that the circumstances of infantile psychosexual development have changed in any fundamental way since Freud's time. In fact, Freud saw the basic pattern as virtually unchanged since the time human families first came into being; the process itself being seen as virtually impervious to cultural vicissitudes. Below the surface of public behaviour, the depths of private experience were held to be much more resistant to sudden climatic changes. And certainly, in spite of all our new sexual candour, there is still no evidence to show that sexual problems are any less prevalent than they were in the past.

For Freud, the physical biology of sex was the basic substratum of the human mind. And, as our bodies and minds were regarded as inseparable and totally interactive, sexually related aspects of the body must necessarily be regarded as having a peculiarly important psychological role. The connections proposed are subtle and intricate so Freud's own collected works are quite the best source of material to illustrate and explain them, but his *Three Essays on the Theory of Sexuality* is an especially valuable source.

In any case, though, it is particularly desirable in this instance to consult the original material rather than depend solely upon the simplifications or 'potted versions' of others. For, as Freud pointed out, our own repressed anxieties are such that they may easily provoke a defensive rejection of the sexual theory if we are not prepared to sift and weight the evidence carefully, and to face possibilities which might be painful and disgusting, or disturbing to our personal and family lives.

But, having devoted this much space to Freud's ideas can we regard them as having any substance? Behaviourists generally have little doubt that the answer to this should be a resounding 'no' and are likely to point to the demonstrable success of their own approach for both explaining and treating certain neuroses. But, allowing that these demonstrations are more scientifically persuasive than those of the psychoanalysts, one cannot assume that an entire psychological system stands or falls by its treatment applications. Freud always maintained the independence of the theories themselves: even if therapies fail, it may be due to unsatisfactory techniques and technology rather than an incorrect account of causality. Analogously, we may know exactly why a boat sank without being able to refloat her. The theory itself must needs be examined, and judged only on the basis of empirically-derived data.

In his book *Fact and Fantasy in Freudian Psychology*, Paul Kline has assembled the results of literally hundreds of experimental studies which test one or other of the Freudian tenets. However, the great scope and intricacy of the theories tested, plus great variations in the findings themselves, does mean that it is difficult to arrive at any general conclusion. Even so, what does emerge is that though some Freudian concepts, particularly those concerned with instinctive motivations, have proved very difficult to substantiate in empirical terms, a great deal more than it is fashionable to believe holds up very well. Moreover, behaviouristic approaches proved to be widely compatible with many of the verified psychoanalytic explanations.

Oedipus and castration complexes, though not emerging as the universal and central psychological processes which Freud made them, still found some degree of confirmation in experimental studies, as did the mechanism of repression, and the prevalence of sexual symbolism within and outside dreams. All in all, recent research has done much to put psychoanalysis on a much surer scientific footing than it was left by Freud himself, though not all aspects have fared equally well.

Behaviourists have often been guilty of overlooking or underrating research findings of the sort assembled by Kline: being dismissive while adding little of positive value to theories of sexuality themselves. By default, psychoanalysis remains one of the few systems which does attempt to trace exactly how the physical self, and particularly the sexual structures and drives, mould and pattern the mind in certain predictable ways. No doubt, like any scientific theory, it needs to be constantly checked and revised and, as is also usual, we must expect to discard it as better formulations emerge. However, this has not yet happened and it seems that the critics of psychoanalysis may have been somewhat premature in proclaiming their own right of succession.

Still, having claimed the destruction of their old enemy, behaviouristic theories have proliferated in all directions, though they have proved completely unsuited to dealing with the body's part in mental life. More specifically, all aspects of sex, perhaps because of their particular connection with Freud, were noticeably and studiously ignored. As a result, scores of basic psychology texts were, and still are, produced without a single reference to human sexuality, and precious little even about animals' sexuality, except in so far as it had been used as a reward or reinforcement in a learning experiment.

On the other hand, as was mentioned earlier, there has been a growing clinical interest in the application of conditioning techniques to the treatment of certain sexual dysfunctions. But, valuable as this sort of repair-technology undoubtedly is, it is very little concerned with mental events or explanatory psychological theories. The result is that vast areas of study related to sexual behaviour continue to be ignored. Even so, though there is little likelihood of any significant *rapprochement* between behaviouristic and psychoanalytic theorists, there is a growing realization among the more eclectic that a good deal more body-related research must somehow be incorporated into future psychological thinking, and that these new approaches must take greater account of sexual aspects than tends to have been the case in the past.

One frequently overlooked or underestimated aspect of psychosexual thinking is the body's biochemistry. And, regretfully, it must again be passed over here, except to acknowledge that hormonal changes and individual differences in their basal levels are extremely important as physical causes and effects of sexual arousal and behaviour, and also of differential physical development. But, apart from the fact that the endocrine processes involved are extremely complicated and still the subject of much controversy as to their behavioural consequences, such a discussion would lead us too far away from our own touchstone of the physical structure themselves.

By contrast, an extended treatment of Freud may be justified by the fact that, abstract as so much of his thinking was, psychoanalysis is always finally rooted in the physical body. Quite specifically, he has done a great deal to illuminate the psychological significance of those mucous-membrane lined orifices which, under appropriate circumstances, can give rise to such a surprising amount of mental tension, delight, or conflict; as well as to the more ordinary physically-based pleasures or discomforts.

So, though an understanding of the place of biochemical processes in sexual behaviour is extremely important, it does refer to a different level of mind-body analysis, and one which must unfortunately be left for the interested reader to pursue elsewhere. An excellent starting point for those willing to do this might be Corrinne Hutt's *Males and Females*, in which she summarizes the subject very succinctly and presents some of the better research dealing with erotic behaviour and the structural differentiation of the sexes.

Hans Eysenck, in his *Biological Basis of Personality*, also considers the role of the body's biochemistry but he does so with the activity of certain palpable structures in mind. His theories do not require that any particular hormones be identified, though correlations are emerging; instead, he is more concerned with identifying the organs which mediate what he sees as the major underlying psychological dispositions of mankind. Again, though, it is not possible to do much more than draw attention to the fact that such theories exist, and that they have proved to be remarkably powerful in generating further research and explaining otherwise difficult to interpret statistical associations.

Eysenck's experimental and mathematical analysis of personality has yielded an elegantly clear picture of personality in which two principal dimensions, *Introversion-Extraversion* and *Neuroticism-Stability*, can be used for plotting the relative position of any individual or sub-group against a psychologically or psychiatrically appropriate norm or larger reference group. Deceptively simple self-administered questionnaires, giving no indication of the extensive sampling, item selection, and correlations which underlie them, have been developed to measure these characteristics – the results of which may be used to add to our knowledge of either individuals or groups.

However high or low we may score on these questionnaires, we can all be plotted somewhere: and though most of us, being average by statistical definition, cluster towards the centre of the scale while smaller numbers fall nearer the extremes of one or other dimension, predictions can be made about the likely behaviour of all. But of far greater scientific importance, data deriving from large groups can be correlated with other characteristics, mental or physical, so that the possibility of causal relationships can be explored. And, as a result of a considerable amount of research, it now seems likely that the level of people's introversion or neuroticism is closely connected with certain identifiable structures of the nervous system.

The dimension for introversion-extraversion denotes a continuum which has as its main characteristic the opposing tendencies of preference for solitude, restraint and reflectiveness at the one extreme and sociability, activity and a more free and easy reaction to life, at the other. Eysenck's theory is that people who choose such different levels of social and sensory stimulation do so because of differences in the functioning of a particular physical structure – the reticular formation – a neural 'booster' sited in the brain stem which also modulates the level of cortical activity.

Most of us are ambiverts, being neither extremely introverted nor extremely extraverted, but we are likely to lie more on one side of the average value than another. This being so, Eysenck's theory is of a very broad applicability, even though the principles are more easily described in relation to extreme cases.

Introverts are held to manifest high levels of cortical arousal because their stimulus inputs are boosted by the activity of the reticular system. They therefore avoid external events which would create markedly higher levels and result in pressure or confusion. By contrast, extraverts, who normally operate at a far lower level of cortical arousal due to the fact that they receive far less stimulus augmentation, tend to seek out a far greater degree of external stimulation in order to optimize their overall level of cortical arousal. In other words, the introvert tends to limit stimulus input whereas the extravert actively seeks to feed a 'stimulus hunger'.

Predictions based on the general theory suggest that response to the powerfully stimulating qualities of sex will be very different for the two types – it being hypothesized that extraverts will seek out more partners, have intercourse in more positions, exhibit a wider variety of sexual behaviour, and indulge in more intensive and extended pre-coital stimulation than will introverts.

The neuroticism-stability dimension denotes rapid and strong emotional reactivity and, in those with high neuroticism scores, is marked by a tendency to develop neurotic symptoms when under strong emotional stress; to be touchy, and prey to sleeplessness, anxieties, and inferiority feelings. So, in view of the powerful emotions and ambivalences stirred up in sexual relationships, sex-related moral and aesthetic conflicts were, quite correctly, predicted to occur more frequently and forcefully in the attitudes and feelings of those scoring above average on the neuroticism scale. As in the case of extraversion, a considerable body of evidence has been marshalled to show that the psychological dimension of neuroticism reflects the activity of specific structures – in this case though, the autonomic nervous system, and that part of the brain which integrates its various activites.

Eysenck's book, *Sex and Personality*, is mainly an account of just one of his own major studies. Its subject matter is, naturally enough, limited to sexual adjustment but, as Eysenck himself says, it exemplifies the application of his theories and methods in the study of many other aspects of psychological adjustment, and particularly those involving body-mind relationships. The approach has certainly proved a very successful one: measures of introversion and neuroticism being extremely discriminatory when it comes to identifying personality of differences relating to an apparently almost inexhaustible range of human activities. In the present case too, the predictions already referred to were again clearly borne out by the results of this particular study, which involved more than 400 males and a similar number of females. Those who are introverted or tend towards neuroticism do indeed have a very different pattern of sexuality from the exploratory and lusty activities of the extravert.

Accounting for these differences partly in terms of the functioning of actual physical structures, the case was then made that such differences have a demonstrable genetic origin. The evidence presented would take a chapter for itself, and those who wish to examine it in detail should refer to Eysenck's *Sex and Personality*, but a strong case has been made that even the degree to which one seeks variety in sex may have a good deal to do with the sub-microscopical genetic 'switches' which control the functioning of our bodies.

It seems, then, that whether one considers such macro-aspects as body size and shape, major surface features and individual organs, or structures lying entirely out of sight, bodily characteristics are important influences on our sexuality. Some may attract, others repel, and yet others prove relatively neutral in our attempts to achieve sexual relations with others but, one way or another, they all influence our level of libido, desire for variety in partners and practices, and our very attitudes and feelings about sexual behaviour.

Of course social and cultural moulding, as well as manner and other personal characteristics, are of immense significance in determining sexual, as any other, behaviour. Similarly, a person's ability to attract and arouse another through physical means has never been in doubt, even though we may still have a great deal to learn about what is attractive to whom. Psychological characteristics, and bodily ones such as symmetry, texture and movement are all obvious terms in the equation of sexual attraction. But work on pheromones, or Freud's psychoanalytic and Eysenck's psychophysiological and genetic investigations, have each shown that the equation is even more complicated than we may sometimes suppose.

Below the surface of apparent rationality, our responses and impulses are nudged along not only by the values, standards and attitudes which we have absorbed, and which may have become a major part of our unconscious dispositions but also, apparently, by equally inaccessible biological determinants. We may have the illusion of freedom to choose but, if any such exists, it is obviously subject to many unconscious or subliminal influences which, being unaware of them, we cannot take into account when we exercise our seemingly free choice.

Later in the book we shall be looking at the theories of one of Freud's one-time colleagues, Wilhelm Reich, and adding yet another dimension to our understanding of the ways in which an inadequate sex life can mark both the body and the mind: drawing them into mutually damaging interactions, and our whole being into discontent and failure. This, however, because of its wider implications for health and illness, is a matter best deferred until later. Yet, as we shall see, it may be that even our physical appearance itself is heavily dependent upon our orgasmic opportunities and capacity.

Freud's view that the mind, and culture itself, is virtually the unconscious tool of biologically determined sexual processes may be going too far, but evidence from many different sources makes it quite apparent that many aspects of our mental and behavioural activities do have their origins in sexual-reproductive drives, and that bodily states in ourselves and others are important unconscious determinants of our supposedly unconstrained actions. As this and the previous chapter have attempted to show, whatever theoretical viewpoint we may prefer, there can be no escaping the fact that a very broad perspective is needed to understand even the basics of human sexuality.

The sexual drive may or may not be the mainspring and *raison d'être* of society, but we can hardly disagree with Freud's conclusion that, for a full understanding of its working, some appreciation of its great significance in all human activities is essential. The relative balance of operative forces will vary from time to time and person to person, but even the most rudimentary and ordinary sexual encounters can be seen as the confluence of not only physical and psychological vectors, but of sociological, cultural and evolutionary ones also.

In the past, gross overestimations of the importance of one's sex and sexuality were frequently matched by equally extreme underestimates. The true balance probably lies somewhere between the two but, wherever this may be, it is now much more generally recognized that this is an area where mind and body meet and interact in ways which have profound significance for psychological understanding.

Chapter five

PERSONALITY AND PHYSICAL MALFUNCTION

That the mind and behaviour are always finally dependent upon the brain's integrity may seem so self-evident as to require no further comment. Anything that damages either the structures or the delicate biochemical balance of the brain is likely to have obvious psychological consequences. Haemorrhages, tumours, or any other form of mechanical damage all bring about changes not only in people's sensory-motor abilities and their intellectual and emotional control, but in their entire range of personal and interpersonal adjustment as well. This aspect, at least, of the mind-body equation is not likely to be disputed.

However, predicting the specific psychological consequence of a particular injury is far from being a straightforward matter. For a start, accumulating cases which can be matched with one another is made unusually difficult because no two injuries are likely to be absolutely identical; not even where lesions have been intentionally and methodically induced, as in the case of a frontal lobotomy. This type of surgery, which involves cutting nervous connections between the front of the cortex and certain lower brain areas, was once widely used to treat severely anxious and disordered mental patients. Its virtual discontinuation was due to a combination of reasons, but not least that therapeutic outcomes were distinctly inconsistent, even when the surgical procedures used were identical. Some patients improved considerably, some were only mildly changed, while the personality of others deteriorated seriously.

One cause of this variability in outcome was undoubtedly due to the fact that, though surgical procedures might be constant from operation to operation, the position and extent of the many specialized areas which constitute the brain itself are as subject to individual differences as any other part of the body. Unfortunately though, they are not as visible as most of the others. As a result,

X-rays and other externally made assessments of the tissues affected by the surgery were seldom more than rough approximations.

Prediction of outcomes therefore proved to be so unsatisfactory that this type of psychosurgery is now generally limited to the most intractable cases; a final court of appeal only to be approached when all else has failed. So, despite some spectacular successes resulting from each of the numerous surgical modifications to the technique, most people have come to feel that limitations in our knowledge of both brain structures and the likely mental consequences of tampering with them is still too rudimentary to justify irreversible treatments in any but the most exceptional circumstances.

Data from psycho-therapeutic brain surgery may be getting scarcer but cases involving accidental brain damage are all too prevalent, and their consequences always available for study. Whatever their source though, whether the result of traffic accident, cerebral tumour or an acute disturbance in the brain's metabolic functioning, all types of organic brain damage suggest that psychological consequences are as dependent upon previous personality as they are upon physical causes.

For example, though someone's response to LSD or one of the other major psychedelic drugs cannot be predicted from the dose given, a much more accurate forecast of their reaction can be made if something is known of their previous state of mind and personality. The same is equally true of any form of permanent brain damage: no simple and mechanical relationship between cause and effect seems to obtain. But then, one could hardly expect it would: such relationships are virtually unknown in human beings, the effect of our unique developmental histories ensuring that we all respond differently to just about everything, other than an instantaneously fatal attack upon our person. Anything and everything which allows for variety in response allows for the effects of previous experience and different dispositions.

Those whose personality and social adjustment were well established and satisfactory prior to sustaining brain damage may not escape any of the impairments which attend their particular type of neurological disorder, but they are more likely to be able to cope with them. Where previous adjustment had been tenuous, the brain damaged person may not have consolidated relationships and routines sufficiently well to be prepared for the great demands made in adjusting to his handicap.

Another problem is that brain damage frequently impairs people's ability to plan ahead by undermining their capacity to foresee all the consequences of their own actions, even in the most everyday circumstances. Also, they are likely to miss many of the implications in the words or deeds of others: their thinking being more than usually determined by concrete rather than abstract processes. Unappreciated subtleties in the behaviour of others, leading to unanticipated actions, can easily lead to great exasperation and anger on the part of handicapped individuals, much to the further detriment of relationships upon which they must depend. And, where emotional or impulse control was relatively poor prior to an accident, it is likely to become relatively even more substandard afterwards. Such accidents not only add substantially to pre-existing problems, but seem to multiply them; it often being a case of the psychologically poor getting poorer while the resources of the better off continue to give them an advantage.

One further consequence of the many forms of brain damage is that the individual concerned may also develop physical incapacities. For example, a serious cerebral haemorrhage, resulting in what is commonly termed a 'stroke', frequently causes a more or less permanent impairment on one side of the body. This, or any other form of brain damage resulting in marked physical, expressive, or sensory disorder must be regarded as even more than a double disaster. Such a person not only has to cope with a physical handicap but must do so while also suffering from mental handicaps which make the coping process infinitely more frustrating and difficult than for those who have full use of their mental capacities, and full control of their emotional expressions.

Disorders of verbal expression or comprehension, visual or auditory recognition problems, amnesias and epileptic fits are hard enough to live with, but associated sleeping disorders or intractable pain, when coupled with problems of mood, memory, or mobility may put insupportable strains upon an individual's personality, and upon his or her relationships. When or if this happens, a certain amount of specialized psychological or psychiatric help may be needed in addition to that which can be given by family, friends, or those providing medical or social services. The problem often being not so much one of restoring what has been damaged, but working out optimal new strategies of adjustment.

Sometimes the most pronounced physical disabilities brought about by brain damage prove to be less serious than they at first seemed. Even severe paralysis may respond so well to treatment and exercise that it is ultimately only marginally disabling, and the person concerned is then able to resume most, if not all, previous activities. But such events almost always involve far more than just a period of more or less permanent mechanical injury to the body: the mind too is always involved, and not always either as much damaged, or as much recovered, as the body. In this respect, the situation is similar to that in which physical disability is due to mechanical damage which does not involve the brain.

Serious malfunction of the nervous system may, however, produce no obvious forms of physical incapacity, even though the end result may be as disabling as quadriplegia. For example, the so-called 'functional' psychoses, of which schizophrenia or manic-depression are the most prominent, are probably of this kind. Genetic research now makes it virtually certain that an underlying physical disorder is present in most cases, and that the observable psychological disorganization is primarily a manifestation of biochemical malfunctions in the brain.

In Chapter one we referred to the pioneering work of Ernst Kretschmer, and to his demonstration that schizophrenia tends to be linked with a narrow and linear physique, whereas manic-depressive psychosis is more likely to occur in those who tend towards a rotund constitution. Later research has refined and made more precise both the physical and the psychiatric criteria, as well as making substantial improvements to the investigatory methods used. The result is that, though the connection now appears less pronounced than it first seemed, the association is still apparent. There is no question of an invariable relationship but it does seem reasonable to conclude that particular physical characteristics are, in some way, linked with these types of mental disorder.

Of course, it is quite reasonable to suppose that a given psychosis may have any of many different origins, or that it results from a multiplicity of predisposing or precipitating causes. In some instances, psychological events alone may be sufficient to induce schizophrenia but, in view of the sort of findings previously outlined in *Personality and Heredity*, it seems probable that a somatic disposition exists in most cases. But, though there is now every reason to conclude that the 'functional' psychoses are as influenced by heredity as bodily forms themselves, the exact processes by which genetic materials work their effects remain highly speculative.

Few nowadays feel that the observed correlations between body type and psychosis constitute a useful, or even a very safe, starting point for causal theories. Instead, most emphasize a genetic disposition affecting brain metabolism: a process which may or may not have wider consequences for the development of bodily structures. The most widely accepted causal explanations of schizophrenia and manic depressive psychosis (and some other conditions) incline to the view that these illnesses are generally the outcome of two interacting factors; psychological stress and a genetic disposition, or *diathesis*. In view of the substantial, but not overwhelming data supporting genetic causality, such a theory seems to be readily compatible with evidence drawn from both hereditary and psychological sources.

Most *diathesis-stress* models propose that diathesis should be regarded as genetically caused variability in people's neurochemical functioning. The presumed consequences of any such imbalance or deviation from the norm may be quite diverse, but one of the effects most commonly ascribed to these changes in brain chemistry is a change in the level of mental arousal, and a resulting inability to tolerate the powerful levels of stimulation met with in everyday living. Additionally, it seems that some of the neurochemical events, and their associated psychological states, are so similar to those caused by drugs of the psychedelic or psychotomimetic (i.e. psychosis mimicking) type as to suggest that the mechanisms involved are almost identical – though intrinsically caused in one case and extrinsically in the other.

As discussed in an earlier book, *Psychedelic Drugs*, the ingestion of even a few millionth parts of a gramme of certain substances is quite sufficient to disorganize the brain's activities grossly. Such drugs, which are commonly very similar in chemical structure to some of the naturally occurring neurochemicals, can cause so much disruption in the functioning of nervous pathways as to undermine an individual's grasp on reality almost completely. And, judging by the results of current research, it seems likely that the scale of naturally occurring metabolic errors leading to psychosis may be of no greater magnitude. The mind is clearly highly dependent upon an extremely delicate balance of bodily events, if it is to function at all efficiently.

But, whether disabilities are predominantly mental or physical in their effects, a great deal depends upon the age and stage of life in which they occur. Not that it is possible to generalize a great deal; much depends not only upon the disability itself and the personality, temperament and life-experiences of the person concerned, but also upon economic, cultural and social fortunes, and upon locally prevailing community and medical services. Nevertheless, there are *some* characteristic differences in the problems likely to be encountered, depending upon the phase of life in which incapacity occurs.

Congenital deformities and disabilities, or those occurring early in childhood, tend to present a particularly wide range of difficulties as the individual's entire developmental history takes place within burdensome and limiting circumstances. In the case of congenital disability, from birth onwards the family may be under an unusual degree of strain. Mothers may even find that the congratulations, presents and cheerful companionship which usually mark the arrival of a baby, and which can do so much to renew a woman's zest at a time when she may be both physically and emotionally drained, are not forthcoming. Instead, she may experience avoidance, a brittle and artificial optimism, or frank gloom: any or all of which can add to her emotional problems, often helping to reinforce her suspicion that she is somehow to blame.

Infants beginning their lives in this way are in a difficult psychological position from the outset: guilt frequently give rise to rejection, perhaps resulting in the child being put into some form of residential care where this is practicable. If this is not possible, nor an acceptable solution, the consequences have to be worked out in the family's relationships. Alternatively, guilt may be transformed into an unusually powerful sense of obligation and the need to serve in order to atone for the blame which parents have assumed. The outcome of this may also be damaging to the child's development, particularly if their parents' behaviour includes over-protectiveness which inhibits their child's efforts to achieve an optimal degree of normality and autonomy. Add to this the fact that multiple handicaps are common in cases of serious birth defect, and it becomes apparent that early-occurring disability can have much more serious consequences than is often supposed.

Special education or residential care can be a mixed blessing: and when it involves parental choice, it can often be an additional cause of anxiety or guilt, and an additional strain on family relationships in general, and those directly involving the disadvantaged child more particularly. To feel that they may be withholding opportunities from their child if they decline, or that they may be taking the easy way out of their responsibilities if they accept, can be an agonizing dilemma. It is easy to see the problems of disability entirely from the point of view of the disabled person, but the psychological strains on both parents and other members of the family can be very severe, and merit an equal amount of practical help and counselling. Unfortunately, this is often not available and families must do the best they can to preserve their own self-esteem and the esteem of others too.

If the child is markedly deformed, disgust and self-hatred for responding this way, is always a possibility, though familiarity will often change such feelings, or else take the edge off them. However, some degree of embarrassment often remains and makes completely natural encounters with people introduced into the family from outside quite difficult. Brothers and sisters are by no means always accepting: in fact, they may become quite hostile or rejecting because of their jealousy over attention given to the disabled child. Sometimes, the discipline problems created within the family are so trying as to make everyone so tense that it would be hard for any child to develop normally within its emotionally taut and potentially friable atmosphere.

In her book *The Psychology of Handicap*, Rosemary Shakespeare gives particular attention to the problems of handicapped children, and to some of the consequences of selecting either the home or the residential care option. Her treatment of the psychological stresses encountered by parents shows how conflicting the aims and impulses can be. For example, keeping a child in the home may deny him many practical advantages in special treatment, care and the formation of friendships with similarly disadvantaged children, among whom more realistic adjustment strategies may be worked out. On the other hand, hospitalization or institutionalization can encourage a child to adopt unduly limited aspirations, to feel rejected and inferior, and thus add to his sense of worthlessness and the futility of trying to make the best of himself.

Either way, the young disabled person is likely to encounter special difficulties in all aspects of his development. Sensory input may be severely limited as a result of mobility problems: holidays and games, or just getting about the neighbourhood may be very restricted, with a consequent limitation on things to talk about. Blindness and deafness not only isolate in quite obvious ways, but they result in such a different experience of the world that it can be difficult for such children to communicate easily with those who are non-sensorily handicapped. Unfortunately too, it can be very taxing to hold a conversation with, say, a deaf or partially hearing person as the pitch and level of one's voice changes, often leading not only to self-consciousness but also to the rather unnatural changes in expression and posture which generally seem to accompany it. To a lesser extent, there are equivalent barriers in communicating with blind people, whose lack of eye contact often seems to weaken the impact and satisfaction of conversation. Of course, such reactions are far from inevitable but they are common enough to significantly reduce many children's contact with other people and to reduce the quantity and quality of their participation in social events.

As Rosemary Shakespeare points out, though it is extremely difficult to compare the mental development of those physically disabled children who are kept at home or provided with special day facilities with those who are taken into residential care, it does seem as though the latter are more susceptible to secondary, or adjustive, forms of handicap. A strict matching of cases is virtually impossible in view of the many physical, psychological, environmental and selection variables involved but children in institutions are much more likely to have secondary deficits in manipulative and sensory-motor skills, as well as manifesting greater intellectual, verbal and emotional disadvantages.

Exactly how far this is a consequence of living in what may be, psychologically speaking, relatively impoverished surroundings is impossible to say without being able to compare cases which are identical except for the fact of institutionalization, but much of the available evidence does suggest that those children who are raised in their own homes may have a number of advantages. It may simply be the case that those children who enter institutions tend to be more difficult in themselves, or are more likely to come from homes where family support is weaker, but this is no more than a possibility for investigation.

A conclusion that more research is needed on this subject tends to be something of a cliché but it does seem in this present instance that the literature concerning the consequences of different types of care is so sparse as to make informed policy decisions exceedingly difficult. One of the few conclusions which does seem reasonably safe is that, serious as are the psychological problems encountered by the physically handicapped and their families, they are far less likely to receive specialized psychological or psychiatric support and aid than many other groups in which social or mental maladjustment is the primary cause of their disadvantage.

Very young children seem capable of accepting even the most marked differences in themselves or others with relative equanimity. But, as the years pass, this acceptance generally diminishes so that, by the later school years, an astonishing degree of intolerance towards others may have appeared, even among children from the most liberal families. Such prejudice and cruelty is by no means uncommon, though it may take the form of neglect rather than a more blunt rejection. Children with 'marginal' disabilities, those able to attend ordinary schools yet who require special academic help or are prevented from participation in the full range of non-academic activities, face a good many obstacles to acceptance. Even the special concern shown for them by adults may make them less likely to be identified as admissible members of their peer group.

It is also difficult for, say, a child in a wheel chair to join in the ordinary hurly-burly of school life, or to find that special companion with whom to share adventures, leisure activities and confidences. Deprived of these opportunities, school can be a lonely, and even hostile, place. Even compensating intellectual gifts can, in some schools and circumstances, make matters worse rather than better. On the other hand, if marked intellectual weaknesses also accompany the primary physical deficit, school life can be made even more unsuccessful and disagreeable.

Of course, many handicapped children meet with fewer trials and tribulations than some of their physically sound contemporaries; not only succeeding well in their school work, but enjoying satisfying friendships and wide popularity as well. Whether the relative proportion who achieve this is comparable with children who are not incapacitated is very difficult to judge as it involves qualitative analysis and the kind of subjective assessment which tends to be avoided by most researchers – who find that such results are, in any case, rarely published by scientific journals. However, research into the attitudes of other children towards the handicapped reveals considerable negativity: a state of affairs which experiments involving information, education and contact with the disabled show to be quite resistant to change.

Whether or not we feel it inevitable, prejudice against people different from ourselves seems to be an all too common fact of life. Children are no different from adults in so far as they seem prone to adopting stereotyped categories which, once applied, may serve to define, and severely limit, people and their roles in life. The individual is no longer seen as a unique personality: instead, all the characteristics of the 'cripple', 'blind', or 'spastic' stereotype are projected onto them and they come under pressure to fulfil the role created. Apart from its other characteristics, the prevalent stereotype of generalized handicap and weakness often results in the disabled person being treated as though they were either childlike or mentally retarded. Conversation is frequently insultingly banal or patronizing: people in wheelchairs not uncommonly being addressed as though they were, or should be, in a perambulator. Indeed, despite so much protest of late, the healthy companion of a disabled person is still likely to be asked something like 'Does he take sugar?': the assumption being that the physically handicapped person must also be mentally inadequate.

Talking with severely disabled people can certainly take a little getting used to; particularly where speech or sensory incapacities make conversation awkward or laborious. Sadly, it seems that most of us are not prepared to make that extra effort as studies show that conversations with handicapped people tend to be not only shorter than with others, but they are also likely to be more conventional, inhibited and trite. How dispiriting it must be hardly needs comment; the way in which it is likely to deepen a sense of rejection and alienation being obvious enough.

The transition from school to adult life is always more difficult than it may seem from someone else's viewpoint. It involves, among other things, taking some of the most momentous steps towards self-definition: our choice, or our fortunes and misfortunes, in establishing a career have ramifications that are likely to affect the entire course of our lives. Through training and jobs, normal people find intellectual and economic opportunities; the chance to travel, be independent, and establish their future social role. But for many disabled people this transition is hardly made: the openings available may be extremely limited and, if the young person's aspirations have been high, bitterness and depression are very likely unless help, support and counselling are available.

The adult who has always been incapacitated has many problems of a special kind, but not least are the consequences of never having been able to compete on fair terms and so to find out just what they are capable of achieving. As a result, all manner of fantasies may be entertained: some being sustaining beliefs about intrinsic worth, while others lead to a feeling of having been cheated and serve as a focus for regret and bitterness. Either way, without opportunities to test themselves, the chronically disabled person's self-concept may be substantially distorted; their view of themselves, and their actual potential, being quite unrealistically superior or inferior.

Nevertheless, most of us are prone to valuing ourselves and each other in terms of achievements: a measure which very much disadvantages those who are congenitally incapacitated, or disabled from an early age. In their case, many of the rules and norms which helped guide the development of self-esteem, and the esteem of others, are inoperative. It is therefore extraordinarily difficult for many handicapped people, unless their accomplishments are equivalent to, or above, the general norm, to achieve mental and social equilibrium.

To have been a pilot, journalist, nurse, lorry driver, teacher or sales person is not only to have had the opportunity to see one's self as integral to society, but is also to have an identity which persists beyond one's capacity to do the job. Moreover, having worked for some time, will not only have allowed for a more natural developmental sequence, it will also have provided the opportunity to make normal friends, meet and perhaps marry, and acquire property. In such circumstances, the chances for two equivalently disabled people achieving and maintaining a good deal of autonomy heavily favour those who have become incapacitated later in life.

There may, however, be equally heavy psychological penalties. For example, disabilities which occur later in life can, if they make work and important leisure activities impossible, take away what has become one's reason for living. Never again being able to be part of a work team, to climb hills, go fishing, or act with the local dramatic group, can be so traumatic a realization that entertaining alternatives can only be achieved with a lot of help. Unhappiness at the sense of loss is easily transformed into the bitterness of an innocent victim and the despair of one who sees no end to the problems created by irrevocably lost or damaged bodily parts.

In addition, those who are suddenly disabled may find themselves helpless to cope with mortgages, hire purchases, school fees, other pressing financial burdens, or the care of children and the running of a home. Others must now take on these responsibilities and there may occur a shift in role such that it may be difficult, or even impossible, for either or both of the partners to adjust satisfactorily. Guilt at not being able to discharge one's customary duties, or resentment at having to ask for, or give, more service to the other can all occur within a matter of weeks, precipitating acute psychological strife in the unprepared.

Lifelong friends and acquaintances may begin to drop away at this stage: after all, it may no longer be possible to sustain the common interests and activities which once cemented relationships together. Memories alone may prove completely insufficient. Marriage itself may falter, especially if its physical aspects become unsatisfying, unappealing, or even impossible. In the case of sex, such manifestations of disability as burns, scars, or amputations sometimes make the prospect of intercourse so unappealing to either or both of the parties concerned that they experience considerable guilt and embarrassment or else make other arrangements. Quite clearly, both outcomes may prove equally damaging for a relationship upon which a handicapped person is so much more dependent.

Establishing and maintaining satisfactory sexual relationships is one of the most problematic areas of disablement. Of course, there are many other basic requirements also to be met – finding some form of employment or source of money, finding somewhere to live, and some way to organize cooking and cleaning – but sex urges, and the need for tender companionship, are as pressing in the disabled as in anyone else. Achieving them can, though, be extremely difficult: and particularly so in the case of those whose disability goes back to childhood.

Without a lot of help or encouragement, the disabled person may lack both the skills and the confidence even to begin courting. Deafness and blindness, whether total or partial, present difficulties almost as obvious as paralysis. And, even where both are disabled, the demands for care which each may later place on the other, or questions of pregnancy or raising a family, make the prospects daunting for all but the most courageous or unwary.

Yet, whether or not they form part of marriage, the need for some kind of sexual relationship remains. In his book *Disabled We Stand*, Alan Sutherland draws on his own experience with epilepsy, as well as on the experiences of other disabled people to show what is implied for the individual. It seems that, in the face of the prevailing negative and censorious attitudes, it continues to be inordinately difficult for anyone with a handicap to be seen in any way but as a representative of one medical disorder or another, in whose case most natural aspirations, including sexuality should properly be curtailed.

However, sexual urges are not easily denied: they occur as frequently and insistently in the disabled as in anyone else, and must somehow be accommodated if additional mental distress is to be avoided. Masturbation is the main solution available to anyone without adequate interpersonal sexual opportunities but, even this can present practical difficulties in some cases, and require either the understanding and acceptance of others, or their actual cooperation. If this is not forthcoming, even this avenue to relief and pleasure may be impracticable or inadequate. In any case, guilt feelings concerning any erotic behaviour or fantasy are more than usually likely to occur in view of the prevailing attitude that the disabled have no business to be interested in sex, and that they should maintain a dignified fortitude and asceticism.

Even the simpler pleasures and solaces of alcohol are often thought shocking in the handicapped, as are many other small indulgences like smoking or gambling. While not making a case for any of these activities, they are among the most popular pleasures of ordinary people, and the fact that there are often such obvious and discriminatory reservations when it comes to a handicapped person does call for some explanation.

It may be that those who are so severely disabled as to be unable to find or perform paid work are seen essentially as 'charity cases', who should be grateful for care and attention, and not expect luxuries. Maybe the old convention that pain, illness and misfortune are in some sense the result of sin still operates at a more or less unconscious level. Certainly the attitudinal connections between evil and disfigurement or deformity are far from defunct, even today. So, in addition to the ordinary problems of living and maintaining self-respect, all too many disabled people have to cope with often completely unconscious prejudices and stereotypes which have the effect of limiting their opportunities and activities in many important ways.

Fortunately, there has recently been an increasing recognition of many of these problems. In fact, 1978 saw the launch of *Sexuality and Disability*, a journal devoted to the study of sex in physical and mental handicap. It was an event which brought hope that the research and interchange of ideas and experiences which it contains might mark the opening of a much wider and more accurate understanding of disabled people's needs. At last, it seemed, there was a respectable platform from which to debate subjects ranging from the ethics of involving volunteer 'sexual samaritans' to policies concerning sex education and birth control. All of this has happened, but it has also led to an increase in factual and background studies which may or may not confer any benefit on the people involved. Concern about this kind of research has often been expressed but was well put by a handicapped author, Gunnel Enby, in her book *Let There Be Love*.

In it, she expresses her misgivings about the purpose of so many questionnaires, probings and statistics, and poses the question:

> Is it because of a real concern for the disabled, a genuine wish that we should at last be allowed our sexual freedom? Or is it because this is a new and hitherto unworked field which can afford the investigators great distinction?

No doubt both occur to some extent, and perhaps without the incentive of some personal reward the amount of research done would be far less. But, if the work done only enhances the reputation of the research worker and does little or nothing to help solve the problems of disabled people, then serious moral issues of exploitation are involved. Much research in other areas is quite certainly of this kind, though whether this is so in the present instance is difficult to judge as the guidelines as to what is likely to prove useful information are still very indistinct in this very new area of study. All that can be said with certainty is that the sexual and emotional problems of the severely incapacitated are very acute, and all the help, sensitivity and understanding that can be mustered is needed, whereas any unnecessary probing of their sex lives, or lack of them, only adds to the burden.

Serious physical disability leading to bed or chair care, or to severe sensory losses, is always likely to result in sexual problems. However, many physical conditions affecting sexual behaviour are not particularly disabling: at least, not in the sense of the individual requiring care or being unable to work. Serious burns or skin conditions, the scars of accidents or operations and damage to the genitalia – all come into this category. But perhaps one of the most obvious and common of these relates to the consequences of breast cancer: a condition which occurs in about one out of every seventeen women in Britain, and causes the death of as many as one in thirty.

The mortality rates could be much lower than they are but many women are so fearful of the diagnosis, the reputation of cancer as a killer, and so terrified of what they consider sexual mutilation, that they put off seeking medical help until beyond the point where they can be helped by radiotherapy or a mastectomy – the surgical removal of all, or part, of the breast.

There are sometimes other reasons too, even including embarrassment at allowing the breast to be examined by a doctor. But research has shown that, for many women, their fear of becoming sexually repellent is greater than their fear of dying. Of course, as the illness progresses, these priorities tend to be reversed and, in any case, sexuality and the ideal feminine beauty for which the sacrifice was made must succumb even more surely and dreadfully to the disease. How often this sort of thing happens is difficult to say, but it is far from infrequent.

More usually, women seek treatment as soon as they or a physician observe the symptoms, but this in no way suggests that the choice is uncomplicated. Fear of dying, coupled with the well publicized favourable prognosis for breast cancer, are strong inducements yet, such is the significance attaching to women's breasts as emblems of their femininity, that the choice is often delayed in a dangerous fashion, or else permission is given for only exploratory investigations, even where the surgeon is emphatic in his diagnosis and the dangers of any delay.

This theme of the great importance women attach to their breasts has been the subject of several recent books – including Daphna Ayalah and Isaac Weinstock's *Breasts*, and Karin Gyllensköld's *Breast Cancer*. The keynote in all is the remarkable psychological consequence of this type of cancer for in addition to threatening its victim's life, it also seems to strike at the very root of their sense of identity, and at their ability to sustain intimate relationships with the people they love.

Of course, all forms of cancer create great anxiety and ruminations about self-destruction if the position should become hopeless. However, studies of those women who have had a presumed completely successful mastectomy still reveal that about half suffer from post-operative depression and anxiety, and that about one quarter contemplate suicide. In many cases, the neurotic behaviour and greater dependence on tranquillizers, sleeping pills and alcohol seems to be specifically connected with sexual concerns rather than the more usual forebodings related to a possible recurrence of the disease.

Depending on the operation, some scars may be decidedly unsightly but, even in the more usual case where the excision has been neatly accomplished and a virtually undetectable prosthetic device moulded to fit the bra, the sense of having lost all feminine appeal, and even of being grotesque, may be difficult to relieve. It seems that some women are so convinced of their own off-putting appearance that they isolate themselves from husbands or lovers, effectively provoking the break they so much fear. Others find the reactions of their mate so discouraging, incompetent, or immature that they too withdraw from the relationship to some extent. And as the sexual cement of relationships crumble, and self-confidence declines, anxiety about recurrence is likely to increase. At this stage help is urgently needed though, unfortunately, it is not always easy to find. Surgeons and other doctors often feel that their job, and indeed the limit of their competence, lies in saving lives. But, important as physical health care and the preservation of life undoubtedly is, its ultimate value must also be judged in terms of the quality of life achieved.

Whatever the disability or disease, and whether it strikes in mid-life or infancy, more than sympathy and physical ministrations are necessary if people are to be helped to attain their optimal level of adjustment. This, of course, involves adequate economic, educational and occupational provisions but, in addition, it may frequently imply the need for specialized help through counselling and psychotherapy. Most marked forms of disfigurement or physical disablement create stresses and ambivalences, including anxieties concerning failure or rejection, which can lead to neurosis or an unduly limited emotional life. Damage to the body is only a starting point: the disability which follows is just as real a social and psychological phenomenon as it is a physical fact. Being handicapped may involve specific bodily limitations but it almost never occurs without their being other restraints also – whether these are imposed by the way in which the physical realities are perceived, reacted to, and treated by others, or by the person himself.

The combinations and permutations of possible ways in which any given physical handicap may be responded to are, of course, infinite. The lives lived are as varied as any others: some crumble or are crushed as a result of their physical ailments, others just get by, and others rise above their circumstances to achieve not only social success but impressive mental adjustment as well. It is, therefore, quite inappropriate to imply some sort of 'handicapped personality'.

Franklin D Roosevelt and the legless fighter pilot Sir Douglas Bader have long been favourite examples of just how disability can be overcome, physically and mentally, by those with the determination to do so. Bader even managed to get his golf handicap down to single figures, making him exceptional even when compared on equal terms with the great majority of golfers. But one of the greatest examples of unshakable resolution in the face of disability must surely be the 'Marathon of Hope', run in 1977 by a young Canadian student, Terry Fox, to raise money for cancer research, and to show just what can be achieved in spite of a severe physical handicap.

Fox's right leg had been amputated as a result of bone cancer, yet within three years he had trained sufficiently to attempt a marathon run across Canada on a artificial limb. Sadly, before the end of his odyssey, he was to collapse and later die as a result of secondary tumours in the lung, but his fortitude and dedication to a cause in face of great pain were nothing short of inspirational.

Fox seemed to have found a purpose, even an obsession, through which to live and justify his life as a handicapped person but, though he earned great respect and raised millions of dollars for the cause, it was at enormous mental cost. His was a triumph of willpower; a colossal overcompensation for disability, paid for in terms of happiness and mental adjustment as well as the more obvious physical wear, tear and pain. The great psychological pressures and sacrifices which were inevitably involved in so taxing an undertaking appeared to be even greater than his physical suffering. Often he was reduced to tears of anguish and dejection, in spite of which he drove his body on until it gave way under him: a heroic, though deeply troubled, figure by any standard.

Such great courage, persistence and achievement may be virtually unparallelled but, even so, remarkable fortitude in the face of discouraging situations is probably far more common than is generally recognized. For the most part though, because the personalities and circumstances involved are not likely to be anywhere near as vivid or dramatic as in the well-known exemplary cases, remarkable feats may pass unnoticed by all but a few. In some cases, the result of almost superhuman effort will be insufficient to achieve more than minor additional skills, though even these limited attainments in self-care or self-expression may be quite as impressive in their own way as those of individuals whose potential allows for a much more complete development or rehabilitation. Fortunately, successful adjustments do not necessarily depend upon the restoration of functions: sometimes circumstances combine with special abilities in such a way that new and fulfilling careers can open up, even where the disabilities involved continue to make a person's previous activities completely impossible.

Elizabeth Twistington-Higgins was a young ballet dancer who, as a result of polio, found herself in an iron lung, permanently paralysed from the neck downwards. Developing techniques in order to breath outside the mechanical lung is no easy matter in itself, but to go on and learn how to paint by holding a brush in the mouth, and later to earn a living by doing so, is a remarkable achievement. Since then, and together with others who must use their feet or their mouths to paint, an organization has been developed to produce and market exceptionally fine cards, calendars, and other art work. In terms of the physical handicaps involved, the psychological achievement must surely match the climbing of Everest yet, though the strain was occasionally apparent in her autobiography, and in Marc Alexander's biography, her great composure and positive attitude to life and its problems stand out very clearly.

Multiple sclerosis, occurring at the beginning of what was already a brilliant career, destroyed the future prospects for cellist Jacqueline du Pré. She too had to deal with despair, dependency and depression as she saw her life style and the music-making which had given it meaning slip away, never to return. But instead of giving way to her negative feelings, she too fought back to become a teacher of great artistic and personal gifts, discovering a new and satisfying career in the process.

Nevertheless, important as achievements must be to anyone with chronic or degenerative conditions, it would be wrong to suppose that these alone can be expected to offset all the apprehensions, regrets and vulnerabilities which burdensome and threatening physical illness can bring. After all, even with health, financial security and a job, life can still be very difficult, especially when one's grip on these seems tenuous. When doubts about the new self and the reactions of others crowd in, attainments undoubtedly help, but psychological reconstruction can often be quite detached from material and occupational considerations: these may help or hinder, but many of the major resources and obstacles to successful adjustment remain where they always were – in the disabled person's mind, and in the attitudes and supportiveness of others.

Helen Keller, who lost both her sight and hearing at the age of 19 months and so became functionally mute as well, was one of those disabled people for whom the support of others combined with remarkable inner resources. Taught to speak and develop her mind by another exceptional individual – Ann Sullivan, a 20 year old who had herself coped with blindness until her sight was partially restored – Hellen Keller went on to graduate from university and become a powerful influence on the education of the handicapped. The fortitude of these two women has been exemplary for the incapacitated and their teachers alike during the last eighty years but, though theirs was a success story, Helen Keller's *Journals* and her very early autobiography *The Story Of My Life* gave some idea of the great mental strain imposed by physical dysfunction.

Most struggles with disability, and their associated acts of personal courage, attract little attention: the gains and the losses, many times occurring only within the private thoughts of the disabled person and affecting only a few people within the family and immediate circle of friends and acquaintances. Yet to do justice to those who must live with physical handicap, and in order to contrast various ways in which mental resources may be channelled under different circumstances, more than the usual emphasis on breakdown and inability to cope needs to be considered. Each of the cases described is, of course, exceptional.

Yet, though most outcomes are mixed, and some disastrous, it is quite clear that people can still flourish in spite of extremely limiting and disabling circumstances. However, many of the most intractable problems seem to depend not only upon the type and extent of disability involved, but on there having being little successful adjustment and accomplishment prior to disablement, and where the steps towards them were therefore less well laid. Those who have previously known happiness and good fortune may present daunting problems of reconstruction but, many times, there remains a firm substructure on which to build. By contrast, those with congenital or early-occurring handicaps must build from scratch and, judging by the number of cases in which people resoundingly overcome their difficulties, reconstruction appears to be more readily achieved than construction – unless, that is, more help can be given than has usually been the case.

Taking the broadest view, personality adjustment and integration is obviously closely connected with the pursuit and achievement of those goals characteristic of our species. Opinion as to what these are, and how far each motivational satisfaction must be attained in order to foster mental health is, however, divided. Even so, it seems reasonable to assume that such goals exist, and that the degree to which they are blocked will have important consequences for the growth of personality. There are many more or less relevant speculations about what these may be, but two of the most elaborate and influential motivational theories of particular relevance to the psychology of handicap are those of Alfred Adler and Abraham Maslow.

Adler's theory of compensation and superiority striving has already received some attention in Chapter two, where the links between physical imperfections and maladjustment due to consequent inferiority feelings were discussed. If he is correct when he claims that the primary motivation of all human beings is to attain autonomy, equality and social acceptance, and that any serious blocking of their realization is the primary cause of neurosis, then physically disadvantaged individuals are obviously a psychiatric 'high risk' group. Moreover, this may be a group susceptible not only to psychopathology, but to curtailments in the growth of their personality as well.

The magnitude and significance of this risk is, however, difficult to estimate as statistical data is seldom assembled in a form which allows unambiguous and broadly enough based comparisons between physically disabled and physically intact people. Despair, renunciation and withdrawal may or may not be treated as identifiable psychiatric conditions in the disabled. Instead, they may simply be classified as unfortunate outcomes of difficult circumstances, and treated by a general practitioner with anti-depressants and sleeping pills: palliatives taking the place of therapy.

From an administrative point of view, comprehensive and reliable statistics are specially desirable when it comes to guiding policy and budgeting for services: in this respect, they may be of as much importance as when they suggest causal connections to scientists. However, strictly from the perspective of a handicapped individual, there are matters of greater and more immediate moment. For example, they are more likely to be concerned that the source of their own particular psychological problems should be correctly identified and appropriately treated. But, of even more importance, is the need to be led in the direction of positive personal growth, as well as away from the effects of debilitating conflict or acquiescence.

As has already been mentioned, Adler's special sensitivity and insight into the psychology of disability were partly due to his own experience with rickets. Weakness and dependence were seen for what they are – serious threats to psychological well-being and happiness which, though they can be incorporated into a healthy mental life, will continue to present hazards unless positive self-esteem can be established and consolidated through compensatory adjustments. Adler's presentation of the many possible scenarios for handling inferiority feelings and their outcomes, ranging from neurosis and suicide to successful compensation, make valuable reading for anyone concerned with handicap. The development of self-esteem is, of course, the foundation of healthy survival but, he argues, for 'growth' there must also be some degree of social altruism and public-spiritedness. It is perhaps no coincidence that each of the remarkable people mentioned earlier proved to have an abundance of the characteristic Adler called 'social interest'.

But the route towards such personal and social growth is, if we are to follow Abraham Maslow's line of thinking, very steep and composed of a number of identifiable steps; its higher points being attainable by only a relative few, even among the most vigorous and able-bodied. However, despite the fact that the theory was produced with ordinary developmental patterns in mind, it has nevertheless proved exceptionally useful for exploring the many psychological ramifications of physical handicap. After all, the principles remain the same, only the circumstances differ.

Maslow's 'hierarchy of needs' represents what he believes to be a sequentially ordered priority in human motives, such that the lower ones must be met to some satisfactory degree before progressing on and upwards to the next. The schema is usually drawn in the form of something like the step pyramid at Sakkara: the simile giving the idea of each level being supported upon a more extensive substructure; each step above the two basic survival needs representing a less fully attainable goal. The case made for this arrangement is subtle, elaborate and hedged by exceptions and subordinate principles, so it would be impossible to do it justice in any brief description. Nevertheless, the main features are clear enough:

Maslow's hierarchy of needs:

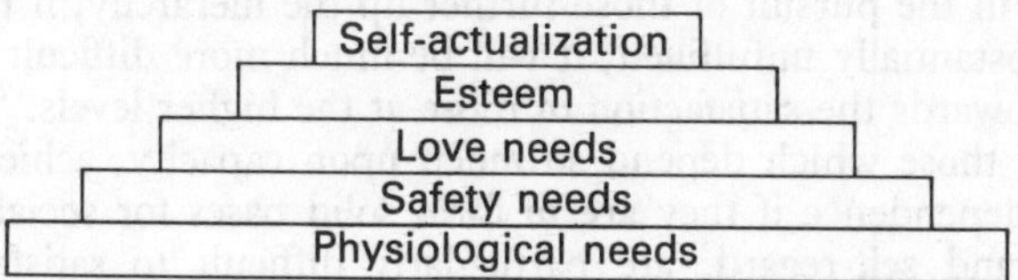

Homeostasis, the process by which organisms maintain the equilibrium of their body processes through motivated as well as reflexive activities, is as basic to mankind as to any other creature. Hunger, thirst or cold reflect physical conditions which, if they should become severe enough, indicate a threat to survival itself. Consequently, these 'physiological needs' have a high priority and so, according to Maslow, they must be met to an acceptable degree before other motives can become salient. In other words, the dangerously dehydrated and thirsty person thinks only of drink: concern with other matters only reappears when this need is no longer physiologically commanding.

In an ordered society, physiological needs seldom dominate as we are unlikely to experience starvation or dehydration, merely appetite and thermal discomfort. Only in exceptional circumstances do civilized human beings encounter acute privation, so other motives are likely to be, in Maslow's terms, 'prepotent' or occupy a foreground place in our minds.

'Safety needs' which, among other things, are activated by

threats to our persons, to our health, and to our economic security, tend to be much more influential motives, even in prosperous modern societies. For example, in tough city areas or in times of war, young people may be markedly susceptible to having much of their available mental energy drained by dealing with safety matters. More mundanely, the economic and health problems which commonly accompany old age make it extremely likely that such needs will become more pressing at this stage of life; in effect putting ordinary people into much the same position as the handicapped. 'Love needs', an emotional hunger for affection and sense of belonging, may also be inadequately met for disabled and old alike; perhaps more often due to a lack of opportunity in the one case, to loss in the other. But, whatever the reasons, age and disability share a great deal in common, in their pressing psychological needs no less than in their physical disadvantages.

The theory proposes that, although complete satisfaction of lower needs is by no means a prerequisite for investing mental energy in the pursuit of those further up the hierarchy, if they are left substantially unfulfilled, it will be much more difficult to progress towards the satisfaction of those at the higher levels. 'Esteem needs', those which depend so much upon capacity, achievement and independence if they are to form solid bases for social recognition and self-regard, are particularly difficult to satisfy when needs lower down the hierarchy are substantially unmet. As Adler emphasized, neurosis, frustration, discontent and compensatory behaviour are typical consequences of low self-esteem, consuming the mind's resources and making 'self-actualization' very unlikely.

Maslow's description of 'self-actualization' is far from clear cut but its prime characteristic depends upon the full realization of potential: that is, a person becoming precisely what they have it in them to be. It involves adopting a life style harmonious with their deepest urges and capacities: an existence usually, though not necessarily, creative and healthily concerned with social, ethical and other cultural matters. Of course, in an imperfect world, few can hope to attain this state, and fewer still retain it over a lifetime, whether the conditions required for self-actualization are sublime or entirely more modest. Instead, most of us move up and down the hierarchy, focusing most of our needs and motivations on the level just above the one sufficiently satisfied.

There are, however, many exceptions to this process. As Maslow himself points out, some rare and creative individuals can achieve self-actualization despite quite minimal satisfaction of their more basic needs. By contrast, there are others for whom circumstance and experience have created such profound doubt about their potential that they behave in quite the opposite way. Whether consciously or unconsciously, they reduce the level of their aspiration, renounce the higher goals, and instead settle for security or comfort.

For those in difficult and limiting circumstances, or with severe physical or mental limitations, such a defensive strategy may well prove satisfactory. By reducing aims and expectations, painful striving and disappointments can be held to a minimum while successes and satisfactions of a more attainable kind can be achieved. The balance is, however, a delicate one, and may be struck at a level far below the optimal if help, encouragement and opportunity are not forthcoming.

The satisfaction of love and 'esteem needs', both of which Maslow and Adler insist are indispensable for positive mental health, as opposed to a tranquillized form of survival, lie very much in the hands of other people: gifts to be disposed or withheld. Unfortunately, though love is not necessarily dependent upon attainments, esteem is, and the disabled person is frequently placed in double jeopardy by the many additional psychological, social and concrete barriers which society erects or leaves in their way.

Despite a good deal of positive legislation related to employment and education, and dramatic developments in prosthetics and bioengineering generally, far too many disabled people are still mentally and physically confined within their families, institutions, or the conventional activities of the handicapped. All indications are that this need not be so; that there are great numbers whose lives could be radically changed if only they had the encouragement and opportunity to dispute the diminished role and inferior status they have been assigned.

The old tendency to school so many of the disabled in resignation and acceptance of, at best, occupational therapy or sheltered work is now being widely challenged. Such a limited objective may well continue to be necessary in some instances, and even enforced in others where, for example, severe economic recession increases competition for all jobs, facilities and services. Nevertheless, the goal of optimization rather that stabilization is now firmly entrenched among most groups working on behalf of the disabled.

Of all the innumerable manifestations of physical incapacity, some of the most widespread and troublesome are those resulting from mobility problems generally, and quite avoidable architectural barriers in particular. Prosthetic devices as well as private and public motor transportation have done a great deal to overcome the difficulty of getting from one place to another, but it often happens that some of the most frustrating difficulties emerge only on arrival at a building or complex.

Since the 1981 'Year of the Disabled' there has been a growing public awareness of these and other problems, so that serious attempts are now frequently made to design and modify buildings with the disabled in mind. Inevitably though, it is going to take many years, and much persuasion, to make the built environment more accessible to the physically handicapped. Of course, cost is part of the reason but, even more importantly, there is often also a mistaken belief that mobility problems affect only a few people. Perhaps thoroughgoing change will only come about when it is fully realized that disability is not a minority concern; that it affects most of us at some time in our lives, whether as a result of temporary injury, pregnancy, or the infirmities brought about by age.

Freedom to move through and between buildings is quite obviously a desirable and sometimes crucial aspect of social and occupational life. More than this though, many of civilized man's most valuable resources are only accessible inside buildings, whether in educational establishments, theatres, cinemas, libraries, galleries, offices or workshops. Just as the mind is dependent on the body for its inputs, so it is also dependent upon a much larger physical body – the built environment – which contains and embodies so many of our cultural riches. Of course, everyone is different in what they want to take from these resources but the complete matrix of a modern mind includes all these things. As with any other element of our culture, we are shaped by the nature of these interactions: the extent and direction of our growth being circumscribed not only by our own potential but also by the way we use, or have access to, what is available. Physical mobility is therefore concerned with positive personal growth just as much as its lack can give rise to negative aspects of development or adjustment.

For those in wheelchairs particularly, travel and simply getting access to other homes or public buildings presents really discouraging obstacles. And, once inside, lifts, steps, toilets and doors may all prove daunting barriers to free movement, while the height of counters or bookshelves may mean that shopping is difficult to do alone. A great many of these problems can be overcome with the help of others, but it does create the dilemma of whether to limit mobility and outings to a minimum or incur the sense of obligation and dependency which requiring a lot of help may bring.

In recent times, the telephone, radio and television have, to an increasing extent, brought the wider world directly into the home. As a result, these devices are now established as inestimably important channels of information, recreation and company for all categories of disabled people. But, significant as their contribution to the quality of life undoubtedly is, radio or TV programmes differ from real social activities in that they seldom lead to more than a passive role: one which has distinct limitations when it comes to forging the personal relationships and achievements upon which self-definition and self-respect so much depend.

There are, however, some notable exceptions. For example, the Open University's use of public media has greatly improved the opportunity for academic and professional attainment among those whose schooling or disability had previously debarred them from higher education. Many physically handicapped graduates have found their degree a passport to work though, sad to say, academic success has had to be an end in itself for others. Nevertheless, even in a grossly pragmatic and materialistic society, the possession of a cultivated mind is still widely acknowledged as an attainment of the highest order so, to this extent, the achievement itself may go some way in helping individuals attain their esteem needs.

Without a doubt, the Open University's broadcast and postal tuition, together with their generally more accessible study centres, have created remarkable new possibilities for many handicapped people. So much so, that some 3,500 disabled students are now counted among its enrolment, and that is twice the number of disabled now studying at all other British universities put together. Naturally, there still remain many problems due to pain and illness interrupting studies, as well as the isolation of those who cannot travel to the centres and there join in tutorials, discussions and undergraduate life more generally. But, because the University is specifically geared to accommodating these problems, and even exploring their extent in its courses, a remarkable amount has been achieved by the students, administrators and academics alike in enhancing the dignity as well as the mental lives of so many disadvantaged individuals.

Clearly though, with or without broadcast material, not all disabled people are sufficiently intellectually gifted or motivated to pursue university level courses or achieve qualifications. Nevertheless, it would be difficult to avoid considerable informal education from ordinary radio and TV broadcasts as the programmes contain so much travel, natural history, literary, scientific and historical material. These media are also great levellers for, by participating in the near universal pastime of televiewing, even the most handicapped can, in addition to stocking their own minds, share common experiences with others and discuss them later on equal terms. It may be a limited participation in wider affairs, but it is participation, and so meets at least one of the most basic preconditions for group membership and the earning of esteem.

Physical limitations may be a necessary, but they are seldom a sufficient cause of someone becoming a 'disabled person'. Usually the process also requires assigning people a constricting and impoverished role, pitying them rather than giving help and respect, thinking categorically rather than in terms of individuals, and failing to recognize that the causes of disability are circumscribed rather than all-embracing. Total incapacity is virtually unknown: in the majority of cases, a vast range of adjustive possibilities remain open so long as encouragement, training and opportunity are provided.

If, however, there is insufficient recognition of the positive and normal qualities of the disabled, and a disproportionate emphasis is placed on their limitations, the consequence may be to create a self-fulfilling prophesy. Withholding social and occupational opportunities can, and often does, lead to a generalized stunting or deterioration of capacities – physical, mental and particularly motivational. Moreover, these avoidable and deplorable secondary handicaps are then likely to combine with the primary one to make people whose lives could have been much more normal disabled indeed.

As Adler and Maslow have outlined in some detail, the conditions necessary to nourish positive mental growth and avoid the polarizing forces which may draw disabled persons towards maladjustive overcompensation, or else acquiescence in the 'sick role', are often in conflict with some of society's most ingrained prejudices and stereotypes relating to handicap. As a consequence of this and other depressing, debilitating or disadvantaging circumstances, physical handicap not infrequently gives rise to psychological problems. But, it should be stressed, many of these difficulties are not a consequence of the disablement *per se*; rather, of pressures which may apply with equal force to members of any readily identifiable minority – for example, homosexuals or black people living in certain white communities. Physical disability may therefore often be associated with psychological disturbances but these are usually a more or less direct consequence of stifling circumstances: ones which apply whenever or however human beings are repressed, treated as inferior, or denied normal participation in social life.

With the possible exception of some neurological and sensory disorders, it can be extremely misleading to assume any homogeneous psychology of handicap and, even here, the notion is of questionable value or legitimacy. Psychological botanizing is always a hazardous business for, whether incapacitated or not, people and their circumstances are infinitely varied: being disabled neither confers nor implies any particular mental characteristics, any more than does the fact of being able-bodied. It may certainly tip the scales against people's chance of making a satisfying life for themselves, and it may even reveal many broad tendencies and considerable convergence of concerns and needs, but the personalities and mental lives of disabled people are as diverse as those of any other aggregate of individuals.

Even so, though a generalized treatment of psychological problems relating to 'the disabled' may be misleading unless it is constantly borne in mind that its purpose is only to provide a context for more particular and specialized thinking, it is still an important stage in reviewing and conceptualizing the type and range of material to be encompassed. Moreover, creating a general picture also helps to reveal typical or common elements, and frequently suggests connections or similarities between problems and their possible solutions. Only when such a framework becomes Procrustean, requiring individual cases to subordinate their form to it, does the process become undesirable. Statistics, categorizations and theories are, of course, as fundamental to the study of bodily dysfunction as they are to any other scientific undertakings. Additionally though, because the subject matter is people, the study of disability shares with all other psychological investigations the constraint that it must also treat the experiences and reactions of unique human beings responding to unique circumstances. Yet, obvious as it may seem, it is something that is all too often overlooked, even by those who are professionally involved. However, unless personal characteristics are given greater emphasis in the future than has sometimes been the case in the past, our capacity to understand and help individuals with a disability will continue to be less effective than need be. Worse still, we may even help perpetuate some of the generalizations and stereotypes which are among the most disabling and distressing aspects of physical handicap.

Chapter six
AGEING AND DYING

Like the disabled, old people are commonly seen as a rather distinctive group: sometimes, almost as a separate subspecies of mankind. Yet, rationally at least, we all realize that ageing is a normal part of adult life, and one which we ourselves must pass through if, that is, our lives are not cut short by illness, accident or some other calamity.

Ageing and dying are, of course, quite obviously and intimately connected. However, youth is no guarantee against having to endure not only death itself, but many of the long and drawn-out processes which lead to it. A distressingly large number of both young and middle-aged individuals still have to experience the physical and mental burdens which are more familiar in the elderly – particularly when cancer or some other wasting or degenerative disease is involved. For this reason, though much of what follows is conveniently presented in a form which presupposes the statistical norm of death occurring in old age, a great deal applies equally to younger people.

Yet despite the fact that the majority of us have a great many years in which to prepare for what lies ahead, many remain demonstrably and hopelessly unready. Instead, we keep busy, blot out disquieting thoughts and, as a consequence, are often not only inadequate in coping with our own problems, but also lack the insights necessary to help others with theirs. Even in loving and caring families, failure to deal with the mental and physical facts of ageing and death can lead to a quite avoidable lack of communication, understanding and help; robbing each generation in its turn of the support which those who must endure, and those who must attend, will one day need.

But, though ultimate collapse is unavoidable, the trajectory of growth and decline has no fixed properties, some people seem to escape most of the effects of decay and enjoy a vigorous and lively old age, succumbing in a brief terminal state, whereas others show all the signs of decrepitude and senility for a great many years. So, though it is perfectly possible to generalize from what is statistically normal, it is also necessary to recognize that there are great individual differences in mental as well as bodily ageing. Nevertheless, we are all equally subject to the underlying processes which give rise to physical ageing.

Even from the very earliest stages of life, vast numbers of cells die every day: in fact, the growth of the body and nervous system sometimes requires that this should be so. But, however unplanned and unfortunate it may be, the process continues throughout adult life, and not all cells can be replaced by the usual mechanisms of cell division, or by any other method. For example, those of the muscles and nervous system are simply lost to the organism, with obvious long-term consequences for both physical and mental effectiveness. Rates of loss of these irreplaceable cells have been estimated to average 100,000 per day throughout adult life, though there are obviously practical problems which make it difficult to determine how far the process is gradual and how far it depends upon stages and changing conditions.

The fact that many people show quite marked mental and physical changes over a short period of time may make it tempting to assume that these cell deaths occur in phases, but motivational and other physical factors are changing too, making any such assumption questionable. All we can be sure about is that the process is progressive and irreversible.

However, many cells can be, and regularly are, replaced as part of the body's normal restorative functioning. Without this maintenance activity, the major organs of the body would soon wear out and senescence and death would occur very much earlier. Unfortunately though, the process of replacement through cell division allows the possibility of errors due to imperfect transcriptions and translations of genetic material. And, as the number of copies being made increases, the possibility of error becomes one of increasing probability. Add to this the effects of radiation or other agents which accelerate the rate of cell mutation, and the fact that mammalian somatic cells have a definite limit to the number of times they can survive divisions, and it becomes apparent that the impetus towards physical decay is an increasing one. In fact, though experiments with otherwise healthy human beings are impractical, work with other mammals shows just how extensive this problem can be. For example, the liver cells of old mice have been found to have gross chromosomal abnormalities in 70 per cent of cases.

So, ageing may be seen as very largely due to the gradual accumulation of defects resulting from errors and failures in the cellular repair system. Its consequences are familiar enough: a loss of strength and elasticity in the muscles, arteries and skin; decline of the sensory and nervous systems, and progressive inability of such organs as lungs, liver and kidneys to function efficiently. Moreover, even the body's defensive mechanisms become impaired so that illnesses, and the damage they create, continuously add to the decay. Death may be fairly swift if the damage is focused on some critical life-support function but it may be considerably deferred if it is more diffusely spread.

Disease, famine, accident or warfare may obscure the fact and produce very fluctuating morbidity statistics but human beings, like every other species of animal, have a characteristic life span, with women living somewhat longer than men. Even so, there are great individual differences and, even under ideal living conditions, people differ considerably in the age they attain: illness and accident aside, bodies wear out at a different rate. Why this should be is not yet clear. It may well prove to be mainly a matter of genetics as the actuarial evidence which is so precisely and pragmatically assembled by life assurance companies, as well as by scientists, makes it quite evident that the progeny of long-lived parents are themselves more likely to survive longer than those of parents who died at an earlier age. Nevertheless, although there is a *prima facie* case to be answered, the effects of occupation and life style cannot be ruled out. Genes certainly control every aspect of our constitutional development and physiological functioning so are likely to be significant in determining life span and vigour, but children inherit more than genes from their parents. Social factors are also part of our heritage, and these effect such health-related things as diet and choice of occupation, whether physical or sedentary, as well as such dispositions as those towards smoking or drinking. So, both physical and life-style factors are likely to be involved.

The recent epidemic in affluent societies of heart conditions which accelerate the ageing process and death itself, has been responsible for what might almost seem a war on those ancient enemies. Exercise and diet have, for many, even become the basis for a new quasi-morality: rectitude being judged in terms of miles jogged, cholesterol avoided, or martinis refused. Mankind's total life span may well never be much affected by such rigorous practices and abstinences; after all, its upper limits are still where they were a hundred years ago, and perhaps thousands before that – when the Bible set it as being about three-score-years and ten. But for all that, bodily care can certainly ward off circulatory and many other disorders, helping to ensure that the individual achieves his own maximum span, and that he does it in the best possible health.

Of course, health and ageing are two closely integrated ideas, particularly when considering the question of when and how middle or old age begins. The widely held, though somewhat arbitrary, convention is to consider middle age as lying somewhere between 40 and 60, while old age is commonly counted from about that time onwards. But, given good health and appearance, such an arithmetical notion may seem to have very little utility and, in fact, they indicate a dangerously stereotypical way of thinking which may only serve to trap or limit the individual. Fixed retirement ages can be as distressing for someone in robust good health as they can for those whose strength and vitality have been more severely drained by the same number of years.

The notion of 'middle age' is, though, not so much an important fact of biology but of social attribution, convention and outlook. Some people have what most of us would regard as the misfortune to be seen as middle-aged while they are still comparatively young: wrinkled skin, hair loss, turning grey and other such manifestations of antiquity may lay in the genes and appear regardless of health and vigour. In themselves, they may have no physical significance yet, unless they can be concealed, they may very well lead others to behave somewhat differently towards that person, nudging them along more rapidly than need be into accepting an elderly or sedate role. It is upon the way people see themselves and are, or think they are, seen by others, that some of the most notable consequences of physical ageing depend.

'Middle age' is very largely a state of mind. The Victorians seemed to embrace it as soon as they could; the women hiding youthful hair and bodies under heavy bonnets and skirts, while equally young men would adopt venerable beards and sticks. Our own generation wants none of this precocious ageing and solemnity; generally preferring an extension of youth. But for those who lose their youthful hair, complexion or shape at an early stage, the transition into psychological middle age may be difficult to avoid. This is likely to be particularly so when their social circle is very restricted, or composed mainly of people who are significantly younger or older.

So, the process of ageing is a bio-social one: cell death, and accumulating errors in those which remain, may be all that is necessary to cause decrepitude and death, but social and psychological factors are also of great importance in determining when and how the facts of decline shall be allowed to shape feelings and activities. Fortunately or unfortunately, there is no necessary correlation between the decay of the body and that of the mind: indeed, though certain faculties may decline, mental power sometimes continues to grow long after physical erosion has begun to be quite apparent. The philosophical and literary fruits of age are many times some of the richest borne in a lifetime, and even scientists have been known to be extremely innovative well into chronological old age.

It is, though, sometimes difficult to avoid the restrictions which the years may bring. For example, like the disabled, older people are not supposed to be interested in sex. Yet, though boredom and lack of opportunity may inhibit interest and outlet to some degree, sexual urges can remain extremely powerful at an age when younger people often consider it ridiculous or even degrading.

Women are under more pressure than men to refrain from sex, even though their appetites can be greater after the menopause than they ever were before. Instead, most women are presented with, and accept, the idea that the ageing female body is particularly unattractive: that not only should they give up any idea of entering new sexual relationships, they should also acquiesce with the general view that physical love is only for the young, at least so far as women are concerned. Of course, this is nonsense: though older women's bodies no longer retain, if even they possessed it, the line and grace of youth, they fare no worse than men. But men are far less loaded with guilt and prohibitions at engaging in the sort of relationships which help to keep people feeling young, and which may lead on to even more sustaining companionships for the future.

Above all though, middle age is typified by contrasts: a time of achievement and regret, of stability and change. Again, there can be no hard and fast rules, but the period from about 40 to 60 can be very much more golden than the traditional 'golden years' of old age. By these middle years the costs and stresses of raising children have often passed, mortgages paid, homes made comfortable and careers well-developed. Health and vigour are frequently excellent and, if it ever comes, this should be a time of authority, success and financial security. At about 50, many of us have reached the crest of our lives: an interlude of freedom like the weightlessness of space-flight; a period between the euphoria of upward ascent and more sober feelings during the inevitable downward journey.

Existentially though, the view of life from this apogee can be extremely disorientating: the self-assessments which are typically made at this time and which often feature so large in 'mid-life crises' are often far from comforting. Once the course of life seems fairly predictable, even the most successful and well-adjusted life style can be seen as a 'rut' – and one which has lost much of its point when the children have been raised and nearly everything that will be done has already been done. Pensions, lack of other skills, or the prevailing job situation hold people where they are while they reflect on what might have been more worthwhile, or what they had hoped for but will now never happen.

In men, this is often referred to metaphorically as the 'male menopause' – which, though it has no equivalent physical basis – is used to indicate the depression, anxiety, self-devaluation and general moodiness which often accompany a woman's physical changes during the menopause. At this mid-life point, a woman's body passes through a number of degenerative changes in the reproductive system, as well as considerable hormonal upsets which have their effects in a great many other systems. Additionally, both sexes are likely to be aware of considerable general deterioration of their bodies: men frequently experiencing this stage as one where their masculine virtues, strength and vigour, are beginning to ebb noticeably; while women see their special feminine characteristics of sexual attractiveness and maternal potential falling away. To the extent that both men and women experience psychologically important doors closing behind them, and the gateway to old age opening before, it seems at least understandable, if not accurate, to group their mid-life crises together under some such general term as the 'menopause'.

Beyond 50, not only is health and vigour declining in most people, but other signs of mortality are also becoming more obvious and ominous. From this time onward, the death rate begins to show a markedly steepening increase: cancer and heart disease begin to take their toll among one's contemporaries, and the death of parents, aunts and uncles removes the front ranks – revealing the old enemy, dead ahead. Of course, many people are relatively unreflective or have experiences which tend to insulate them somewhat from the mental and physical exigencies of this period. But, for a great many, there comes a turning point during which awareness that time to come has been largely supplemented by time left, and a recognition that serious questions about one's identity and life's meaning are still to be answered.

The developmental psychology of middle and old age is surprisingly little investigated compared with, say, that of infancy and adolescence. But, of those who have made important contributions, perhaps the greatest navigator of the ontological shoals awaiting us all in this stage of our journey is Carl Gustav Jung. Many psychologists would strongly disagree with this assessment, arguing that not only are his methods highly subjective, but that his data source is highly selective. Certainly it could not be denied that the sort of people Jung treated or analyzed were typically highly intelligent, and probably already sympathetic towards his own well-known and deeply entrenched metaphysical tendencies. Nevertheless, though his observations and interpretations may be have a far less than universal applicability (as are most worthwhile psychological insights) many have apparently found them accurate and relevant to their own lives.

In *The Stages of Life*, Jung considers the characteristic ways in which, at each of them, we channel our limited supply of mental and physical energy more emphatically into one sort of activity than another. In keeping with his 'Principle of Equivalence', he then argues that when, and only when, energy expenditure in one or more areas is reduced can a greated amount be made available to others. So, in theory at least, as the ageing body's energy requirements decrease, a relatively greater amount is made available for psychic activities. As a result, the middle years frequently see the appearance of a 'radical transvaluation', or turning away from materialistic activities to those concerned with spiritual matters. Increasingly, religious, social and philosophical speculation and values gain prominence, though more concerned with understanding than with the activity commitments which characterize younger people's interest in these things.

Of course, Jung recognizes that these potentials for energy reinvestments are no more than the opening of new possibilities: for many, more mundane objects will absorb these available resources. Yet, he argues, the combination of mental and physical events which occur in mid-life lead a substantial number of people to use an increasing proportion of their mental energy on questions of meaning and value. Unfortunately though, the result can just as easily be confusion and despair as growth and the re-definition of existence: outcomes depend very much upon people's circumstances and previous mental development, not just their energy investment and personal needs. In view of the sort of questions posed, it could hardly be otherwise for, of all the religious and philosophical themes demanding attention in later life, none are more pressing, or more impenetrable, than those connected with death and beyond.

We may try to avoid posing these questions, but few can do so entirely. Even if not consciously framed, our hypotheses and conceptions form anyway, resulting in an accretion of conscious and unconscious ideas which are both amorphous and ambiguous. So, what people say about dying is no sure guide to what they think or feel; and studies, particularly of the questionnaire or formal interview type, are always likely to have difficulty in dealing with such subjects, about which people tend to have markedly unformed and contradictory ideas, beliefs and emotions. And, of course, the difficulties are likely to be even greater when, as in the present case, the subject matter is a sensitive or disturbing one, and one which is capable of generating great embarrassment. Stereotyped and flippant responses are entirely to be expected: mental defences often being busily at work avoiding a confrontation with subjects consciously or unconsciously repressed, while additionally protecting the ego from being revealed to others as weak, perplexed, immature or superstition-ridden. Prayer in the face of death and danger is common enough, even among those who assert atheism and ridicule the supernatural before and after the threat. It is therefore an extremely delicate and, practically speaking, often impossible task to judge or anticipate people's mental reactions to the prospect of their impending physical death and dissolution.

Even so, the inexorable physical changes of ageing, the death of friends, relations, or spouse, all confront us with practical as well as philosophical problems of adjustment – which crush some but are successfully handled by others. There have been a number of interesting psychological studies along these lines, but one of the better known ones was published under the title *Aging and Personality* by S. Reichard and his colleagues. Taking a group of American men in the somewhat wide age-range of 55 to 84 they undertook an unusually thorough programme of interviewing, rating and testing, followed by a search for statistically identifiable categories of response to age and retirement. This present book, being more specifically concerned with mind-body interaction is not the place to discuss Reichard's work in detail, but the five categories identified in their analysis have created a very useful descriptive framework within which the interdependence of mental and physical characteristics can be explored.

Naturally, any categorization of human beings is likely to be achieved at the cost of simplifying and therefore, to some extent at least, distorting reality. It may be that no single human will meet all the characteristics of a statistically-created category, but they can be extremely helpful in showing which features tend to go together. The system developed by Reichard and his colleagues proved to be one of the more satisfactory ways of grouping, though even then it was only able to accommodate two-thirds of the people involved in the study: the remaining third, who had also contributed the data from which the correlations were made, did not fit well enough into the typical patterns created. The categories ranged from the most positive – those people who were mature, optimistic and with few regrets – through to those who were more passive and accepting; 'rocking-chair' types, and those who developed an 'armour' of habits and activities to shut out anxiety and fears. Then there were those who were angry at life, resentful of age and fearful of death; those whose own failures and economic or other misfortunes had made them self-hating and, at the extreme of nihilism, those who (claimed at least) not to be concerned about death as it would be the vehicle of their release. Reichard's categories certainly reflect stereotypes, but they are also a useful starting-point for exploring the ways in which personality interacts with economic, social or health considerations to shape the pattern of ageing. What is needed now is more information about the principal direction of causal relationships.

Despite obvious similarities, there are also a good many sex differences in patterns of ageing. Amongst other things, a number of significant landmarks differ, making it harder to identify a point at which old age might be said to begin for men and women. Even those women who have outside careers tend to retire some years before their male counterparts and, in any case, have a longer expectation of life: forward planning is therefore much more practicable in their case. Retirement from one's job is probably a fairly crucial moment for both sexes, though women are probably more able to adapt to being at home, more capable of filling their domestic hours contentedly, and less likely to find themselves an intruder in the domain of someone else. Moreover, whether or not this may change in the future, men are much more likely to define themselves in terms of their occupation and so be more disorientated when they no longer have one. At 65, with a further life-expectation of only a very few years, men are often tempted to begin the mental letting-go process long before it would be likely, or appropriate, for a newly-retired woman.

For either sex though, people's response to retirement will be equally variable – from garden or rocking-chair contentment to regret, depression and foreboding – depending on the individual's unique combination of personal characteristics and their circumstances. Of course, much depends upon health and economic factors, but much too depends upon whether there will be anyone to love and care for one as disability increases, either through a steady deterioration of mobility, sight, hearing and strength, or else the more rapid and alarming effects of stroke, cancer or cardiovascular disease. Personality, health and circumstances are all involved in coping with old age, and these interact one with the other, never remaining constant. Plateaux of apparent stability can, and do, occur but the pattern is essentially a changing one: the foundations of this stability are inevitably insecure and slips may be expected to occur as dependence increases, illnesses develop, or spouses die.

During the prime years, past, present and future may each seem to contain a more or less similar balance of pleasant and unpleasant things. In old age though, the present is likely to include feebleness, poor health, a decaying body and the loss of friends and family. The future contains the likelihood of either a fairly sharp death as a result of the several equally disagreeable terminal diseases, or else a more gradual decline into dependency. For many old people, it is the latter, becoming incapable and a burden to others that presents the most alarming prospect – even if they can rely on there being some loved person on whom they can depend when the time comes. Not surprisingly then, a great many old people choose to spend the latter part of their lives in the past: endlessly reminiscing about people and events set in a time of greater personal security and hope.

Withdrawal into the past may be a matter of more or less conscious choice, or it may be the result of largely unconscious processes but, either way, there does tend to be a quite marked reduction in contact with matters of the present. Cars, mortgages, education and jobs are often of primary interest to an elderly person's children, but, for the old, these things are largely matters of the past. 'Generation gaps' are created in many ways but not least by the fact that things which are of compelling interest at one stage may have little relevance at another. Some people manage to span these rifts through continuing to live more positive and evolving lives but the progress of ageing will usually limit these possibilities in due course, leaving affection and shared memories as the principal common bond holding people together.

Working wives and the dispersal of families and friends which modern job mobility has done much to create has meant that, for old people in the home, gossip and casual visitors are likely to be much less frequent than they would have been in the past. In their place radio and television programmes bring news and entertainment; the 'soap operas' even providing access to large surrogate families whose doings, like a real family, can be shared with others as a useful basis for further human contact. Unfortunately though, sensory or intellectual impairments often cause old people some difficulty in following their radio or television programmes. Even a modest degree of deafness can be surprisingly alienating if it causes the old person to miss the point of programmes watched by the rest of the family. Shared experiences are likely to be few enough and, if even these common denominators of modern living cannot be discussed, points of contact will be seriously reduced.

Having lost one's husband or wife, and become an appendage in someone else's world, or living alone most or all of the time, can leave anyone with very little concerning the present or future to discuss. As a result of these or other forced limitations, withdrawal into the past may be the only tolerable option left open. One of the dangers of this strategy is, however, that retreat from reality allows people's thought processes to become progressively more detached from logical sequences or relevance to others, with the result that social alienation may become more profound while dependence upon recollections, daydream and fantasy becomes ever more powerful.

Garrulous old age, with its wandering thoughts, confusion and memory losses is a common enough occurrence, as is the more serious decline into senile psychosis, where delusions of persecution and unfounded charges of mistreatment often bring such embarrassment to families that they are glad to be rid of their aged relative. In fact, the social and psychological burdens on those who care for the old are often almost as acute as those of the old persons themselves. Rows, accidents, the consequences of incontinence, guilt about ungenerous though perfectly natural feelings, the lack of privacy and the irritating ways and demands of many elderly folk can wreak havoc with family life and the mental equilibrium of all those concerned. Of course, this scenario is by no means inevitable: many families live happy and mutually respecting existences.

Nevertheless, both old people and their families have a very natural concern that things will become more difficult as time goes by and both sides must somehow adjust to the reversal of parent-child role which dependency tends to bring.

When the ageing person is in comfortable financial circumstances and has always had a vigorous mental life, conditions tend to be easier. Many anxieties are reduced, opportunities for travel, entertainment, and so on are greater, and the well-stocked and well-exercised mind may continue relatively unimpaired despite the limitations imposed through physical incapacity. In such cases, the old person is less likely to experience the isolation and despair which is so often brought about by other people's avoidance. It may seem cynical, but old people who own property, valuable possessions, and are financially well off, are also far less likely to be ignored than those who are not so comfortable.

Loneliness is one of the greatest afflictions of old age: without others, many of the most basic conditions for sustaining the will to live are removed. As Eustace Chesser points out in his book *Living With Suicide*, without love, meaning, hope and purpose, self-destruction becomes entirely more likely, whatever one's age or state of health. Contrary to what is often supposed, suicide is by no means a prerogative of the young. Certainly many of the same existential problems mentioned may effect young people as readily as the old, but age allows fewer possibilities of rectification, and brings a surer recognition that death is approaching rapidly anyway. The outcome may be suicide in some cases, but it may also be the almost comparable act of abandoning the will to live. Most doctors have seen cases of rapid decline and sudden unexpected death following a loss of will to continue – for example, after a beloved husband or wife has died – but the complex circumstances involved almost defy the possibility of obtaining adequate statistical data. The syndrome is, however, becoming much more widely acknowledged, understood and researched, as can be seen from recent books like James Lynch's *The Broken Heart: The Medical Consequences of Loneliness*.

Illness, pain, uselessness and loneliness are all hard things to bear, whether old age and the prospect of death are factors or not. Also, whenever or wherever the body is seriously enfeebled or diseased, a number of additional tribulations occur; particularly through the violation of one's sense of shame. Smells and bedpans, signs of decay and ugliness can all be difficult to live with. Having someone else dress and undress us or supervise our defecation and urination, contravenes the sense of shame and modesty experienced to some degree or another by all peoples of the world. Yet, though physical care may be a necessity, it is often given without due consideration of the feelings of those most directly involved.

At a time when my own mother lay dying in a hospital, I used to give lectures at a staff college for senior members of the nursing profession. Inevitably, such a preoccupying event found its way into several of the discussions which took place at and around that time: in particular, the barbarously blunt way my father had been informed of her forthcoming death, and the almost equivalent distress which she, in her ignorance of the prognosis, was suffering as a result of what were actually quite unnecessary infringements of her physical modesty. Some matrons and assistant matrons on the course completely understood the significance of these often-flouted needs for screening and privacy while body functions are attended to, but others simply felt that physical shame is completely out of place in a hospital. Yet, fundamental as medical care undoubtedly is, there surely remains a responsibility not to humiliate other human beings but, instead, to show respect and consideration when tending the body. Few people like being treated as an object: a clinical and inert thing to be handled. So, even though certain embarrassing things have to be done when caring for the old or sick, these should be performed with full recognition that people are more than bodies; that their sensibilities and sense of propriety need to be studied quite as closely as their temperature charts.

Although the great majority of people in English-speaking countries will ultimately die in a hospital, there are often important conflicts of interest which raise serious questions about the effectiveness and desirability of current practices and institutions. One of the central problems is that death in a ward can be very distressing to other patients and visitors alike: consequently, the dying are likely to be segregated or avoided, and thus isolated at their time of greatest psychological need. Moreover, hospital staff have been trained with physical healing at the very core of their education and ethic, with the result that death may come to seem like personal failure, thereby encouraging the use of quite futile tests and treatments. Many of these are uncomfortable or exhausting: they may help the professionals to obtain greater peace of mind at having done everything possible but, unless there is some improvement and extension of human, as opposed to biological existence, the main consequence of so-called 'heroic' methods may be to weary the patient, distress and impoverish the relatives and make the process of dying a mechanical affair robbed of psychological or spiritual significance for any of the people concerned.

Dying has always been one of mankind's most sacred occasions but a technologically advanced society may, almost by accident, lose contact with this aspect. People are admitted into hospitals so they can receive the best physical therapy available, and there they are met by professionals specialized in the healing of particular bodily disorders. For most illnesses this is probably an excellent system, particularly as modern medical and nursing training contains an increasing amount of normal psychology and some psychiatry. But, for those who are quite predictably destined to die in hospital, such a place may be far from ideal for the purpose: they are, after all, huge bureaucratic institutions geared to the throughput of temporarily sick people.

Most importantly though, being admitted into hospital removes the dying person from the reassuring presence of family and friends. Instead, they are surrounded by strangers, patients or staff, whose own presence in the ward is only an interlude or duty period in their ongoing lives. Beyond hospital topics and the odd joke or sign of compassion, the dying patient may find few real points of human contact either with other patients or the medical staff. Worse still, the artificiality imposed by ward-visiting may so inhibit friends and relatives that they are quite unable to do more than fill the time with gossip or other empty talk. So, for patients aware of their impending death, confinement in hospital may reduce their end to an experience of great loneliness and desolation: surrounded by people, yet unable to share with them, or tap the comfort and strength they need to face their end.

Of course, by no means all who die are very aware of what is going on. Some slide into a clouded state of mind due to age-related deterioration; others hope to recover from an illness until their condition, or the drugs used to control it, have carried them beyond the point of fully grasping what is happening. Many doctors and relatives regard this as merciful good fortune and often go to great lengths to keep this knowledge from those who are dying. In many cases, this restraint or suppression is motivated by pure concern for the person dying and, no doubt, often maintains the semblance of normality for a while longer, making the end of life less stressful or depressing than it might have been. However, motives underlying keeping quiet about foreseeable death can sometimes seem to serve the purpose of survivors more than the dying person, though either party may be equally responsible for the holding back.

Relations may be simply too immature to handle the kind of situation which terminal illness brings; perhaps rationalizing their witholding of the prognosis as a positive or protective action. Even doctors are not always prepared or very competent at entering into the difficult, and what may sometimes be extremely emotionally taxing, dealings with the dying. Instead, they see it as entirely the affair of relatives, who may also be given the task of deciding how, when, or if, the news is to be broken to the patient. This is perhaps often a wise and well-considered strategy, but so important is the management of this event, from everyone's point of view, that all decisions should be carefully worked out in terms of the various personalities concerned.

It sometimes happens that when people discover that knowledge of their forthcoming death was withheld from them by relatives and doctors, they become extremely angry: however, by no means everyone would choose to receive this piece of unwelcome news before it was necessary. It depends very much upon the personality of the individual concerned. Some people evidently feel that they should know in order to prepare themselves and use their remaining time appropriately as the precious commodity it has become: others quite clearly prefer to defer, or even deny, acceptance of their extinction. For some, the ideal death would be an unexpected heart attack; for others, though, mental and spiritual preparation, settling practical affairs and taking proper leave of ones counts for much more. The difficulty lies in identifying the particular disposition of specific individuals: getting it wrong can be a great misfortune, yet most of us have little experience and few guidelines to go on. Statistics and scientific studies are of little help in this, as in most situations touching existential matters, and our anticipations, speculations, or prognostications about the reactions of ourselves or others to impending death may well prove very wide of the mark.

Understanding the needs and feelings of those who are dying is made excessively difficult because of the great embarrassment which tends to affect almost all concerned. Conversations are typically artificial and guarded, with fears on each side that they will either display or provoke a distressing emotional outburst. As a result, either the dying person or their family may opt for hospital care as the easiest way out of a tense and painful situation: the former perhaps rationalizing the choice in terms of not being a burden or not wanting the family to witness their suffering or ignominious deterioration, whilst the latter may conceal their true motivations and justify their behaviour by stressing the medical advantages of being in an institution. Of course, these are good reasons for such a choice, and may often be the real and salient ones, but it is also apparent that impending death can alienate members of even the most loving families, resulting in the psychic abandonment of the individual who is dying, and the guilt of those who are not.

In the case of the very old, the emotional content of contemplating and discussing death may have diminished very considerably as a result of having plenty of time to come to terms with the idea; no longer feeling much connection or sympathy with the present time and, in any case, feeling that the pleasures of life are not substantially outweighed by tribulations, tedium and tiredness. Of course, there are no age limits in these matters but younger people, with more to have continued living for, may be expected to react to their annihilation more sharply, and many more of these may be expected to experience a great deal of resistance and anguish before being able to accept that they must die.

Of all those currently working on the psychological aspects of death, perhaps the most remarkable and influential is Elisabeth Kübler-Ross, a psychiatrist of German origin, now living and working in the United States. Her early voluntary work with the victims of wartime oppression and death camps not only determined the direction of her subsequent career, but added substantially to the qualities of insight and compassion which has enriched her work with ordinary people dying in ordinary circumstances. As a doctor, she has had considerable influence on other members of the medical professions; markedly affecting attitudes and approaches to the counselling and management of those who are dying. Quite as significantly though, the ideas contained in her *On Death and Dying*, and many other books and articles besides, have now reached huge lay audiences and have begun to make acceptance and handling of death, a more open subject, and one treated with far greater sensitivity than has been usual in the past.

Like life itself, Kübler-Ross has shown how the process of dying has its own typical psychological ups and downs, and how understanding and anticipating these transforms what may seem a purely negative phase of life into a very positive and even pleasurable one. The situation with which she is most particularly concerned is where terminal illness is diagnosed and the patient has some time to consider the course and outcome of their condition. Naturally, there can be no invariable pattern of events: personalities, circumstances and the illness itself allow for infinite shades of difference, but it is possible to pick out the typical stages in dying as in any other developmental phase.

The initial response to a diagnosis of terminal illness very much depends on how it is broached – whether hope of recovery is emphasized, allowed, or realistically discounted – and how long hope remains a part of the patient's perception of his illness. However, from the time a person learns they have a lethal condition, Kübler-Ross traces the typical reactions which follow – from the shock and denial of the first stage, to anger, and the feelings of meaninglessness, loneliness and depression which come later. But though there are great individual differences in this, depression ultimately bottoms out and, from then onwards, there is the possibility of moving towards greater self-awareness, more enriching relationships with others, and acceptance of the fact of dying and parting. Religious beliefs undoubtedly help some people to achieve this last stage, but frequently even those who have them can benefit from some sort of alternative or additional secular counselling at this time.

But, though the work of Kübler-Ross and others like her is focused upon last things, it nevertheless emphasizes the importance of coming to terms with the idea of death as soon as we are able. This is not just so we shall be of the greatest help to others, or well prepared when our own time comes, though both would happen; rather, coming to terms with the inevitability of physical death increases our potential for living effectively. In her view, death is not the enemy of the living but, on the contrary, is an integral part of our life cycle, and one which helps give it shape and meanings. Like Dickens' Scrooge, it may require a long time and some presentiment or foretaste of death to stimulate the will to live fully and well, but it is never too late to begin again, or too early to come to terms with the precious and fleeting nature of personal time. As Kübler-Ross puts it:

> It is the denial of death that is partially responsible for people living empty, purposeless lives; for when you live as if you will live for ever, it becomes too easy to postpone the things you know you must do. (*Death: The Final Stage of Growth*)

Viktor Frankl, another German psychiatrist, who had himself survived in a death camp though all his family and most of the people he knew died there, also turned his horrifying experiences to positive effect. In the development of his 'logotherapy', or existential psychology based on the need to find meaning in life, he also discusses (in *Man's Search for Meaning*) acceptance of life's transitoriness as fundamental to mental growth and health: 'At any moment, man must decide, for better or worse, what will be the monument of his existence.' The monument does not have to be imposing in the usual social sense; it may simply be one's children, or difficulties faced and surmounted. But it does depend upon actively pursuing worthwhile aims, rather than being carried along on an aimless, even though comfortable way to the edge of extinction, there to find despair or even panic because life has been squandered pointlessly and cannot be changed.

The tendency to sermonize is very marked in the work of both Kübler-Ross and Frankl and, for this reason, is unpalatable to many behavioural scientists. None the less, though much of what they have to say about living in such a way that there shall be no regrets about things done or undone can be construed as purely philosophical or moralistic, their conclusions have been based upon an unusually wide experience of people dying. In fact, Kübler-Ross has spent most of her working life observing and counselling the dying, and so could be said to have an empirical basis for her views which can have few, if any, equals. For some, like Kübler-Ross, the distillation of experience is wisdom rather than statistically-based conclusions and it is this more than anything else that lies at the heart of the modern hospice movement.

In some underdeveloped countries, there are still special places where the moribund are left in the company of others with an attendant to feed them, until they die. The West has probably very little to learn from these particular Eastern practices: the people taken there may accept their fate with little outward sign of emotion but such psychological discarding of the helpless has little to commend it, however congruent it may be with a particular culture. There is one respect, though, in which modern Western hospices resemble their Eastern counterparts; they are places specially provided for the dying, and where there is no question of attempting to cure the patient. The great difference is that the hospice provides intensive medical and psychological care for the dying person; taking every advantage of modern drugs and other treatments to minimize pain and incapacity while maximizing the quality of mental life during these remaining days.

For many, the very notion of entering a place to die is unacceptable: they would prefer to continue with treatment in a hospital, however hopeless their case may be. Others may be fortunate enough to have all their mental and physical needs willingly met within the home so, unless there are practical reasons for doing otherwise, they often prefer to meet death within their families. Even so, a growing proportion of all types are beginning to discover that a hospice can provide the kind of support not easily found elsewhere.

Whatever other emotions beset people when they know they are dying, and these can range from relief to rage, fear is seldom likely to be absent. Of course, there are many types of fear: there is fear of becoming a burden; fear of losing control of the mind and physical functions, thereby becoming grotesque and losing love and respect; fear of eternal separation and of the unknown, and so on. But studies have also shown that, very high on this list, is a dread of pain and facing terminal agony.

Naturally, hospital and family doctors are not at all lacking in the skills necessary to control pain, but their practices and resources are geared to treating the living, not relieving the dying. By contrast, doctors in a hospice can and do become highly specialized in the control of pain *per se*. Moreover, they can use drugs without considering the possibility of dependency and, unlike the general practitioner who must always consider the wisdom of prescribing powerful drugs to people who may, intentionally or not, lethally overdose themselves, can always administer optimal levels of pain-killing substances.

Euthanasia, though illegal, is probably quite common in the later stages of harrowing terminal illness. Again, for obvious reasons, there can be no usable statistics to suggest how frequently overdoses are mercifully administered by the doctor himself, or how often he allows the people concerned possession of a sufficient quantity of a drug so they can choose the point where irreversible suffering has made the prolongation of life unacceptable. Such a course may involve legal danger to the practitioner or considerable guilt for a relative so, for the most part, one only knows about these things from personal experience or conversations among friends. Nevertheless, it is quite clear that many families have reason to be grateful for the courageous intervention or help of their family doctor in limiting pointless and cruel pain. The problem is, though, one cannot always rely upon doctors to provide or permit a humane end to the suffering: after all, their own ethical views, as well as their careers, are involved. And there is always the point, which applies to all concerned, that the choice made may not always have been the same as that of the dying individual.

For those and many other reasons, the hospice is now becoming increasingly popular with doctors and patients alike. There at least, pain will be kept to its absolute minimum and the patient can depend upon constant and immediate attention. In his book *Care of the Dying*, Richard Lamerton carefully considers both the psychological and practical implications of euthanasia, but comes to the opinion that it is generally a hazardous and undesirable solution to the problems of terminal illness. Instead, he argues, careful preparation and management can make death in the home or in a hospice a unique opportunity for mental and spiritual growth. Parting from the body, perhaps facing absolute extinction, must always be frightening: yet this fear can be very much decreased, and even transformed into something more positive, if the person concerned has adequate mental preparation and support. Religious beliefs and loving families can be of enormous help but, with or without them, it has been found that the sort of specialized psychological care which is being developed in hospices can also substitute for, or supplement, these.

Under ideal conditions, the end of bodily existence may be transformed from a time of desolation, sham relationships and regressive denial into a final enriching experience for the individual concerned, and for others too. But the pain of impending parting often prevents honest interchange between people who are emotionally very close. To prevent grief in the other, each may talk about getting better, summer holidays, or other patently unrealistic plans for the future. Instead of supporting the dying person, they isolate him and, instead of giving mutual comfort and exchanging affirmations of love and meaning, the opportunity is wasted. This realization, if it comes after the patient has died, may remain as a lifelong feeling of guilt that, emotionally at least, one turned aside and slunk away, without even taking a proper farewell.

'Growth through death' approaches, such as those developed in Kübler-Ross's own institute and now throughout the hospice movement generally, are concerned with making sure that the reasons for this kind of guilt do not occur. Counselling with the dying person and their family, the presence and support of others who are also dying, and a context in which to feel and express emotions fully and honestly, are all specifically geared to achieving a positive state of mind in which each remaining day will be valued. All the evidence suggests that this aim is widely achieved where such specialized help is available, and that education for dying is as desirable as preparation for work, marriage, child-birth, retirement, or any other stage of life.

In previous centuries, when the sudden death of children and relatively young people was common, there was a greater taste for daily reminders of mortality. Gruesome *momento mori* in ornaments, jewellery and decorations, as well as tombstones, drove home the lesson that one should always be prepared for death. Even beyond the Victorian era, preoccupation with funereal themes and practices continued to emphasize the imminence of death and its importance as an event in both our mortal and immortal existence. More recently though, belief that death marks the beginning of another form of life has waned somewhat and, as a result, new responses to it have had to be worked out. For some, it seems to have resulted in a denial of death – whereby bodies are either frozen in cryogenic capsules for later resuscitation, or else are stylishly dressed and covered with lipstick and powder before being placed in 'comfortable' hermetically sealed caskets. The motivations involved are obviously very mixed: some disparage these ostentatious funerals as indicating a neurotic denial of reality; creating out of these human effigies a psychologically undead who are less threatening to those who cannot themselves face the reality and inevitability of either their own deaths, or those upon whom they are still dependent.

But there are alternative, more charitable, interpretations of these mortuary practices; ones which may be applicable at least as frequently. For example, long after a body has grown cold, it may still seem quite unbelievable that it is now completely inert and devoid of any human presence; that words addressed to it cannot somehow be heard; or that life might not yet miraculously return, physically or as a spirit. Even the most sophisticated are not necessarily exempt from such feelings as rationality is easily suspended in the face of great emotion. It is therefore hardly surprising that considerable concern for the care and preservation of the body is usual.

The mental pain, disorientation and desolation felt by survivors can be just as great as that which was experienced by the deceased: so much so, that it has been proposed that the 'post-mortem psychology of survivors' should receive as much attention as is given to the problems of the dying. And, high on the list of important subjects, are funeral arrangements and mourning – where it has been argued, even fulsome displays of respect and grief can be comforting to some; affirming the value of the dead person's life, and greatly helping the healing process. Rituals and ceremonies have proved universally helpful in the handling of solemn moments in human existance and it is by no means inappropriate that any close reminder of the deceased person, and especially their body, should be treated with loving care. Though whether the scale of some of the more expensive and elaborate interments is always set by such simple notions is something to be wondered at.

The mystery of death cannot be overstressed: it puzzles and fascinates us much more than life seems to do. For example, a very considerable proportion of the world's great poetry, literature, painting and philosophy seems to be either a search for meaning, or reassurance in the face of death. At an apparently more superficial level, for they seem more concerned with blunting painful reality than adjusting to it, crime stories and films endlessly repeat their stylized and banal scenes of killing. Cowboys, policemen and criminals simply crumple and fall when shot, stabbed, or clubbed: death is stripped of fear, anguish and grief, and of the distressing and prolonged suffering usually involved. Dying is thus diminished, dehumanized and subordinated to thrills and pleasure: the anxieties of all concerned are temporarily suspended; death is presented as an exciting, instantaneous and generally fairly painless mechanical event, devoid of all profound existential meaning. The significance of all this, and the needs served by these various art and entertainment forms may be very diverse and difficult to specify, but the unflagging and compelling fascination exerted by death is obvious enough.

From early childhood onwards, events like the death of small animals, pets, or elderly relatives, all add to ubiquitously circulating tales of ghosts and spirits to stimulate both our curiosity and our fear of personal destruction and decay. Nightmares and other signs of existential anxiety may be quite pronounced for a while but tend to disappear as the child absorbs the cultural myths or beliefs which structure the fearful uncertainties of our own or our dear ones' survival. The nature of this structure is variable, and dependent upon innumerable social and cultural influences but, according to Jung, the process by which most of us come to terms with the transience of physical life is implicit in our very nature.

As has already been discussed, Jung's theory of the 'collective unconscious' is based upon inherited mental predispositions to perceive and react to certain events in a typical way. The repetition of impressive experiences throughout human evolution, Jung argues, consolidates and fixes them so that the human brain itself is programmed to respond in certain ways when appropriate circumstances occur in individual lives. Of all the impressive recurrent themes, death is the most certain and intense: it is therefore one of the most highly energized 'archetypes', or more circumscribed dispositions of the collective unconscious. Over thousands of generations, mankind has observed the death of others and experienced the anticipation of his own. And, over a considerable proportion of this time, analogies drawn from the annual regeneration of nature, plus his own denial of death's finality, have given rise to the associated archetypes of rebirth and a creator god. So, impressive emotionally-laden myths and ceremonies have continued to grow around dying, giving rise to powerful religious and philosophical ideas which have become basic to the very fabric of individual psychic life, and society itself.

But, Jung argues, archetypes of the collective unconscious are relatively unformed and virtually identical in all people; they only give rise to broad tendencies and dispositions which are then expressed in a variety of cultural forms. Moreover, within this cultural diversity there are great individual differences, depending on people's unique circumstances and experiences. This may be due to fairly straightforward processes of education and learning but, when traumas and sources of anxiety are repressed in the personal unconscious, an archetype may form the nucleus of a complex, thereby giving rise to a unique and intensively focused form of mental activity. Death and religious complexes may therefore express themselves in an unlimited number of ways – from morbid ruminations or apprehensions to a dedication and ordering of life around the prospect of death and rebirth. But, whatever the outcome, all complexes share the common property of organizing the mind's activities so that they give selective attention and prominence to any event connected with them.

People are often unaware of complexes; their own, or those of others and this is especially so when, as with death, they are widely shared and can be easily related to such familiar and everyday activities as belonging to a church or enjoying articles, books or films about murder, war, catastrophe, ghosts, or cosmic destruction. In such cases, and particularly where the content reflects what is actually the bulk of most people's recreational reading and viewing, we may dwell on death almost interminably without the significance of this behaviour ever being questioned. Just as the best way to hide a pebble is to leave it on a beach with millions of others, it seems that the best way to camouflage personal fears or fascinations is to express them within circumstances which are so commonplace as to provoke the minimum of attention or need for justification. But so great is religious, artistic and recreational interest in death that one can be in no doubt about its psychological significance, even for those who seldom speak of their fears or beliefs directly.

One of mankind's greatest ambitions has always been to see into the future but, curiously enough this is one of the easiest precognitions we can make. For those spared an early fatal illness, accident, or other disaster, there awaits the slow decline into age and thus death. Not surprisingly then, we tend to close our minds to such personal foreknowledge: allowing it might cast such long and dark shadows over the present. Yet repression is a very costly strategy, and one that must be paid for in psychic energies which could be more usefully deployed. Moreover, because of their special nature, complexes connected with physical dissolution are particularly durable: unlike some others, they are unlikely to weaken and dissipate over time. Quite the reverse, they gain strength as death comes to those we love, and ever closer to ourselves. Finally, there is always the likelihood that traumas or life's attrition may weaken defences and allow unconscious material to flood into consciousness at a time when we are least able to deal with it.

The problem is, however, more multiplex than simply accepting the inevitability of death, then living with that knowledge: it also involves coming to terms with whether there is life after physical death. The two issues are so closely interwoven that it may even seem paradoxical that, though mankind's only absolute certainty is his bodily extinction, his greatest uncertainty has always been whether some part of the self survives. This is not just a matter of religious or philosophical significance for, in a sense, death is the anvil of personality; the base upon which the hammer blows of experience fashion the individual. Whatever our beliefs about a creator god, our final judgement, or rebirth, we seem obliged to develop some sort of cosmic view. It may be completely materialistic or it may involve a personal god but, however conceived, it modifies experience, suggests a moral framework, influences our values, and helps fashion our sense of life's meaning.

In many respects then, the psychological significance of death lies more in the way it moulds feelings and attitudes throughout life than the way it affects the final phase. For this reason, Jung argued that death is, psychologically speaking, a matter of as much significance as birth. The contemplation of physical death may be as depressing as the idea of psychic survival is bewildering, but our conclusions on these matters are critical: together they constitute the framework within which we must shape our lives and make many profound decisions which have far-reaching consequences both for ourselves and for our dealings with others.

Chapter seven

MIND OVER MATTER

With the possible exception of a small number of seriously mentally disturbed individuals who see themselves as completely determined by things outside themselves, mere observers of their own bodies and lives, almost everyone else shares the feeling that we can exercise choice and that we do have mental control over a great many bodily actions. However, this common-sense belief is not without its critics: the problem being how to account for a formless, non-space occupying, non-substance like mind acting in a cause-effect relationship with matter. After all, whereas the breaking of a window by a cricket ball may be fully accounted for in physical terms, one cannot conceive of cricket balls breaking ideas, or ideas shattering windows. Mental events are simply of a different order of being: having no weight, location, shape or mass, they cannot be treated in causal accounts as though they have.

The whole area is a philosophical minefield from which no one has ever escaped unscathed. A theory that even attempts to show we can make conscious decisions which cause the body to move according to our will is immediately in trouble. Yet, I have no doubt at all that I can choose whether or not to tap my desk, and that my arm and fingers will obey my conscious wish. Of course, this is what philosophers call a naive belief, though there can be very few people indeed who are not equally sure that their 'voluntary' movements are just that. Fortunately, this naivety is at last becoming somewhat more acceptable as scientists and philosophers begin to draw together, each widening their own conceptual systems.

The joint efforts of physiologist John Eccles and philosopher Karl Popper have been especially important in making a scientifically-based case for admitting conscious choice as a causal element in an otherwise mechanistic universe. Their argument that consciousness must serve some important behavioural purpose because only characteristics with marked survival value could be selected for as highly as it obviously has been, has proved extremely influential. Nevertheless, a great many people remain unconvinced, and the very fact that controversy continues to rage makes it clear that any theory which allows mental events as causative of physical ones must still be considered to lack any broadly accepted theoretical rationale. After all, we are still no closer to solving most of the strictly philosophical problems inherent in the notions of free will and dualism. And scientists too must continue to live with the fact that mental causes must always, even if they are accepted, remain as unobservable elements in any cause-effect sequence which originates with an idea and terminates with a bodily movement or response.

Yet, allowing that our present understanding of the way in which mind and body might relate to one another is still in a very confused state, and that we have many more questions than answers, the range of problems continues to extend far beyond the relationship of conscious ideas to purposive muscular activity. As we shall see presently, unconscious and non-consciously motivated activities have also proved to exert a remarkable amount of control over bodily events, often in what seems to be complete opposition to our conscious wishes. In some instances though, purely physical principles have turned out to be sufficient to explain what seemed to be incredible feats of mind over matter: 'fire-walking' is an excellent example of this.

The practice of walking barefoot across a pit of glowing embers is of ancient origin: it was known in classical India and China, and has been widely performed in such different cultures as those found in Malaya, Japan, New Zealand, Bulgaria and Spain. Variations, including a 'fire bath' of red-hot cinders, and self-flagellation with a red-hot torch, are also recorded as inexplicable or even supernatural events for, like the fire-walkers, adepts usually contrived to accomplish these activities without the agony or burns which would be expected. Europeans have witnessed such events on many occasions and in many different parts of the world but, in 1935, the London University Council for Psychical Investigation arranged for a demonstration to take place under controlled conditions in England. There they observed an Indian adept, Kuda Bux, walk unscathed through an eleven foot trench filled with coals glowing at over 800°F and, though careful checks failed to reveal the use of any chemical or other physical protection, he emerged quite unscathed at the other end. Encouraged by this, an Englishman attempted the same, only to be burned and forced to jump for safety within two steps. No doubt the two men differed in thickness of skin on the sole of the foot, but this alone is not a sufficient explanation: even the most calloused feet are not impervious to fire at that temperature.

For many, the explanation lies in supernormal powers achieved as a result of meditation, ecstasy or other unusual states of consciousness. There is, however, a more prosaic explanation for the whole phenomenon of fire-walking based on the simple observation that, if a surface is sufficiently hot, a drop of water will seem to hover over it, trembling and skidding around for some little time before vaporizing. It does this because the tiny zone of vaporized liquid acts as a barrier between the drop and the surface. The effect does not last long before the remainder of the liquid is also vaporized but this so-called 'Leidenfrost effect' was tested by American physicist Jearl Walker as possible explanation of fire-walking and similar phenomena. He even went so far as to demonstrate that, with damp feet, he too could walk on white hot coals without sustaining any damage, and that after dipping his fingers in water he could then submerge them in molten lead at 500°C with equal impunity. In each case, a tiny envelope of vapour was all that was needed to protect him. Incantations and mental preparation are quite redundant.

The feet of the fire-walkers, like those of everyone else, sweat; moreover, adepts tend to drink a good deal in their preparations, and often walk or stand among the damp soil dug out in order to make the pit. So, an imperceptible barrier of vapour protects them, but only so long as they judge and time the placing of their feet correctly. What was once regarded with awe should now, it seems, more properly command only our respect for those whose safety depends entirely upon their delicate timing, and an infinitesimal and continuously evaporating barrier of steam which causes the damp foot to hover fractionally above the coals themselves. Though remarkable, such achievements do not fundamentally affect our understanding of the usual relationships between body and mind. But there are other, even more outlandish and mysterious happenings which do tax our psychophysiological theories much more.

One such oddity concerns the appearance of 'stigmata', or wounds similar to those said to have been suffered by Jesus at his crucifixion, which occur on the bodies of some rare and pious individuals. It should be said at the outset that many such seem to have been due to nothing more than self-inflicted wounds which, whether consciously or in some unconscious or dissociated state, were caused in order to achieve a completely bogus importance and sanctity. Proving deception can, however, be a difficult matter; particularly when access to the stigmatic is restricted by members of their religious community. Such happenings are generally regarded with considerable ambivalence by the Roman Catholic Church, which has had a virtual monopoly on them since the thirteenth century when St Francis of Assisi set the pattern followed by nearly 400 since then. But the possibility of a miracle is acknowledged: in fact, more than 60 have, like St Francis himself, been canonized – though only when it was felt that their self-sacrifice or piety alone would have justified such elevation anyway.

Even today, there are still stigmatics: one of the best known in recent times being Father Pio Forgione, an Italian Capuchin friar. For half a century, from its sudden and traumatic onset in 1918, 'Padre Pio' bled from wounds in his feet, hands and side. The lesions neither healed nor turned septic, despite the distinctly unhygienic mits and other clothing with which they were usually covered. By contrast, there have been other cases in which the stigmata regularly heal and reappear. For example, at around the turn of this century, St Gemma of Galgani was being afflicted by wounds which would not appear until Thursdays, yet which would heal again by the Friday. By all accounts, her lesions were deep and blood-filled; the wounds on the back of the hands seeming to penetrate almost as far as those on her palms. Yet, within a matter of hours, they would be normal again.

The stigmata of Therese Neumann of Konnersreuth were also cyclical – usually occurring on Fridays – though, from the start, hers were regarded with deep suspicion by religious and lay investigators alike. In his book, *Psychical Research Today*, Donald West voiced the not infrequently held view that she was a 'trickster', yet at least as many other people seem to have concluded that, if she was a fraud, it was almost certainly not a conscious deception. Rather, many psychiatrists have seen her as simply a pious and imaginative nun who was also the victim of severe and persistent mental disorder. Her medical history is certainly compatible with this view for, by the age of 20, Therese suffered from attacks of hysterical blindness, paralysis and gastric disorder. Then, in 1926, she started to develop astonishing symptoms, beginning with a blood-coloured serum flowing from the eyes but, later that year, turning into the classic stigmata. Furthermore, she went on to claim that she took neither food nor liquid; the sacrament alone being sufficient to sustain her. A Church investigation in 1927 was inconclusive and she refused further examinations when they were proposed in 1932 and 1937. Since 1962, when she died, there has been a continuing argument about the cause and status of her wounds; some holding that they were simply the symptoms of an hysterical disorder, whilst others hold that there is more to it than that.

In *The Physical Phenomena of Mysticism*, Herbert Thurston explores some of the many ways attempts have been made to understand and explain the stigmata. For example, the Roman Catholic Church's view is presented as now being rather close to that originally expressed in the seventeenth century by St Francis of Sales. St Francis speculated that God sometimes creates, in chosen individuals, an extraordinary state of identification with Christ's passion; but the stigmata themselves are produced by unusual, though conventional means. Of course, this begs the question as to the 'conventional' processes involved, and there is no built-in acceptance that all stigmatic phenomena are divinely inspired. On the contrary, many are seen as being, at best, the consequence of hysterical states of mind and the Church has been at some pains to make sure that bogus and pathological phenomena are kept separate from those they regard as miraculous.

We may have every reason to remain sceptical about anything which seems at variance with well-established observations and theories, but there can no longer be any doubt that our unconscious minds are quite capable of producing bodily changes which could not possibly be induced in ordinary states of consciousness. Moreover, the physical effects are quite well attested in many cases; the blood of stigmatics has proved to be real enough and, in some instances, the haemorrhages have been observed under laboratory conditions. For example, the Belgian Academy of Medicine investigated the case of a Louise Lateau, whose arm was isolated within a sealed glass cylinder. In due course, there occurred a spontaneous oozing of blood through the skin of the hand; an event observed and verified by several medical witnesses.

A rather more informal investigation of the stigmata was conducted on another young woman a decade later by another physician, Dr Adolf Lechler. After seeing a film about the passion, on Good Friday 1932, one of his patients developed severe pain in the hands and feet. Suspecting hysterical motivations, and in the spirit of enquiry, Lechler decided to adopt the widespread convention of treating her with hypnosis. But before attempting to remove her symptoms, he decided to intensify and objectify them by suggesting that actual wounds would appear where the pain was felt. The girl responded well to the suggestions, bleeding from sites on her hands and feet, and showing the 'crown of thorns' and sagging (cross-bearing) shoulder-marks as well. After photographing, Dr Lechler used further suggestion to remove the symptoms, having made his case that stigmatic effects, though rare and extreme, conform to the general pattern of hysterical and potentially hypnotically-induced behaviour, and are therefore more likely to be psychophysiological phenomena than supernatural ones.

On the whole, religious bodies nowadays tend to welcome careful investigation of apparently supernatural happenings: overcredulity has done more harm than good to people's faith when subsequent events have revealed that what has been hailed as divine action was actually due to either naked fraud or quite natural causes. Even during the last few years, there have been some remarkable instances of events which might previously have been accepted as miraculous, but which instead have been revealed as trickery. For example, right up to the end of the 1970s, articles and books like Nona Coxhead's *Mindpower* describe the astonishing cures being affected by 'psychic surgery' in places as far apart as Brazil and the Philippines. The practitioners, who range from labourers to ministers of religion, use a variety of techniques, from simple manipulation to empty-handed imitations of surgical procedures, apparently reaching into bodies to repair damage, often bringing out blood, tumours and other tissue. For a long while observers, including many doctors and scientists, failed to see any signs of palming or any other form of hocus-pocus, but analysis of the blood and tissues removed has since shown much of it to be of either animal or manufactured origin. As with Victorian seances, not all practitioners have been caught out, and it is not possible to prove that all 'psychic surgery' depends upon trickery, but it seems reasonable to assume that it does.

The important thing, though, is not so much that the so-called 'surgery' often demonstrably involved conjuring tricks, but that a great many patients seemed to have been cured as a result of it. Some have urged that, in spite of the regrettable use of flim-flam, the healing was real enough because the practitioners really are conductors of psychic energies which lie outside themselves, or the patient. They are, the argument runs, tapping the same powers as those used by people like Harry Edwards in Britain or Oral Roberts in America, or indeed any of the other familiar and successful healers operating in the Western world. If so, the argument continues, then the theatricals can be forgiven as, at worst, irrelevancies and, at best, aids to the patient's faith and positive state of mind.

In Britain alone, the National Federation of Spiritual Healers claims a membership of over 2,000 though it estimates that perhaps four times that number actually practice some healing and that, in all, up to 80,000 people a week are now being treated. Some, like George Chapman, work in a deep trance, allegedly acting as a psychic medium for the powers of a dead Scottish surgeon, 'Dr Lang'. Most, however, perform their healing in more conventional states of mind, though mindful of being used as a 'channel' or 'transmitter' of outside powers which they claim can actually be felt flowing through their body and into that of the person being treated.

The subjective feelings of the healers are as inaccessible to outside verification as is the power-source itself, yet it cannot be denied that spiritual healing has resulted in some remarkable cures. Success in the treatment of cases ranging from persistent headaches to well-advanced cancers has been widely claimed, and not infrequently corroborated by physicians. Moreover, many of the patients involved were only treated after all else had failed; coming to the healer without any great hope, or any *conscious* faith in their abilities.

Jesus had himself healed the sick by spiritual means, and encouraged his followers to do the same. As a result, the church once again finds itself caught in a dilemma: having to support the principle while doing its best to steer clear of practitioners, all too many of whom have turned out to be fraudulent. The patients too have often proved not to be what they seemed: 'miraculous cures' have, like the stigmata, often rebounded to do more harm than good to those who have accepted them. So faith tempered with a considerable degree of scientific scepticism is now the formula, however preternatural things may at first seem.

Since 1858 when St Bernadette had her first visions of the Virgin Mary, the Grotto at Lourdes has become an increasingly important place of pilgrimage: particularly for those in search of a cure for their illnesses. Over the years, vast numbers of people have regained their sight, their hearing, the use of their limbs, or have recovered from some other serious physical condition. So celebrated have these 'miracles' become that bus and plane loads of sick people are constantly arriving in the hope that they too will be healed. To accommodate them all, the underground basilica has had to be expanded so that it can accommodate as many as 20,000 at a time: people crowding together in faith and the hope that they will be among those miraculously cured.

Yet despite the great reputation of Lourdes, and the abandoned crutches and wheelchairs which attest successful outcomes, the Roman Catholic Church itself is anxious to make it plain that Lourdes is not a miracle factory: that miracles, though they happen, are extremely rare and the gain from a pilgrimage to Lourdes is far more likely to be spiritual and mental than physical. Quite realistically, they point out that many people die in Lourdes, or deteriorate, and that most of the apparently miraculous cures which take place are more of the mind than the body, despite discarded crutches or white canes. Nevertheless, it has been predictably difficult to get this message home while not, at the same time, destroying people's faith or hope.

Among the cures seen by doctors at Lourdes, a small proportion has defied what was considered any reasonable naturalistic explanation. Some of these, though by no means all, may one day be regarded as miraculous but by far and away the greatest number of spectacular cures are considered to result from the shedding of hysterical symptoms. In these particular cases, what happens at Lourdes is, in some respects, very similar to what happens in the case of psychic surgery, spiritual or faith-healing, or under hypnosis. The patient, in a state of emotional excitement and expectation responds to the suggestion of a cure, whether this is made explicitly or implicitly, and abandons what is an unconsciously simulated illness. The outer manifestations of physical dysfunctions are in these instances only the external evidence of a mental disorder and, as relapses or the adoption of new symptoms may show, psychological adjustment is not necessarily fundamentally changed despite a remission of symptoms.

'Hysteria' as a diagnosis, is not one which is lightly communicated to either the patient himself or to others in his circle. Far more than, say, depression or anxiety state, such a diagnosis is likely to be misunderstood; to seem a frivolous or a contemptible way of avoiding responsibilites, while enjoying the considerations and privileges due to those who really are ill. Consequently, the therapist is usually very careful to avoid any sort of premature disclosure which might result in unnecessary damage to the patient's self-esteem, or to the interpersonal relationships he must depend upon during and after his treatment. In any case, the hysteric is not faking illness: his disabilities are real enough, even though their origin and continued existence lie in the mind rather than in physical systems.

Despite the apparently physical nature of many hysterical symptoms, all attempts to identify organic causes have so far failed. Similarly, statistical studies of families and twins have also failed to reveal any clear genetic predisposition, though psychological studies have identified a 'hysteroid personality' which seems particularly vulnerable. The distinguishing characteristics of hysteroids have been described as tending towards vanity and self-centredness; being emotionally shallow, though dramatic and labile in emotional expression; and being sexually frigid, yet emotionally demanding on their partner. It must be said, however, that although such a picture may be broadly typical of those who later develop hysterical neuroses, by no means all fit this simple and tidy pattern.

But, though there may be a good deal of variety amongst the personalities of hysterics, the diversity of their presenting symptoms can seem nothing short of bewildering. The study of symptom selection, tracing the personal and contextual circumstances which lead to the unconscious process of adopting one set of neurotic symptoms rather than another, is a fascinating subject in its own right. However, since the time of Freud, it has become widely accepted that the underlying cause of hysterical behaviour is broadly the same for this, as for any other form of neurosis-tension due to intolerable conflict or stress. Freud's further conclusion, that the origin of this tension is almost invariably due to the repression of sexual drives and memories, is no longer widely held, though sexual conflicts are undoubtedly a prime factor in many cases. Often though, as the psychiatric casualties of two world wars have shown, externally created sources of anxiety not only precipitate the condition itself, but mould its form into a coping strategy for handling problems which are felt to be both insupportable and insoluble within the limitations of legally or morally acceptable behaviour. Soldiers, for example, may find themselves terrified by the prospect of death or injury but almost equally fearful of the shame and punishment that desertion might bring. In these circumstances, illness is a perfectly natural unconscious wish: it is, after all, virtually the only solution which will avoid the prospect of either mental or physical destruction.

Conventionally, the symptoms of hysteria are categorized as being of the 'conversion' or 'dissociative' type. They may seem widely different conditions but, as Freud quite soon realized, they differ only in the externals, not in their fundamental psychodynamics. And, as a matter of fact, the two forms are actually somewhat similar in that they each mimic physical disorder: one suggesting dysfunction mainly in body systems, the other apparently implying some sort of brain damage or disease. Either would meet our soldier's need, and both have fulfilled it on many occasions.

Dissociative hysteria is characterized by amnesia: by lost periods of time when people may wander off, having 'forgotten' who they are. Sometimes, as in the film story *The Three Faces of Eve*, they even develop double or multiple personalities – distinctive and contrasting 'selves' – which share very few important memories in common. Much more usual, however, are relatively straightforward disruptions of consciousness: amnesic symptoms which are in reality only a pale imitation of the real clinical and neurological conditions. In wartime, soldiers may be found miles away from their frontline unit, unaware of how they got there and confused about their identity. If they are lucky, medical causes are sought: if not, they may be shot for desertion. Explanations in terms of their possible proximity to an explosion or having received a bump on the head may be invoked, but hysterical amnesia is a purely psychological phenomenon: the unconscious mind has simply dissociated itself from unbearable conflict and simulated a mental state which will, if successful, have desirable outcomes – the primary gain being that it removes the individual from an unendurable situation; the secondary being that illness or injury leads to care and sympathy, leaving self-esteem intact, or even enhanced.

More obviously connected with our present subject of mind over matter, are the bodily disorders of conversion hysteria, in which psychic disorders are converted into apparently physical ones. In the nineteenth century, one of the most common forms was 'convulsive hysteria' which, as its name implies, is characterized by convulsions. On the surface at least, attacks have a good deal in common with epileptic fits – involving gross musculo-skeletal spasms and the loss of voluntary control. But here the similarity ends for, unlike true epileptics, the hysterical patients does not lose consciousness, does not lacerate the tongue or collapse violently onto concrete or against other dangerous and painful objects; does not lose control of the bladder or bowels but, instead, characteristically flails his arms and legs while running through the gamut of emotions – laughing, crying, screaming, and so on. This may, perhaps, be regarded as the archetypal form of hysteria, though it is one which is far less common nowadays, perhaps because it has become so widely recognized as such.

However, less exotic manifestations of hysterical conversion continue to appear in a kaleidoscope of forms, including simulations of appendicitis, tuberculosis, or pregnancy. More frequently though, they involve specific dysfunctions in the skeletal musculature or the sensory systems: paralysis of the whole or part of limbs, total or partial blindness or deafness, and loss of sensation over areas of the body, being some of the more common manifestations. Again, wartime brought a steep increase in these conditions: often, as in cases involving paralysis of the trigger finger only, symptom selection making their origin remarkably obvious. More often though, the presenting symptoms were less naïve, though they would seldom be any more convincing to an alert doctor.

Malingering cannot always be ruled out, particularly when the symptoms involve such things as severe lumbar pain or recurrent headaches – for which there are no invariable clinical signs to act as criteria. Differential diagnosis may be difficult in some instances, but it should be stressed that hysterics are not malingerers: they have no conscious control over their symptoms: in their case, they just occur and certainly cannot be shed at will. The psychiatrist's task of identifying the true hysteric, though not always easy, seldom presents insuperable difficulties: it is, however, very much a matter of experience and skill.

Medical examination of hysterics may nevertheless be very much complicated by 'somatic compliance' – a tendency to produce symptoms related to weak or previously diseased or damaged systems. Disentangling the organic from the overlayed hysterical element can, as a result, sometimes be an involved and laborious business. Moreover, brain and vascular diseases commonly occur in association with hysterical disorders so that diagnosis, aetiology and treatment are by no means always as self-evident as some simple accounts would suggest. But, in spite of these exceptions, the majority of cases can soon be shown to be neither consciously feigned nor due to organic causes.

A pistol fired unexpectedly behind the ear of someone faking deafness will produce a marked startle reaction: not so with a hysteric. The same sort of thing is equally true in the case of body anaesthesias – where pins can be jabbed into the insensitive parts without apparent effect. Malingerers are not likely to welcome painful or extensive exploratory surgery, but hysterics have no such qualms. The differences in reaction are considerable, but then so too are they when hysterical symptomatology is compared with organic impairment. For example, an hysterical patient may completely lose his voice yet still continue to cough normally. Similarly, a chronic case of writer's cramp may still permit the shuffling of cards or performance of other dextrous tasks involving the apparently impaired muscle group. Loss of feeling in the hands or feet is common among hysterics but, when the areas of insensitivity are mapped, unless the patient is a neurologist, the pattern is likely to be what might be covered by a glove or stocking. Such a neat result is just not physically possible: the nerves which serve the hands and feet are part of complex systems which also serve other parts of the arms and legs. The area of an hysteric's anaesthesias therefore tends to correspond with a layman's idea of how nerve nets might be distributed, not with any form of anatomical reality.

Earlier on, when discussing stigmata, the possibility that they may be hysterically induced was mentioned, and certainly stigmatics have shown virtually the full gamut of conversion symptoms. But bleeding wounds go beyond the dysfunctions conventionally recognized as hysterical as they involve actual organic disorder and so cannot be explained in terms of hysterical processes alone. Nevertheless, the purely mental origin of many stigmata seems beyond doubt: a conclusion which is additionally supported by the fact that their form is variable and, like hysterical glove and stocking anaesthesias, owe more to conventional beliefs than material fact. Only in recent years has research shown that crucifixion must, for totally practical reasons, have involved nailing through the wrists rather than the palms: something which, whatever its provenance, is also apparent in the Shroud of Turin. Bleeding palms echo a tradition in medieval and renaissance painting much more closely than the actual events which took place far earlier in Jerusalem.

Discrepancies which indicate the essentially subjective nature of hysterical disorders are to be found everywhere, including the patient's bedroom. Watching movement during their sleep has often enough revealed the fact that apparently paralysed limbs are quite capable of operating normally when the individual changes position or turns over. Less often, but far from unknown, have been cases of sleepwalking among those who, by day, are confined to a wheelchair. But one of the simplest ways of checking actual disability is by hypnotizing the patient and, while they remain in a tranced state, suggesting that they will be able to perform a series of tasks which will tax the areas of malfunction. For example, the hysterically blind may be asked to select objects from the desk; the paralysed to move around; and those with skin anaesthesias to respond when they feel touch, heat, or whatever. In most cases, the procedure is quite straightforward, so long as the patient can be hypnotized.

The relationship between hysteria and hypnosis has long been recognized: in fact, prior to Freud, the only effective treatment for hysterical states was hypnosis, and even Freud himself began his career by using direct hypnotic suggestion to remove symptoms. Perhaps if he had continued to practise medicine in this way, he would always have remained a respected and orthodox physician but the frequency with which hypnotically removed symptoms returned, or others were adopted, persuaded him to try other methods. That his apostasy was, in the short run at least, so damaging may seem curious: after all, hypnosis was still trying to live down the unsavoury reputation bequeathed it by its notorious forerunner, Franz Mesmer. Yet as Freud was to see while in France studying with the great Jean-Martin Charcot, hypnosis worked. Moreover, its methodology was now more in keeping with the consulting room than the music hall, and its remarkable ability to restore physical functions to the hysterically impaired almost as remarkable as the way they could be induced in others.

Charcot maintained that hysteria and susceptibility to hypnosis were linked in so far as both indicated a 'weak' nervous system. Freud disagreed, and has since been proved correct; at least in so far as it is now apparent that susceptibility to hypnosis is quite normal, no characteristic organic inferiorities having been discovered in even the most deep-trance subjects. There are, however, individual differences in susceptibility for, although studies show that about 90 per cent of European adults can be hypnotized to some extent, only somewhere between 20 and 30 per cent can be put into a somnambulistic or deep-trance state. Another parallel with hysteria appears here too, as it transpires women are again significantly more susceptible than men. In addition to being female, the characteristics which correlate with heightened susceptibility include above-average intelligence and emotionality, having vivid waking and dream imagery, and having positive and confident attitudes about being hypnotized. Contrary to old beliefs, the most difficult type of person to hypnotize is someone with either very low intelligence or with a psychotic mental disorder.

As with susceptibility, the ability to hypnotize is not inherently limited to a minority. Most people are quite capable of inducing hypnosis in others provided they have sufficient confidence, do not create anxiety or suspicion about their motives in prospective subjects, and have taken the trouble to study, understand and practise the techniques of induction. The methods finally adopted can be extremely varied: some use a torch or suspended object to tire their subject's eyes while encouraging total relaxation of the rest of the body. The advantage of this technique is that when the hypnotist suggests that the subject's eyes are becoming tired, and that the lids are fluttering and so heavy they want to close, the physical facts actually help to create the illusion that the process is working and, as a result, make further suggestion easier. There are many such little tricks of the trade which can be used to deepen the trance state but, above all, the hypnotist must use suggestions of total physical relaxation and heaviness as he encourages his subject to attend only to his voice. When successful, this deep physical relaxation, narrowing of attention, and acceptance of the hypnotist's role as guide, provide the basic requirements.

Beyond this early phase, suggestions that the trance is becoming deeper and deeper may be tested by such things as first suggesting that the subject will not be able to open his eyes or raise his arm when asked to try. Inability to do so reinforces each stage and leads to further suggestions of relaxation, deepening trance and attention to the hypnotist's voice only. In the case of particularly susceptible subjects, one session may be sufficient to reach deep-trance states – perhaps even somnambulism, in which the subject can open his eyes and move around while still remaining hypnotized. This, however, is exceptional even for the most responsive subject: generally, a number of sessions are required to attain such remarkably altered states of consciousness and physical functioning.

As a demonstration of the effects of mind over body, there can surely be no more convincing demonstration than some of those which can be produced under hypnosis. There are, of course, some equally interesting mental phenomena as well – including age-regression, post-hypnotic suggestion and the creation of hallucinations – but it is the most specifically somatic effects which are of immediate concern. And these can be quite startling, particularly the way in which voluntary muscles can be temporarily paralysed so that a subject may not be able to stand, speak, move their hands, and so on. These effects can, by the use of appropriate suggestion to suitable subjects, even be sustained beyond the hypnotic trance so that, just like the hysterical patient, no amount of conscious effort will overcome them.

Of more potential utility though, is the way in which hypnotic suggestion can be used in the control of pain, permitting even the most major of painful surgery to take place without an anaesthetic. As a matter of fact, some of the earliest surgical uses of hypnosis occurred because it was just about the only alternative to alcohol or 'biting the bullet' a century and a half ago when British surgeons began to use this technique for limb amputations and other radical procedures. The results claimed were distinctly satisfactory for their time but, once available, the quicker and more predictable effects of ether and nitrous oxide were quite understandably to oust a technique which seemed to have no rationale and was, in any case, closely identified with the mumbo-jumbo of Mesmer.

The development of anaesthetics has surely confirmed the wisdom of that choice, even though it is no longer seen as an all-or-nothing alternative. Nowadays, hypnotism is often used side by side with modern anaesthetics in certain areas of modern medicine and dental surgery: for example, babies are born and teeth filled or extracted with nothing more than hypnotic suggestion to control the pain. And, judging by the reports of patients and the rapidly growing number of clinical users of hypnosis, the procedure is not only successful in inhibiting feelings of pain, it does so without the dangers and unpleasant side effects which can accompany the use of anaesthetic injections or gases. In some mysterious way, it seems the mind can block the usual feedback from pain receptors and even inhibit certain withdrawal reflexes, greatly reducing though seldom completely abolishing even the most severe pains of dentistry or terminal cancer.

More surprisingly still, hypnotic suggestions can cause marked changes in physical systems over which we have absolutely no control in normal states of consciousness. Hunger, for example, gives rise to stomach contractions and changes in gastric acidity which no amount of will-power can affect. Yet hypnotic suggestion of eating a meal can not only accomplish this, but can also affect the biochemistry of the gastric juices themselves. Depending upon the type of food suggested in this purely imaginary meal, changes in the relative balances of pepsin, trypsin, lipase and maltose will occur to match the protein, fat or carbohydrate nature of the food. In other words, the body's chemistry can be matched to the digestion of purely imaginary foodstuffs.

Medical researcher Stephen Black has spent a great many years experimenting with and describing the great variety of phenomena which can be created under hypnosis and, in his book *Mind and Body* leaves no doubt about the unexpected powers of mental and physical control made available through hypnotic induction. Accounting for them in medical or physiological terms is, though, another matter. He can trace their phylogenetic and evolutionary origins through lower animals but, like everyone else, Black has found the problem of identifying physical mediating mechanisms virtually insuperable. Of course, this tends to presuppose that hypnosis involves unusual neurological states: a hypothesis which is not acceptable to all researchers.

Theodore Barber, an American researcher and one of the most active experimentalists in this whole area, doubts whether the concept 'hypnosis' is even a useful one in most cases. He certainly does not deny that hypnotic procedures can be, and are, effectively used to control pain, labour contractions, digestive and cardiovascular functions, etc. However, he does question whether the cause of these effects is due to anything very much more than a harnessing and heightening of such ordinary processes as suggestibility, relaxation and the use of fantasy or other imagery. With these, we can quite unremarkably influence such involuntary somatic events as salivation, penile erection, fluctuations in heart rate, blood pressure and many other autonomically regulated activities over which we have no control through simple will-power. In support of this position, Barber argues that relaxation alone can quite demonstrably greatly affect labour contractions in childbirth while placebos, or simply the reassurances and attentions of a doctor, can bring about marked reductions in feelings of pain.

Essentially, what Barber is suggesting is that much of what we ascribe to 'hypnosis' or 'trance-behaviour' is more appropriately conceived as suggestibility and role-playing. This is only part of his account and, it must be said, he has much more difficulty when it comes to dealing with cases where, for example, the hypnotic suggestion of receiving a burn results in inflammation and blistering of the skin. This sort of example of mind over matter requires a more elaborate and wide-ranging explanation than can be provided in psychological terms alone. Suggestibility and highly motivated role-playing may well be a necessary part of the causal sequence but they are not sufficient: tissue changes demand neurological and other physiological elements as part of any complete account. Not that Barber should be criticized for not producing such a comprehensive theory; if he had been able to bridge satisfactorily the causal gap between psychological states and nervous system activity, he would also have done what no one has ever been able to do – solve the ancient philosophical problem of how non-material mental events can effect very material bodily ones.

Unfortunately, monitoring gross physiological functioning during hypnosis has added very little to our understanding of the process, beyond showing that it is neither a sleeping nor an ordinary waking state of consciousness. Instead, both modes seem to combine: vegetative measures of blood pressure, oxygen consumption and reflexes are more like the wakeful state, whereas electrical brain wave activity has more in common with the lighter stages of sleep. Apparently quite compatible with these observations, is the theory of the Russion physiologist Ivan Pavlov, who proposed that hypnosis involves some degree of generalized cortical inhibition in which small pockets or islands of neurological activity continue to function as in the waking state, but they are no longer co-ordinated within the normal waking pattern. These 'islands' were thought to correspond to such restricted areas of psychological attention as remained active after an induced narrowing of attention had shut down much of the broad-band scanning activity which is characteristic of the brain during its alert wakeful state. But, even with today's electronic sophistication, we are still a long way from being able to identify, monitor and interpret such delicate changes of activity in the human brain. Consequently, Pavlov's theory remains unconfirmed and hypnosis continues as a puzzling fact. From time to time newer theories, like Donald Hebb's, suggest alternative models more in keeping with recent observations and developments in neurological thinking, but essentially it is still an area in which scientists find more to despair than to rejoice over.

So far, we have rather tended to assume that the unusually heightened states of suggestibility we have been discussing as 'hypnotism' can only be achieved through an external hypnotist. In fact though, self-hypnosis is perfectly practicable and can occur as the result of conscious intention or, it has been argued, unconsciously in the case of hysterics. The complete clinical picture of hysterical disorders may well involve far more than the unconscious effects of hyper-suggestibility, but this is certainly a prominent part of most of them. Even people who might otherwise never be considered as 'hysterics' can temporarily find themselves in a state of heightened suggestibility and may, in appropriate circumstances, even become caught up in a group hysteria – where mental and physical dysfunctions of a kind which can readily be induced by hypnosis spread 'contagiously' through a group.

Often, the people concerned are young girls or women, not infrequently living or working in close proximity within a school or convent. The characteristic outbreak of jerks and spasms, fainting and paralysis, is sometimes quite spectacular, though if the group is broken up fairly quickly, the 'epidemic' can fairly quickly be brought under control and 'cures' brought about by simple tonics or any other convincingly presented nostrum. Even medical personnel are by no means immune: for example, there was just such an epidemic in 1955 at London's Royal Free Hospital, involving abnormal reflexes, convulsions and loss of limb control. It struck down 292 members of staff, 255 of whom had to be hospitalized. In due course, the outbreak was given the diagnosis of 'encephalomyelitis', though no specific pathogens were ever found and the staff 'patients' recovered as the emotional wave of anxiety and high emotion which had swept through the hospital subsided. There have been a number of broadly similar cases in other institutions, before and since, and these too have been given a medical diagnosis, though it is widely felt that all the evidence points to outbreaks of group hysteria.

Given a model on which to base our behaviour, together with a heightened or claustrophobic emotional context, and it seems that group pressures can cause a great many otherwise quite normal people to 'think themselves sick'. Outbreaks of actual disease often provide just these conditions, and doctors are well aware that many of the patients they see are the victims of suggestion, not pathogens. Though less obvious, a substantial proportion of the minor and everyday 'illnesses' seen by general practitioners are believed to have an almost purely psychological basis, a conclusion based not only on the lack of medical indications, but also upon the fact that such patients respond equally well to virtually any treatment given.

But, though the symptoms of illness are often unconsciously self-induced, the use of certain quite consciously applied techniques sometimes allows sufferers to self-correct them. Indeed, Christian Scientists, following the teachings of Mary Baker Eddy and Phineas Quimby, regard this as a basic rule. In their view though, *all* disease originates in the mind and its cure lies in seeing it as illusory. Disorders of the kind we have been discussing are likely to respond well to this sort of positive thinking but, alas, it can result in unnecessary tragedies where physical disorder or pathogens are at work. Nevertheless, the fact that purely mental attitudes seem to work so satisfactorily for much of the time suggests that not only are the body's normal restorative functions often underrated, but so too is the incidence of psychologically induced symptoms.

The use of direct hypnotic suggestion to relieve hysterical symptoms, control pain, inhibit addictive behaviours and depress stress-creating autonomic activities is familiar enough to most people. But to other than Christian Scientists, the idea of taking personal mental control of one's illnesses is quite unfamiliar. Yet during the first decades of this century, the practice of autosuggestion was very well known, and quite well thought of in many quarters. As with so much concerning hypnosis and medical uses of suggestion, the origin of this fashion was France. Emile Coué had studied hypnosis under some of the most outstanding and medically respected practitioners of his time, but one of the most influential events in the development of his own ideas occurred when, as a pharmacist prohibited from prescribing drugs himself, he concocted a convincing-looking placebo mixture for a customer and found that it worked very well. As he wrote '. . . the mental image can, within certain limits, substitute itself for the virtue of a drug; and the imagination possesses a power capable of directing certain life activities, restoring us to normality'. On the strength of this, and, of course, other episodes, Coué concluded that the power of hypnosis was not dependent upon the suggestions of an outside facilitator and a mysteriously changed state of consciousness but, instead, upon the power of autosuggestion which the hypnotist was only instrumental in strengthening and guiding.

The fame of Coué's method of autosuggestion spread rapidly as a result of the remarkable treatment successes achieved in his free clinic for working people at Nancy. Some of the time he used direct suggestion, though without hypnosis, to treat patients. But his main efforts were directed towards teaching people how to heal themselves through autosuggestion. The general formula, 'day-by-day in every way, I'm getting better and better', was to be repeated often and confidently in receptive moments, not as an instrument of willpower but as a countervailing force to oppose the negative and apprehensive feelings which give rise to mental and physical disorders.

More specific formulas of autosuggestion were recommended for particular problems. For example, tension and other nervous states were countered by constantly repeating such words as 'calm' and imagining scenes and feelings of calmness. Pain was controlled by the continuous use of such phrases as 'I have no pain' or 'It's going, going . . . (until) it's gone –'; the mind not so much combatting the pain in any direct way but blocking its expression and replacing it with positive suggestions and positive emotions.

Hypnosis was already a demonstrably quite satisfactory treatment for many such conditions and, in these cases, the only advance made by Coué was to replace the external locus of control by an internal one. In itself, this was no mean achievement, particularly for poor people unable to afford specialist fees, but the treatment also went further in that it was applied to a number of physical conditions not readily treated by conventional hypnosis. By means of his own confident suggestions, and those he taught patients to use for themselves, Coué claimed that even many organic disorders could be rectified. In a popular summary of the work, which carries an introduction by Coué himself, Harry Brooks lists some of the unusual cases successfully treated. They include not only those of an obviously psychological nature, like depression and headaches, but others – like asthma, appendicitis, rheumatism, skin ulcers, dyspepsia and even a prolapsed uterus – which were then more usually regarded as purely medical problems.

Positive thinking and visualizing the process of improvement may have worked in practice, but the way it came to be misinterpreted, corrupted and lampooned ultimately destroyed confidence in it. And, without confidence, there was nothing left: Coué's methods simply melted in the face of distrust and disbelief. Yet, even as this was happening, others were also beginning to stress the importance of mental processes in both the creation and treatment of bodily illnesses. As early as 1917, George Groddeck, who came to be acknowledged as the 'father of psychosomatic medicine' wrote in his journal 'I consider it a basic and dangerous misconception to suppose that only the hysteric has the gift of making himself ill for whatever purpose'.

Psychosomatic conditions differ from those of hysterical origin in that the disorders of hysteria are purely functional whereas psychosomatic illness, though also dependent upon psychological causes, gives rise to actual organic dysfunction or damage. Hysterical symptoms of paralysis or sensory loss may be far more spectacular in appearance but, unlike some psychosomatic conditions, they are never deadly. In fact, hysterical reactions are often very effective in protecting the patient from many of the more dangerous stress effects which give rise to psychosomatic illnesses. By dissociating consciousness, or producing simulated illnesses which effectively remove them from stressful circumstances, replacing anxieties with the cossetting of nursing care, hysterics can often reduce mental or environmental stress in such a way that their endocrine and autonomic nervous systems are not under the same psychophysiological pressures met by those who do not adopt these strategies.

Of course, whatever the degree of environmental stress, it will be perceived and reacted to differently by different individuals. Those whose emotions are evoked easily, respond strongly and subside slowly will naturally be more frequently and powerfully subject to emotional tensions – with all that this implies in neural and biochemical terms. By contrast, those of a more phlegmatic temperament may be expected to experience considerably less psychological stress in equivalent or similar circumstances, and therefore suffer less physical stress too. In their case, those endocrine activities which form so central a part of the typical mammalian 'fight-or-flight' preparation, are less likely to be powerfully activated: consequently, digestive, cardiovascular and muscular systems will remain relatively quiescent. No doubt a highly reactive system is more adaptive than a sluggish one in primitive conditions of living – where threats appear and are dealt with, successfully or not, in a relatively brief time-span. In modern circumstances though, perceived threats to the self and ego are somewhat different in kind and persist over many years and, in such cases, strong emotional reactivity ceases to be an advantage and becomes instead a source of vulnerability.

Chronically constricted blood vessels, increased blood pressure, rapid heart rate and respiration, all place additional burdens on the constitution, and all very obviously threaten the individual's survival. But the system most vulnerable to the disruptions of emotional stress seems to be the gastrointestinal tract: as observations of bloodflow, acidity and surface rupturing show all too clearly, the stomach and its connected ducts are among the most sensitive imaginable indicators of emotional strain. Animal studies have been particularly helpful in confirming just how susceptible the digestive system is to stress, and how dangerous mental states can be to life itself. For example, rats subjected to random and uncertain punishments were generally found to die within as little as 24 to 36 hours of their being placed in these stress conditions. 'Executive monkeys' put in an experimental situation where they could operate a lever to prevent electric shocks, lived longer but they too only had a life expectancy of weeks before they also died of a perforated duodenum due to the build up of acidity in their digestive systems.

Human beings, particularly those unable to escape an executive or decision-making role in ordinary life, also commonly suffer from severe gastrointestinal disorders. Peptic and duodenal ulcers – open sores due to chemical change resulting from excess pepsin and hydrochloric acid in the oesophagus, stomach or duodenum – not only debilitate but sometimes even kill. Long-term feelings of anxiety, anger and resentment give rise to fight-or-flight autonomic activity which, in turn, produces the muscular tension and endocrine changes which are both directly and indirectly damaging. Ulcers, colitis or gastritis are only part of the medical hazard created by biochemical changes brought about in the digestive system.

Overeating is sometimes a more or less unconscious response to elevated levels of acid secretion and hypermotility of the digestive tract. Soft foods do not scratch ulcerated surfaces and creamy or fatty products may act as a balm, but they may also lead to obesity and high cholesterol levels which increase pressure on heart and circulatory systems already subject to the same emotional stresses as those disrupting the gastrointestinal functions. The situation may become even more dangerous if, as part of their life style or strategy to handle emotional situations, the individual concerned uses alcohol or tobacco. Cigarettes and spirits are particularly likely to result in additional pressures on the cardiovascular system, and alcohol has a strong tendency to irritate and strip away the protective surface from ulcers.

Bleeding ulcers, or fear that they will perforate, naturally elevates stress levels even more. Detectable cardiovascular symptoms, even relatively harmless heart-rate fluctuations or palpitations, may have the same effect – indeed more so in view of the dread created by the prospect of heart failure. The result of this physical feedback can then become an ever-intensifying vicious circle in which physical disorders created by emotional stress give rise to additional emotional stress, and so to further physical symptoms and so on.

Unless they are handled with great care, the outcome of this kind of psychosomatic-somatopsychic vicious circle can be disastrous. *Somatopsychic* feedback, including attention to the tiniest and most normal bodily events, easily becomes a compulsion. Fear provides the motivation and, particularly in early middle age when expected signs of deterioration begin to appear, the over-anxious readily overreact. Some tend towards invalidism, a strategy which may have high hidden costs in the quality of life, not only for the individual concerned, but also for those close to him. It may, however, be a successful adjustment from the point of view of physical health if it brings about a less stressful life style. But if it merely results in continuous and apprehensive monitoring of body functions, it is more likely to exacerbate stress feelings and reactions. Overweight joggers whose psychosomatic problems have led to hypertensive or cardiovascular effects are at particular risk: as with squash or any other sport which can make occasional demands in an otherwise fairly sedentary existence, the results of overzealous attempts to regain health and vigour can be fatal if bodily systems are already in poor shape.

Among the other well-known conditions which can be partly or wholly psychosomatic in origin are quite a number of less dangerous, though still very disagreeable, illnesses. The connection between tension of the neck and scalp muscles and headaches is familiar to us all. Migraine, a much more severe form of headache which also involves nausea and impaired vision, and which may persist for hours or days is also a tension illness likely to be triggered by such things as quarrels or work pressures. Emotional stress causes arteries in the head to dilate and pulsate, thereby stimulating free nerve endings and giving rise to pain. Neurological and genetic studies suggest the existence of hereditary predisposition in many cases, but it is the physiological consequences of emotional stress which actually trigger attacks.

Bronchial asthma also presents a picture of mixed causality: histamine reactions to an allergen can, by themselves, readily bring on an asthmatic attack in some predisposed individuals. The events involved – excessive mucus secretions, constriction or collapse of airway walls, panting and wheezing and the associated fear of choking – all seem to arise from purely physical causes. Yet studies which have involved separating parents and children, while keeping the children's physical environmental conditions constant, have shown how important some mothers can be in precipitating their offspring's attacks – whether or not the youngsters otherwise have strong reactions to particular allergens. Typically, such mothers emerge as being both hostile and emotionally unstable, the atmosphere within the family itself being characterized by anxiety and frustration.

So, an allergen may be a necessary and sufficient cause of asthma in some cases, only a necessary one in others, and perhaps neither in yet others. In cases where an attack is brought on by stress or argument, and when there is no reason to believe that allergenic substances occur or have increased in the environment, it is not unreasonable to suppose that the necessary and sufficient cause in some instances is psychological. In fact, psychoanalytic causal explanations generally consider the child-mother relationship as central – particularly the love-hate ambivalence of the asthmatic towards his mother. The very symptoms, choking and crying, are held to suggest the conflicting emotions of fearing emotional suffocation on the one hand, abandonment on the other.

Freudian theory has also been used to account for another major grouping of psychosomatic disorders – skin diseases – including eczema, hives and neurodermatitis. All are disfiguring and experienced as shameful and are often thought by psychoanalysts to be outward and visible manifestations of inner masochistic or self-hating tendencies. Moreover, Freudians regard the site of infection as symbolic and significant. For example, infections of the hand will both punish and inhibit masturbation, whereas those of the pubic or genital area may serve similar ends with regard to exhibitionism or promiscuity. Certainly, repulsive skin eruptions can be both personally distressing and socially limiting. But whether they are seen as often, or ever, the means by which the unconscious mind inhibits or punishes the body for its own morally unacceptable impulses, must ultimately depend upon one's view of the psychoanalytic argument and the case material used to support it.

Warts and many allergies of the skin may or may not fall into the same category, but their mental origin is frequently in no less doubt, particularly when they can be banished by equally subjective means. Despite all the advances of modern medicine, 'wart charmers' continue to practise their ancient art because, very often, they do a far better job. All that seems necessary is faith in the charmer and sometimes, though not necessarily, the carrying out of a few quasi-magical directions – which presumably strengthen the belief that mysterious forces are involved. These may take the form of leaving some highly improbable offering to who knows what in the local churchyard, but whether or not a particular charmer employs such mumbo-jumbo, prestige suggestion seems to be all that is needed to bring about the rapid and complete disappearance of dozens or even hundres of warts at one time.

Hypnosis can also be used with great effect to banish warts. As a refinement, some studies have even shown that only those warts on a particular part of the body, or occurring down one side or the other, can be removed by simply planting the suggestion that they will go. But, impressive as these demonstrations of mind over body may be, the power of suggestion in the control of allergic responses is more so. For example, in some studies first conducted by Japanese researchers, blindfolded patients who suffered from an actual and specific plant allergy were touched on one arm by what they were told was the allergen: they responded with an allergic rash, even though the material used had previously been established as neutral so far as they were concerned. Then the other arm was touched with the plant to which they were allergic but, this time, they were told that it was quite neutral foliage: the allergic rash failed to appear. The same results cannot, of course, be reproduced for all allergies: many if not most are probably purely chemical reactions, but it does show how important mental state may be in affecting the body's most basic biochemical activities.

Psychosomatics is now a rapidly growing area of medical understanding: the catalogue of conditions once thought to be of a wholly or mainly physical pathology but subsequently shown to have a major psychological component in their causality is increasing all the time. So too, it seems, is the number of patients as stress diseases rise ever higher in the list of serious disorders. During World War I, the work of Freud and others came very much into its own, showing just how frequently hysteria was the underlying cause of apparently physically-based illness. Perhaps mainly as a result of our developing understanding, World War II highlighted the far more widespread nature of psychosomatic illnesses. They may differ from hysteria in the reality of their organic damage, but each demonstrates something about the many ways in which mental states affect the body. The relationship between mind (psyche) and body (soma) may continue to present philosophers with metaphysical problems but, for doctors, the psychosomatic link is demonstrably a clinical reality.

No one would now doubt that stress can lead to physical disorders but the fact that it does so only in some cases suggests that personality may also be an important causal factor. Some people can accept, and even thrive in, the sort of circumstances which are intolerable to others. For some, a gentle rebuke from their employer can cause stomach-knotting tension and distress that others would not experience even when sacked, and the same pattern of differences can occur in relation to virtually all of life's problems. The sort of genetically-based emotional lability referred to by Eysenck as 'neuroticism' and discussed in earlier chapters is obviously an important feature, but it is only one developmental element among many. Without necessarily being sympathetic to Freudian or any other analytic approach, it is quite apparent that forgotten or repressed childhood experiences are also remarkably influential in modifying later learning, shaping our expectations and actions, and so exerting a powerful influence on the development of adult temperament and personality.

So, genetically determined constitutional differences interact with even more varied developmental and environmental conditions, giving rise to unique individuals, living in unique circumstances. This is a state of affairs which may not seem to augur well for those whose interests are primarily concerned with the identification of fairly clear-cut personality types, which can then be correlated with specific psychosomatic illnesses. And, in fact, such work frequently does lead to serious methodological objections though, since Helen Flanders Dunbar pioneered the field some 50 years ago, research has become increasingly sophisticated. Even so, as Barclay Martin points out in his *Abnormal Psychology*, problems arise even now when investigators use unquantified descriptive terms which could equally well be applied to most of us. Few people, if any, can be absolutely free of conflict, hostility, anxiety, self-doubt, or whatever other adjectives are used and, in any case, there is a good deal of overlap in personality descriptions for the various illnesses.

Nevertheless, it is possible to discern some typical characteristics. For example, migraine sufferers tend to be ambitious and meticulous types; asthmatics fear abandonment, being overdependent yet hostile towards their loved ones; and those with stomach ulcers are more likely to show surface independence yet retain powerful dependency feelings and fears that their own capabilities may not be sufficient to maintain their often high level of socio-economic achievement. All, to some degree, seem to share in having above-average feelings of anger, hostility and resentment about their treatment, though some illness types are more associated with their suppression than their expression. In fact, if one had to pick out one salient trait from the whole of psychosomatic medicine, it would surely be hostility.

In a now famous research into heart disease, Friedman and Rosenman began by studying the personality characteristics of a group of apparently healthy men, and then followed their fortunes with regard to coronary heart disease. They found that, if they divided their sample into two groups on the basis of their personalities, there were marked differences in susceptibility to early occurring heart attack. What they termed 'Type A' individuals were markedly aggressive and challenging in their life style; characteristically impatient, ambitious, tense and fast-moving. By contrast, Type B personalities were less hostile and competitive, more relaxed and more able to allocate time for pleasure or just being. It is, of course, Type A individuals who are most at risk: their personality may appear to confer many adjustive advantages in a materialistic society, but it is more likely to be paid for in terms of physical disability, recurrent and fatal heart attacks.

But, just as physical disorders can be brought about by mental means, so too can their effects often be reversed in similar fashion. However, though psychoanalysis and other forms of psychotherapy may be appropriate and work moderately well in the case of hysteria, the techniques evolved to handle neurosis and other purely non-organic ailments are not particularly effective when it comes to psychosomatic disorders. Nevertheless, psychotherapy can and sometimes does help to reduce anxieties by revealing and emotionally defusing repressed or otherwise troublesome memories, impulses and fears. Also, more direct counselling methods can be beneficial by providing insight into motivations which lead to conflict and tension, and by helping modify those attitudes and aspects of life style which create and perpetuate them. Research reports claim modest treatment successes for conditions as diverse as asthma, vaginal spasm and gastrointestinal disorders, but the results are such that the overall utility of these methods must generally be regarded as somewhat low. Even when psychotherapy appears to be working, the relative value of verbal exchanges – which form the very core of these techniques – is generally indeterminate as relaxation is almost always an important additional component. Sometimes relaxation is a significant by-product of the situation itself, and quite unmistakably so when the patient lays on a couch or is subject to hypnosis. But even where the relaxation element is not so obvious, extended psychotherapy can still be a distinctly relaxing and soothing affair: a passive and narcissistic interlude of calm and reflectiveness in which ideas that would be stressful in other circumstances are softened and neutralized by their context.

Behaviour therapists have argued that, at least in a high proportion of cases, the most important part of 'talking therapies' is not, as claimed, their ability to achieve catharsis, insight, or the realignment of life style. Instead, they point to the implicit, though less evident, counter-conditioning aspects of these situations – whereby the experience of previously stressful ideas and states almost inevitably comes to be associated with relaxation. As a result, anxiety which formally led to psychosomatic disorder is inhibited and replaced by a more positive state of mind: this, in turn, can be expected to produce a consequent reduction in agitated autonomic activity and to correct those unbalanced physiological processes which first gave rise to the psychosomatic illness.

Much of behaviour therapy is, in fact, based on this principle of 'reciprocal inhibition' – a proposition to the effect that tension and relaxation are mutually exclusive, and can be interchanged by means of carefully controlled experimental procedures. It is further assumed that the majority of chronic mental and physical tensions are a result of faulty learning: fight-or-flight reactions having been, or continuing to be, associated with an inappropriate or previously but no longer menacing circumstance. Treatment therefore consists mainly of learning how to remain relaxed when contemplating or confronting these hitherto alarming conditions or events. Once such autonomically controlled activities as heart rate, blood pressure and acid or other secretions in the stomach cease to be seriously affected by such real or imagined conditions, the body's restorative activities can then begin the work of regulating and healing those structures not yet irreparably damaged.

Simple as the goal of mental and physical relaxation may seem, it can be an almost impossible objective to some people; particularly those whose whole life history strongly suggests an innate predisposition towards excessive emotionality. In their case, control may best be achieved in a piecemeal fashion – perhaps beginning with those tension symptoms which are most disruptive or physically threatening. 'Biofeedback' is the name given to one such method which has, since the 1960s, grown at an exponential rate, revealing a potential for the mental control of physical processes which was earlier regarded as impossible. By very definition, the autonomic nervous system was classed as being automatic and involuntary: it being unthinkable that people might be able to regulate functions like heart rate, blood flow, sweat production, or the brain's electrical activity by deliberate and planned mental activity. Yet so it proved.

The feasibility of achieving this type of control was demonstrated by an American psychologist, Neal Miller, whose experiments using dogs and then rats, showed that they could be conditioned to modify several cardiovascular and gastrointestinal activities in response to pleasurable reinforcement. Astonishing as it then seemed, rats proved capable not only of learning to control heart rate and blood pressure, but also the regulation of intestinal contractions, the rate of forming urine and the constriction of blood vessels in stomach, tail and ears. The next step was to see whether it was possible to teach human beings to exert *voluntary* control over some of their 'involuntary' bodily activities. It was, of course, obvious that though the ends were similar, very different procedures and rewards would need to be marked out.

From the beginning, it was recognized that control could only come about if it was possible to reinforce the desired autonomic responses when they occurred, thereby increasing the probability of their recurrence and persistence. But it was also obvious that this could only happen if people were sufficiently aware of their bodily states. Feedback is the key to learning any skill; for example, however long one practises throwing darts, without information as to where they land, improvement will never take place. So the next stage in the development in human biofeedback techniques was to single out particular autonomic activities and develop equipment which would monitor them – providing feedback data that was optimally informative but minimally disturbing to the subject.

Heart rate and blood pressure are very easily recorded, and have the added advantage of being things which many people are highly motivated to regulate. Using a simplified form of feedback by which a tone indicated success or lack of it in bringing them down, Miller found that patients with abnormally and chronically accelerated heart rates and elevated blood pressure were indeed able to achieve a remarkable degree of control. In little more than a decade similar research has taken place with virtually every other autonomic function, and in relation to virtually every form of psychosomatic symptom or disorder – from excessively sweaty hands to asthma and tension headaches. Unfortunately though, gastrointestinal events, particularly biochemical ones, are extremely difficult to observe and monitor continuously under ordinary circumstances, so biofeedback research and treatment is still somewhat weaker in this area than that related to cardiovascular activities and the brain's electrical functioning.

Physiological activities need to be sensitively measured and monitored for biofeedback purposes, but they are usually best presented in as simplified and unobtrusive a way as possible. A tone or a coloured light signal switching on or changing characteristics as the desired physical states are approached or achieved, is a fairly conventional way of providing feedback. The subject's task is to pay particular attention to their bodily states rather than the equipment's activities, so they will ultimately have an improved awareness of how the desirable state feels and be able to dispense with hardware altogether. The process is a passive one: active striving is usually counterproductive as concentration and the exercise of will tends to give rise to tension which, in addition to its unwanted physical consequences, blocks subtle body-awareness.

People naturally find it extremely difficult to say just how they manage such things as bringing down their heart rate, or influencing pulse volume in the extracranial artery to avoid migraine headaches, though the process can fairly easily be taught and learned. The teaching component is clearly very dependent upon the feedback itself, but it is also improved if the therapist provides information as to how the process works, identifies the location, and describes the operation of the organs to be influenced. The individual running the session can also assist by helping create a relaxed state of mind, perhaps also devising word-pictures of situations appropriate to the state of mind being sought. Finally, encouragement helps offset doubts and maintains motivation, while praise given when the subject is successful can provide a useful additional reinforcement for the learning taking place. Teaching, however, is mainly a matter of providing the equipment, instructions and psychological support: the would-be teacher's problem being summed up by Barbara Brown, one of the pioneers of biofeedback, when she noted the marked degree by which our ability to control internal processes exceeds our ability to say how it is done.

In fact, so long as one understands the principles and has access to equipment, a teacher or anyone else, is not strictly necessary: in a sufficiently motivated individual, all that is necessary to bring about learning is the pleasurable reinforcement which comes from feedback showing that goals are being achieved or approximated. In practice though, identifying these goals and determining the best ways of achieving them, is usually much easier and more effective where one has a knowledgeable and experienced helper. This does not remove the locus of control away from the individual and change the situation back to something more like a doctor-patient relationship, but it can be an important consideration when it comes to recognizing misleading recording artefacts and clarifying exactly what is happening.

Even very sophisticated electronic equipment can now be manufactured so cheaply that, once biofeedback principles became widely known, the market was swamped with physiological recording devices. Part, at least, of the reason for this remarkable economic and technological interest seems to have been that, in addition to doctors and scientists, biofeedback proved to have an almost greater appeal for vast numbers of both health faddists and those with religious or philosophical interests in meditation and mind control. Regrettably though, many people's understanding of basic physiology was such that they really had very little idea of what they were doing, and they were so inexperienced in biological recording that they were unable to recognize malfunctions when they occurred. This was particularly so in relation to the brain's electrical activity as recorded by amateur electroencephalographic (EEG) equipment which, like its clinical counterpart, works by amplifying the minute electrical fields which can be picked up between electrodes attached to the surface of the scalp. Much of this electrical activity certainly does originate within the brain but, because the apparatus has to be extremely sensitive to record such minuscular events, it is also highly susceptible to including artefacts due to such things as ill-fitting electrodes or the movement of muscles in the scalp itself. In any case, EEG records are a composite of events of many different types, taking place at many levels and sites, and are so difficult to interpret that except where lesions or other abnormalities are involved, even most neurologists prefer to be no more than tentative about their psychological significance.

Nevertheless, once it was known that biofeedback techniques could be used to increase the very small amount of 'alpha' activity which takes place during normal conscious activities, and that this rythmic 8–12Hz (cycles per second) wave form is specifically associated with a tranquil and pleasant form of relaxed wakefulness, attaining and sustaining these states became something of a fashion. Then, when it became widely known that Zen masters and other meditational adepts regularly produce well above average levels of alpha, and that many of the earlier experimenters reported themselves achieving 'highs' this way, the fashion came to be almost a craze. Some hailed biofeedback as 'Electric Zen'; a technological short cut to spiritual enlightenment – but subsequent experience has shown that attaining enlightenment, or satori, requires more than just relaxed attentiveness.

There have, however, been some small gains from the discovery that biofeedback techniques can be used to modify EEG patterns, and in ways other than augmenting the proportion of naturally occurring alpha activity. Mental relaxation has probably been the main benefit so far but a number of studies suggest that some forms of epilepsy may be helped this way and that headaches and pain may also be ameliorated. Other studies have concluded that behaviours as varied as drug addiction and criminality can be substantially modified by means of EEG feedback but, as William Ray and his colleagues have shown in their review of the clinical literature published between 1968–78, many such claims must still await further verification. What is not in doubt, though, is that biofeedback techniques will permit us immensely more mental control over our bodily activities than could possibly have been foreseen 20 years ago.

Even so, evidence that a great deal of what is usually described as the body's automatic functioning could be brought under mental control, and that this could in turn be used to alter states of consciousness, has been available for hundreds of years. European travellers to India and the Far East found there fakirs, sadhus, monks and mystics practising techniques of body-mind control which were thousands of years old and which might have, but did not, affect the thinking of those other Westerners responsible for formulating the new science of physiology. Instead, they chose to regard the mind-over-body controls practised in the East and elsewhere as curiosities more relevant to the study of religion or magic than to modern science.

It was classic chauvinism but, in recent times, things have changed considerably due to a widespread reaction against materialism and an ever-growing interest in Eastern philosophies and religion. Zen Buddhism and Yogic practices have attracted literally millions of admirers and sometime practitioners, though many rapidly give up once they realize it requires a great deal more than adopting the diet, haircut or dress of their spiritual teachers to become like them. When biofeedback came along, it seemed that achieving the sort of mental control of physical functions which spiritual teachers in the East spent so much effort mastering might help, but this did not work either. Only relatively few seemed fully to understand that the external trappings and remarkable physical accomplishments were only part of the context and preparation for intensive religious or meditational activity, and that spiritual goals might be facilitated but could not be attained this way.

Still, though the number of Westerners who have achieved the Buddhist's ultimate bliss and freedom from the bonds of existence, or realized the Yogis' unity of their own soul with the absolute may be few indeed, a great deal has been learned about the mind's potential to regulate what had previously been supposed involuntary behaviour. Without any of the hardware employed in biofeedback techniques, it was shown to be possible to achieve the same, and even more spectacular, results. The methods varied from place to place and tradition to tradition; sometimes degraded by those who used them to perform profitable or ego-enhancing tricks or feats, and sometimes treated casually as the by-products of spiritual development. But, whether or not the practitioners lost their spiritual way, and whether or not the ideas upon which the practices were based made any sense to the modern scientific mind, the phenomena themselves could no longer be dismissed.

Modern physiologists are not likely to be impressed by the Yogic account of 'Kundalini', a divine serpent said to lay dormant at the base of the spine, yet which can be induced to travel upwards by a channel in the backbone, via six psychic centres, until it unites blissfully with the locus of a thousand petals situated at the top of the head. But the ascetic practices, postures, breathing exercises and intensive body awareness developed as part of this belief system quite definitely do give rise to real enough physiological phenomena, though the serpent Kundalini has yet to be recorded as one of them! Ernest Woods' *Yoga* is an excellent introduction to both beliefs and the practices but, for experimental evidence regarding yogic powers, one must look elsewhere.

During the last few years, the All India Institute of Medical Sciences in New Delhi has been the main centre at which yogic powers have been tested, particularly by researchers B. A. Anand and G. S. Chhina. In controlled laboratory conditions, they have been able to monitor their subjects' heart and breathing rates, body temperature and EEG before, during, and after experiments. One of the better known studies involved Ramanand Yogi, who was placed in an airtight metal box measuring six feet by four feet and told to signal when he wanted to come out. A glass panel allowed visual observation of the yogi, while an air pumping device allowed the researchers to monitor oxygen and carbon dioxide levels within the capsule.

Ramanand Yogi soon went into a deep meditational state, his EEG record indicating a relaxed drowsiness, while both cardiac activity and respiration were calm and slow. During some of the time, he was consuming less than half of the oxygen which previous tests had indicated was the absolute minimum necessary to sustain his basal metabolism, yet he remained in the box for ten hours – until the effect of carbon dioxide suffocation disrupted his meditation and caused him to signal that he wished to be released.

Other studies have also provided striking demonstrations of the degree to which yogis in the state of 'samadhi' (meditation) can sustain persistent EEG alpha activity throughout experimental sessions in which strong lights, loud noises, and immersing the hand in ice-cold water were all used in an attempt to disrupt it. As ordinary people could not hope to block in this way or even produce the persistent alpha state, the results of these various studies must be regarded as providing further dramatic demonstrations of the ways in which mind can exert its influence over body.

Not yet subject to laboratory studies, though widely reported, are the Tibetan feats of 'Lung-gom' and 'Tumo' which, respectively, allow adepts high speed travel and the ability to resist intense cold. On many occasions, Tibetan monks have been recorded as running, over difficult terrain, for distances of around 300 miles in 30 hours. An average speed of ten miles an hour might not, at first sight, seem outlandish but, as any marathon runner would say, it is an almost incredible feat over that distance. Runners in peak condition and training cannot begin to attempt this yet, if the reports are correct, monks – whose preparation is mainly spiritual, and based on breathing exercises performed during three years of meditation in a dark place – can and do succeed in making these epic journeys. How they might do this is uncertain at the moment, though it has been suggested that they use some form of self-hypnosis: synchronizing their pace and respiration with a 'mantra' or repeated phrase, while fixing their eyes on some point of focus – like a distant peak – to further limit their awareness and maintain the hypnoidal state.

Tumo is an even more austere undertaking, involving a long period of meditation and going naked in the ice and snow on high mountains before attempting the final test of mastery. This consists of sitting in the open, in freezing conditions and, by means of breathing exercises and meditation alone, drying a wet sheet that has been wrapped around the body. If the novice can do this at least three times during the night, his reward will be to graduate to an even more harsh life of asceticism and semi-nudity in the snows of Tibet's great mountain regions.

Time alone will tell whether these latter feats, like those of the yogi or Zen master, will one day be verified by science and so require explanation, or whether they will join the ranks of many another marvel which could never actually be tested. I must admit my own credulity is strained somewhat by the Tibetan reports but so, until recently, would it have been by claims that the brain's electrical activity could be brought under voluntary control. Clearly, our understanding of the mind's ability to influence internal bodily states is currently at a very rudimentary stage of development, and it would be unwise to feel sure about anything yet. But all the signs suggest our latent capacity for developing potentially beneficial mind-body controls may be no less than our unconscious ability to induce such unwanted somatic effects as hysterical conversion symptoms and psychosomatic illnesses. If so, we may be on the threshold not only of important new developments in the human sciences, but in the evolution of consciousness itself.

Chapter eight
HEALTHY BODY AND HEALTHY MIND

The belief that good physical health has an improving effect upon all aspects of psychological functioning, whereas illness or bodily sluggishness is apt to result in flabbiness of character, moral weakness and intellectual blunting, has a very long and checkered history. Even its most antique utterance, *Mens sana in corpore sano*, Hippocrates' tenet 'a healthy mind in a healthy body' seems to have expressed a commonplace enough view when it was coined some two and a half millenia ago, judging by contemporary military, social and philosophical traditions in the classical world. Graeco-Roman emphasis on bodily hygiene, exercise and care was not, of course, only connected with the idea of mental wellbeing. Far from it, for though bathing was quite obviously a source of great pleasure and relaxation, and vigorous exercise a way of ensuring good circulation to brain as well as muscle, the healthy bodies created in this way also gave rise to another, less direct, benefit. Strength and fitness bring their own rewards, not the least of which is likely to be self-assurance in the face of opposition or confrontation. But, in circumstances where the outcome of larger scale conflicts are decided more by physical fighting and campaigning than the deployment of missiles, their widespread distribution can also serve to bolster a whole society's self-confidence; reassuring members of their security, and promising success should the time come for their frontiers to be expanded. So long as they conformed to the necessary social requirements, people with sturdy and vigorous constitutions were therefore rather more likely to be regarded as exemplary citizens; their personal qualities heartening others, and encouraging a feeling that society itself was in good shape.

So in Greece and Rome, as in many other countries before and after, mental and physical ideals became closely associated, creating a stereotype which for thousands of years has been developed and reinforced by literature and art. In this convention, physical strength and bodily beauty were almost invariably equated with strength of character, generosity, honour and all things good whereas malice, deception, irresolution of spinelessness have usually been personified in characters with weak, unhealthy or deformed bodies. With few exceptions, the pattern persists to this day, and will quite probably continue to do so, prejudicing relationships, affecting opportunities, or otherwise creating self-fulfilling prophesies. Clearly, the origins and validity of such a stereotype are in need of careful scrutiny and perhaps substantial revision.

Of course, it would be an absurd oversimplification to suggest that pragmatic military considerations might have more than a small part to play in creating this particular expression of the healthy body/healthy mind equation, but it would be equally wrong to overlook the connection altogether. For example, during the nineteenth century, when the British Empire was vast and still growing, there was also a parallel and rapid expansion in the type of school necessary to provide the soldiers and administrators who would control it. The philosophy of many of these English 'public schools' quite explicitly included the Hippocratic tag, and well-nigh glorified sports on the ground that physical health was a virtual prerequisite for the development of a sound and wholesome mind. Naturally, they were following a tradition which involved much more besides: the entire syllabus of history, literature, art and languages reflected many aspects of what they interpreted as the classical ideal.

But it was a tradition suffused with references to the importance of physical health and vitality, whether the source was Cicero – 'in a disordered mind, as in a disordered body, soundness of health is impossible' – or some altogether less urbane voice from Rome's great Republican period. But regardless of origin, the point of view itself is so characteristic of classical thinking that it came to be taken for granted; ultimately becoming a cornerstone of that particular school system. So it came to be accepted among an ever-widening circle of educators that, by giving prominence to physical exercise and strenuous teamwork, they were actually serving their prime objective of cultivating character and mind – as well as producing the sort of people who would be physically and temperamentally prepared for action. Psychologists too, particularly those who were themselves products of the public school system, frequently echoed this view; reinforcing it by adding their own professional authority.

For example, William McDougall's *Introduction to Social Psy-*

chology, written before World War I but continuing to exert immense influence as a basic textbook for educators and psychologists alike until after the next, asserted:

> A well-developed and active muscular system tends to maintain a certain tone of the nervous system that favours an alert and confident habit of mind. Perfect functioning of all the bodily organs not only favours in this way mental activity in general, but tends to an objective habit of mind.

In the event, the great political, social and economic upheavals which came after the World War II created a near-universal transformation of all ideas connected with education – and the conduct of warfare for that matter. Grammar and secondary schools, which by then had absorbed much of the public school ideal, were combined with council schools to create 'Comprehensives'. Specialization was encouraged; curricula were expanded to allow a cafeteria-like selection from what was available, and the policy of maintaining a balance between mental and physical activities discarded in most cases. Nevertheless, for a time at least, the classical principle of *mens sana in corpore sano* permeated a very broad spectrum of British educational thinking – just as it, or its equivalent, has also done in many other countries at one time or another.

It may be coincidental, or seem cynical, but it does seem that wherever and whenever political expansionism or other events create a foreseeable need for fit and disciplined armies or work forces, educational and political agencies alike are especially liable to stress sport, exercise, or physical labour as intellectually and morally improving factors. Classical tenets may or may not be used to justify the way society educates its young and manipulates its citizens, but it always seems to find some vindication.

Japanese workers are encouraged and sometimes coerced into physical exercises which will, it is supposed, add to their energy, concentration and efficiency in some (profitable) way. In Cuba as in China, directed physical work or exercise is, whatever its other justifications, currently still employed to promote 'healthy attitudes' as well as to develop healthy bodies. Of course, there are important differences, but each is a variation on a theme once equally familiar in the German 'Joy Through Strength' movement – where, alas, the disparity between words and deeds, promises and outcomes, theory and practice left many people permanently mistrustful of any claim which links physical and mental excellence. Such things are, of course, exceptional but they do highlight the direction in which ideas can, under certain circumstances, develop.

Allowing though, that exploitation *can* occur, this still leaves completely open the question of whether a healthy body actually does tend to give rise to a healthy mind. Needless to say, the claims, assumptions and testimony deriving from the sources discussed so far must be considered highly speculative, if not downright suspect, as the chain of body-mind interactions involved is necessarily far too long and intricate for specific links to be unequivocally identified and appraised. For example, the healthy body–healthy mind tradition of schooling presents a not entirely implausible case that, by siphoning off all surplus energy through sporting activities, nothing is left over to fuel untoward sexual or aggressive behaviour, or the dark and unhealthy fantasies which their direct suppression can create. Yet the number of links likely to form part of any hypothesized chain of causal events leading from the games field to an adult's mental life beggars the imagination, let alone our capacity to check them empirically in order to see what weight of conviction they might bear.

No doubt the stern and puritanical institutions which promoted these policies of rigorous physical exercise as part of their educational package did have some remarkable successes, and produced their share of fine people with admirable mental health. Though whether such outcomes were at all a consequence of optimizing their pupils' physical health through sport, or whether they occurred in spite of it, is another matter. By the same token, it is no more clear what contribution this hearty approach to education had in the case of those whose school and later lives were marred by unhappiness and maladjustments. In short, simplistic views of the relationship between physical and mental health are generally more notable for their artlessness and panache than for their corroborative evidence. But then, we are dealing with ideologies rather than scientifically based ideas.

Of all the modern ideologies which stress the relationship between a healthy body and a healthy mind, nudism (or naturism as it is often called) must surely be one of the most picturesque and charming expressions. Not that it can be claimed as a totally modern invention as its early advocates even included Benjamin Franklin in the eighteenth century and Henry Thoreau in the nineteenth, but its growth as an organized movement and its widespread acceptance throughout the Western world has taken place entirely in the twentieth.

It began humbly enough in pre-World War I Germany as a somewhat middle-class utopianism, rebelling against a combination of Victorian prudery and the stiff formality of a German society already overly impressed by uniforms and insignia of rank. Jung completely understood this sort of compensatory behaviour by which too great a development in one direction tends to be opposed by equally extreme tendencies in the other. Jean-Jacques Rousseau's 'noble savage' and the impulse which drove people like Gauguin to the South Seas in search of a 'lost' innocence and simplicity are, perhaps, somewhat similar in kind and of a similar origin. But whatever the determining factors, early 'Nacktkultur' (naked culture) was the prototype for a philosophy which has been growing ever since, proclaiming that their way of cultivating a healthy body certainly does help develop a healthy mind.

There is, of course, the obvious argument that sunshine, exercise and fresh air all contribute towards keeping the body toned and supple, consequently leading to greater vigour and zest for life. But it is hard to believe that total nudity is required for this: trunks or a bikini can surely not detract significantly from the benefits of an otherwise similar open-air life. Nudists are the first to agree with this for, though their philosophy stresses the physical advantages and pleasures of going naked, mental health considerations depend much more on the change in relationships and self-regard which this brings about.

From the beginning, nudism developed an ideology in which relationships were inextricably mixed with going unclothed. For example, during the period following World War I, German socialist workers groups were noticeably active in promoting nudism, not as an end in itself, but at least partly as a means of weakening those social and sexual barriers which divide and isolate human beings, particularly disadvantaging members of the working class. Nudity came to be seen as a levelling or democratizing force in that dispensing with clothes was thought to remove not only some of the signs of status difference which divide and disunite people, but many of the impalpable barriers too. Meeting and living in communities, where all traces of outside rank and importance had been left behind, it was thought, encouraged people to treat one another as what they are, rather than in terms of what they do or own.

Of enormous importance to nudists was, and still is, the fact that men and women participate in this sense of comradeship, abandoning the taboos, prudery and stereotypes which perpetuate false mystiques and inequalities in treatment and opportunity. The assumed advantages of this are, first of all, that by breaking down sex segregation, a fuller sense of human solidarity can occur, with members of both sexes coming to see members of the other as *people*, rather than as representatives of an almost alien group. Secondly, anxieties about the size, shape or nature of the body and its parts were expected to dissipate once mutual disclosures had been made in an accepting and, in any case, very physically mixed crowd. But, most of all, all the fears and fantasies about being seen naked, seeing others, and sharing in the sense of vulnerability and unadorned humanity, are believed to prevent or act as an antidote to the sort of anxieties which are still common, and seem to have been immeasurably more so in early post-Victorian times.

In principle at least, it does seem that many sources of mental distress might well respond favourably to this sort of situation. For example, if the circumstances of going nude are positively accepting, it is entirely likely that anxiety concerning body structures or being unclothed in the presence of the opposite sex could be counter-conditioned; relaxation coming to be associated with the idea rather than anxiety. Even alarming impulses towards self-exposure or voyeurism may well be defused in circumstances where reality and its associated emotional reactions displace those of fantasy.

But nudists seldom represent their communities as places in which to deal with mental problems: rather, they stress the positive and wholesome nature of the motives which draw them together. In reply to those who, even now, charge them with indecency they usually reply that, far from encouraging sexual expression, normal or abnormal, they are essentially concerned with maintaining a moral atmosphere appropriate for the family life which is lived in their clubs and settlements. Their vague statistics are hard to check as relative numbers are unknown, but the claim made is that nudists have an extremely low rate of divorce, and that sexual offences and juvenile delinquency are very rare indeed. However, as nudist affiliations are hardly likely to be reported in relation to such cases anyway, there is really no way that an outsider could know whether the claim is true or not.

It is believed that because children become used to the biological realities of sex at an early age and grow up with much less emphasis placed on the sexual organs of themselves and others, they are not so susceptible to the fantasies, guilt and repressions which distort the development of children raised in more usual ways. Instead of schoolyard misconceptions and segregations, they grow up with much more realistic attitudes and less likelihood of regarding the opposite sex as inherently different, strange, or alarming. This at least is the theory, and the principal argument advanced as to why the children of nudists are likely to have certain major advantages in the development of a healthy mind.

There are, however, some who believe that quite the opposite may be the case. Curiously enough, one such was the psychoanalyst Wilhelm Reich, best known for his theories concerning the need for total uninhibitedness in sexual surrender as a major route to mental and physical health. The strange thing about it is that he too, like the nudist movement itself, was closely connected with German socialist worker groups during the period between the wars, each playing a prominent part in the struggle to break down all divisive class and sex barriers and free individuals' bodies as well as minds from morally repressive and socially imposed controls. Reich worked actively in this mildly revolutionary milieu for some time, advocating considerable liberalization in sexual behaviour and birth control yet, though nudism might seem quite compatible with their shared goals of democratization, mental health and reduction of the social barriers standing between men and women, there was one important point of difference which made him actively antagonistic towards nudism. The point of disagreement was not so much that adults would be in any way harmed by nudism but that it contained hazards for the psychosexual development of children. He felt, for example, that inferiority complexes might occur in young boys as a result of the very unfavourable comparisons they would make with the adult organ. But, much more importantly, as a Freudian psychoanalyst, he believed that serious castration complexes and anxieties might be created by very young children seeing vaginas and interpreting them as evidence for the reality of castration.

A British psychologist, J. C. Flugel, has considered the various pros and cons of this argument, and several others besides, but though he is himself fairly sympathetic towards the view that nudism is not the threat that Reich took it for, it is true to say that there remains room for disagreement as to whether mental health is improved or harmed by living out nudist ideals. There is no conclusive empirical evidence either way. But, in view of the fact that literally millions of people in Europe alone now regularly enjoy nudism as part of their holidays, whether or not they have ever visited a nudist club or even heard of the *International Naturist Federation*, suggests that its positive virtues are seen as outweighing any negative aspects. In the event, and so far as I know, there has been no evidence to suggest that there is any increase in psychological disturbances as a result of such disclosures on the beach. But then, it is hard to imagine how one might even begin to show that there are substantive mental health advantages either.

Careful selection and control of diet is another activity which shares with nudism a considerable 'back-to-nature' element, as well as a number of beliefs about its potential for positive mental health. Both have attracted large numbers of adherents though diet, being more obviously fundamental to all aspects of health and vitality, claims far more interest. Indeed, the 'health food' movement is now very big business, and not just in marketing 'natural' products uncontaminated by potentially harmful agricultural or preservative chemicals. There is also a flourishing publishing and broadcasting side, offering seemingly unlimited numbers of alternative regimes and diets, most of which are claimed to optimize the balance of necessary nutritional components while minimizing the intake of supposedly more dangerous refined or high-cholesterol products.

Purely bodily and survival considerations are no doubt at the core of all this interest and activity, but it is probably seldom completely detached from some important mental health related issue. In many cases, it may be no more than the presence or prospect of fat creating a disagreeable self-image, or anxiety that one's appearance might limit social or sexual relationships. Yet, of course, remaining or becoming slim and healthy, and experiencing the sense of well being these and other abstinences may bring, can have decidely worthwhile somatopsychic consequences in their own right, particularly in so far as the results include less unnecessary drain on the supporting musculature or strain on the digestive and cardiovascular systems.

For some people, though, simply avoiding the negative consequences of poor diet is not enough; they are more interested in its potential for *positively* improving mental health.

Vegetarianism has long been associated with the idea that eating 'dead animals' is not only repellent but unhealthy too, as their fat and decay products pollute the body and lead to mental and physical sluggishness. Furthermore, it is argued, the butchering of animals is likely to create decidely harmful conflicts and repressions for anyone at all sensitive to the exploitation and misery that meat-eating brings to other creatures. All in all, and in addition to the fact that meat production is grossly inefficient and therefore unjustifiable in a hungry world, vegetarians are inclined to view the eating of meat as not only an aesthetic and moral issue, but one concerning physical and mental health as well.

There are, however, various degrees of vegetarianism: some make use of milk products and others will also eat eggs but 'vegans', the strictest group, will have none of this, restricting themselves to foodstuffs of purely non-animal origin – whether or not killing is involved. These are the most orthodox and, naturally enough, least numerous members of the movement, but it seems to be the vegans who most clearly express the healthy body/healthy mind ideal to which most of the others subscribe in thought if not so punctiliously in deed. Recently, however, traditional forms of vegetarianism have been meeting with strong ideological competition from those who support George Ohsawa's claim for a 'macrobiotic diet'.

Macrobiotics is a complex mixture of dietary practices, self-awareness development, and heterogeneous Buddhist and Chinese philosophical ideas. Centrally though, all foods are regarded as having either predominently *yin* or *yang* characteristics; that is, exerting an influence towards one or other of the contrasting but complementary principles of passivity or activity which are said to permeate every object, quality and relationship in the universe. The theory is that the food we eat determines our personal balance of yin or yang – for example, joy and sorrow, good and evil, strength and weakness, spirituality and materialism – and that only through careful diet can balance and harmony be achieved. Ten stages of upward development towards this philosophical goal are specified, each with its own dietary prescriptions. The lowest allows for 30 per cent of animal products – with a mixture of salads, deserts and soup – but the highest level allows only 100 per cent brown rice and a limit of eight ounces of liquid per day. Chewed about 50 times per mouthful, such a diet is claimed to prevent disease, greatly enhance mental health, and be invaluable in the pursuit of 'enlightenment'.

As with conventional vegetarians, most who go on macrobiotic diets are not extremists but for those who do go on to the rice-only regime, there are very definite hazards. The early stages of fasting, or any rigorous diet, can give rise to extremely pleasant states of consciousness which may seem to validate the claims made for mental and spiritual enrichment. Unfortunately, though, these 'highs' are usually more closely connected with the warning symptoms of lightheadedness due to blood-sugar abnormalities than anything else. But, just as the early stages of alcoholic intoxication can be so agreeable as to encourage one to go on still further, so too can the metabolic changes induced by a drastically reduced diet: in either case, moderation can have psychologically beneficial effects but excess can be injurious to mind and body alike.

A small quantity of brown rice is perfectly wholesome in itself but, by itself, is insufficient to fuel and repair the brain and the rest of the body: mental and physical malfunctioning is therefore entirely to be expected if the diet is too prolonged. Beyond a certain point, vigour and judgement are both likely to be impaired; sometimes to the extent that people fall ill as the result of deficiencies in metabolically vital trace elements, or as a result of their weakened state and reduced resistance to pathogens. Deaths as a result of malnutrition are by no means unknown.

For those with a pre-existing tendency towards anorexia, such fads are particularly dangerous as they serve to rationalize irrational behaviour. Worse still, being cultish practices, they are likely to be indulged in a context where admiration rather than a more appropriate alarm might be created in others. But such cases are rare: most people on a vegetarian or macrobiotic diet opt for fairly moderate and balanced regimes with, perhaps, occasional fasts or short periods of strict dieting. The typical pattern of both groups is essentially middle-of-the-road, a mixture of popular yoga or other 'keep-fit' activities and a diet of highly nutritious food – honey, wholemeal bread, nuts and fruit, fresh vegetables, natural yoghurt and the like – so warmly and vigorously marketed by the health food stores.

'Naturopathy', the treatment and prevention of disease by correct eating and the elimination of accumulated toxins, is now a growing facet of this type of dietary control. It too emphasizes fresh fruit, vegetables and grains as a basis for attaining or retaining physical health and vitality though, beyond the period of therapeutically supervised habit change and purification, it tends to be assumed that no fixed rules are required as the body, once cleansed, will thereafter recognize its ideal nutritional requirements. Central to the philosophy is a belief that not only are superficial diseases of the mind as well as the body cured as a result of whatever programme of diet, massage and musculo-skeletal realignment may be involved, there is also a 'total effect', whereby the individual becomes more 'in touch' with the natural world, and more able to make use of the energy and intuitive guidelines which make for mental health in the fullest sense.

It must be said though that, so far as positive mental health gains are concerned, we are still discussing claims which are largely anecdotal or impressionistic. Scientific investigations of other than the negative effects of diet on mental health are both difficult and rare, the main exceptions being some studies which seem to show that scores on intelligence tests may be improved with some diets. The context of this type of study is, however, usually either where there has previously been severe undernourishment, or else some specific dietary deficiency.

Yet, even in the best of health, and however well the body is treated through exercise, outdoor living and careful diet, it can never reach and maintain a constant state of functioning. It is not a machine but a community of biological organisms which pass through many differently phased peaks of optimal performance, alternating with troughs of fatigue or sluggishness when fuels are running low, or while restorative or regenerative activities are in progress. *Circadian rhythms*, roughly 24 hour cycles of waking and sleeping, are the most obvious of these periodic variations in our mental and physical behaviour, involving as they do marked changes in consciousness, vitality, alertness, mood and efficiency.

However, that we each vary somewhat in our response to this cycle is quite apparent from the 'night hawks' and the 'early birds' whose meetings at breakfast time can be particularly traumatic. Modifying habits helps to some degree but, except under unusually motivating conditions, these two extreme types tend to remain very different from one another: they both have circadian cycles but their timings are different. Shift work sometimes requires that people reverse or alternate the natural form of their circadian rhythm, in which daylight coincides with optimal functioning and nighttime corresponds with the normal decline in all active functions. As with 'jet lag', where time changes must be accommodated as a result of very rapid east-west travel, rest and habit can offset the initial effects of being awake and active during that part of the cycle usually given to sleep and renewal, but the body must be given time to adjust. Most of us are not subject to frequent disruptions of our circadian rhythm but, when they occur, they do help emphasize processes that are at work in us all.

Throughout each 24 hour period, changes in circulating blood sugar, hormone activity and other metabolic activities are constantly shifting the baseline of our energy, sensory awareness and mood. As blood sugar levels fall, we are more inclined to be irritable while, after a meal when digestive processes are placing additional burdens on blood supply, we are more likely to be contented and lethargic. The rhythm is, of course, very much influenced by our habits: the way in which we divide the period between sleeping and waking, and the way in which we conventionally space our meals throughout the day. But, whatever is imposed by individual life style, the body's circadian rhythm is profoundly important in shaping the daily course of our mental lives.

We may not be able to change this fact but thoughtful attention to patterns of eating, sleeping and activity can certainly minimize untoward effects. And self-awareness about the course of our own cycle can help in deciding when to do certain things. For example, those whose peak of energy falls early in the day are best advised to complete tasks then, if this is at all possible. Unfortunately though, the tendency to treat both ourselves and others as pieces of machinery is firmly entrenched, and perhaps virtually unavoidable in an industrialized society which rigidly parcels the day into standard packages of work and rest. However, the recent introduction of 'flexitime' work hours in some places has introduced a very slight hope that the future will see less ironbound work schedules, even if this particular idea was originally conceived to ease mass transport problems rather than to accommodate individual psycho-physiological differences.

Although the main circadian alternation between daytime alertness and nighttime drowsiness is obvious to all, it is actually composed of non-obvious shorter rhythms, each of which may only become apparent through keeping a detailed diary over a substantial period of time, and recording daily fluctuations in co-ordination, vitality, concentration, and so on. Naturally, very few people actually go to the length of keeping such detailed records but those who do have made it apparent that there are not only marked differences in the overall pattern of individual circadian rhythms, but that they form part of longer periodic changes and contain many shorter ones. The shortest of these, the *ultradian cycle*, is of about a one and a half hour duration and involves periodic fluctuations in digestive, sexual and fantasy activities throughout the day, and recurrent periods of dreaming and sexual arousal throughout the night.

Monthly cycles, connected with the moon's phase, have long been the subject of mythology – the very term *lunatic* being derived from beliefs that the full moon and madness are somehow connected. If so, the scientific rationale is very obscure and, though there have been many reports of increased crime and disturbance among mental patients at the time of the full moon, few serious researchers have been tempted to work in an area more usually reserved for students of the occult. Even if crime and disturbances on the ward are increased during this time, it is always possible that strong moonlight favours criminal activities; and that bright nights keep patients awake and that this leads to more disturbances. Only carefully controlled research will show, first of all, whether any significant increases in these behaviours actually occur and, if they do, what causes them. For the moment, however, it is not known whether the lunar cycle *per se* has any effect on people's minds or bodies.

Coincidentally, for there is nothing to relate them to phases of the moon, the period of about a lunar month often does correspond with marked cyclical changes in body-mind functioning. Following the ideas of Wilhelm Fliess, a Berlin physician whose ideas and friendship exerted a considerable influence on Freud's early thinking, modern proponents of biorhythm research also claim to have identified somewhat comparable cyclic changes in functioning. Fliess's part in the history of psychoanalysis, though not always fully acknowledged, was decidedly consequential. It was he who showed Freud that it was infantile sexual fantasy, not actual events, which lay at the core of most repression and neurosis, and at the root of most subsequent psychosexual development. Whether the conclusion was right or wrong is another issue, but the contribution was of the greatest theoretical significance. However, Fliess also drew Freud into his ideas concerning the mental effects of biological rhythms, which he supposed to occur at 23 day intervals in the case of men, 28 days in the case of women. The male cycle was supposed to be typified by fluctuations in strength, courage and endurance, whereas the female's showed equivalent changes in her emotional sensitivity and feelings. In the event, though Freud at first showed considerable enthusiasm for Fliess' biorhythm theories, a split between the two men over the authorship of some central psychoanalytic ideas led to the biorhythm hypotheses being dropped by Freud, and thus consigned to an oblivion from which they have only recently been recovered.

Nevertheless, the commonplace observation that we all have 'good' and 'bad' days or phases as a result of apparently inexplicable variations in our temper or mood, co-ordination or energy levels has led a number of people to start afresh on keeping detailed records to see whether cyclical patterns of the sort described by Fliess really do occur. It seems that the search was rewarded for it is now widely claimed among biorhythm enthusiasts that there is indeed such a marked periodicity of body-mind activities – though their pattern involves a 28 day cycle for emotions, 33 for intellectual and cognitive function and 23 for such physical characteristics as strength, energy and co-ordination. They emphasize that each of these cycles comprises a distinct peak and an equally distinct trough, the cycle swinging through a lowest point before beginning the upward swing again: the low points, or 'critical days', are obviously the ones to be careful about. For example, one would try to avoid allowing emotionally or intellectually taxing events to occur either on or around the appropriate critical days. By the same token, activities which are unusually physically demanding or dangerous are best undertaken on the upswing or crest of that particular cycle.

The potential advantages of being able to co-ordinate these rhythms with our daily activities needs no stressing: our lives would be transformed if only we could optimize the match between our capacities and the demands made on us, or at least be prepared for those days when we are likely to be below par. Naturally, such pragmatic considerations have stirred a lot of popular interest in the subject, and have given rise to almanacs like Bernard Gittelson's *Biorhythm 1980–81–82* and pocket calculators with which to determine one's likely state at any given time. In fact, the predictive aspect – a form of augury – sometimes begins to look a little like astrology, although the rationale remains firmly grounded in individual biological activities, rather than in some sort of external cosmic process.

Unfortunately though, the number of variables involved in doing this sort of 'real life' research, and the inevitable 'softness' of criteria, make such studies excessively difficult. As a result, much of the work done has been undertaken by those prepared to sacrifice more experimental rigour than is usually acceptable to most scientists. The results must therefore be regarded as at least equivocal for the time being and are, in any case, usually presented as practical guidelines rather than scientific results. Even so, it would be just as wrong to dismiss this kind of work out of hand as it would be to take it at face value. The evidence may be weak, but there is a certain reasonableness about the rationale. Still, the inescapable obstacle to progress and acceptance is that no one has yet been able to identify psycho-physiological criteria to mark the confines of proposed cycles which are even fractionally as concrete and unequivocal as those of the menstrual cycle.

Women's *Once a Month* periodic cycle, discussed in Katherina Dalton's book of that name, is at least as commonplace a thing (for half the human race at least) as the lunar month with which it so closely corresponds in duration. Yet, even its psychological consequences have been little understood until quite recently. There are obvious reasons why women's periods have not been studied and discussed in the way they are now, but there is no doubt that women have always been well aware that their mood and abilities were somewhat dependent upon them. What was much less evident, though, was the extent and detail of this dependence. Our understanding is still somewhat rudimentary, and estimates vary, but it now seems that as many as two-thirds of all women experience marked psychological changes during the few days prior to the beginning of menstruation. Some become depressed or lethargic, others may experience energy peaks and sexual yearnings, but most tend towards more negative states – such as anxiety and 'moodiness'.

Pre-menstrual tension may also being a recurrence of physical disorders as diverse as skin rashes, stomach ulcers and other digestive upsets. Sleeping and appetite are likely to be affected, and performance on all sorts of tasks, from driving to taking IQ tests, can be affected. During the four or five days before menstruation, accidents, arguments, suicide and admission into psychiatric care are all more likely to occur. In very few circumstances are the mental effects of normal bodily functioning seen more clearly but, even here, there is much more to be learned about other stages in the cycle. No doubt the effects will be more subtle as most women are quite unable to specify characteristic changes other than those of the few pre-menstrual days and, without a calendar to remind them, would usually be quite unaware of their stage in the cycle. Yet cycles normally proceed upwards and downwards in a series of inclines, so it is entirely to be expected that future research will present a fuller picture of the gradual rise and fall of the fluctuating mental and physical states, rather than treating them as sudden and discontinuous changes.

In her book *Body Time*, Gay Luce discusses the findings of research dealing with biorhythms of every kind – some scientifically established and some very questionable – including the possibility that men too have periodic emotional rhythms related to cyclical metabolic events. Corroborative evidence for this latter claim is not yet persuasive and it will no doubt be many years yet before adequate evidence for many of the hypotheses presented can be assembled and assessed. But the more general affirmation that mind is often demonstrably influenced by cyclic changes taking place in the normal healthy body, is unassailable and Luce's conclusion, that our mental harmony may well be dependent upon many more biorhythms and geophysical events affecting the body than we suppose, seems a perfectly reasonable one.

According to many biorhythm enthusiasts, the cycles which accompany us throughout life begin their almost clockwork pattern at birth. And so they might, but personally, I regard any such inflexible conception with considerable mistrust. Even the menstrual cycle is far from invariable, responding as it does to health, nutrition and even mental state. Nevertheless, there is nothing inherently improbable in the notion that the course of important mental events is partially set by the physical ones which occur at birth. Of course, forceps deliveries have often enough caused focal brain damage, resulting in later epilepsy. And cerebral anoxia, due to the baby being deprived of oxygen in the birth canal, with or without the umbilical cord twisted around its neck, has all too often resulted in more diffuse intellectual problems. But, it is now being argued, even without organic damage, and where the baby is delivered in perfect physical health, the circumstances of birth may still give rise to unfortunate and long-term psychological consequences.

Frederick Leboyer, a French obstetrician, has been one of the foremost exponents of this view; arguing that the rough and insensitive way babies tend to be delivered in hospitals can cause massive psychological trauma. Milling people, brilliant lights, noise, perhaps even forceps on the head, or being physically pulled out of their mother, then being slapped, weighed, and taken to a crèche in another noisy and dazzling room, certainly does suggest the possibility of trauma. If, that is, newborn babies are capable of registering these events, and can be affected by them. Leboyer and many others since have no doubt that they are aware of what is happening, and that these experiences are harmful. Their solution is to make the transition from womb to room as pleasant and reassuring as possible. The mother too naturally benefits from such conditions as subdued lights and gentle humane treatment but, of even greater long-term significance, she communicates her relaxation and confidence to the unborn child, and so makes the physical process of birth easier and less stressful for the infant. So important is this thought to be, that an increasing number of obstetricians now go to great lengths to minimize the physical trauma: even, for example, allowing mothers to give birth in a warm bath, and control their delivery posture and timing in such a way as to suit themselves and the baby more than hospital practices and routines.

The British psychiatrist R. D. Laing has said that traumatic birth can make someone emotionally autistic for life, turning them into 'primal cringers' whose entire subsequent history is affected by those few hours at the beginning of their lives. This is, of course, an extremely difficult proposition to check: life histories are so varied that it would be almost impossible to identify clear causal links connecting events in the delivery room with mental events in later life. However, there is one way in which this is sometimes attempted – though it is by no means a universally acceptable method among either psychologists or psychiatrists – that is, by encouraging people to recall or relive their birth experiences within a supportive therapeutic setting. Though quite different in many respects, the procedure itself nevertheless does have a generic similarity to the way regressions are induced and emotional abreactions brought about in Freudian and many other analytical processes. The coincidence is, though, by no means purely fortuitous.

There are now several techniques in regular, if not common use, all of which can trace at least some part of their common ancestry back to the pioneering work of one or both of Freud's colleagues, Otto Rank and Wilhelm Reich. For example, as early as the 1920s, Rank was getting certain of his neurotic patients to adopt the foetal position while working towards a reliving of their birth experiences. For all sorts of reasons, such elaborations of orthodox psychoanalytic procedures were always suspect, and frequently suppressed or discarded. Rank's publication of *The Trauma of Birth* in 1926 (later consolidated in *Will Therapy and Truth and Reality*) was no exception: its hostile reception being in no small part the cause of his abandoning psychoanalysis and developing his own system of 'psychotherapy', with its entirely new emphasis on the importance of will and self-determination.

But Rank's beliefs about the lifetime importance of birth trauma – the primal anxiety and repression which fear and the overwhelming sense of loss and separation burden even the most normal person – have never been entirely lost or discarded. His insistance that the major human motivation is to regain embryonic bliss, and that much of our mental life depends on the way we handle the conflict between this goal and the anxiety which birth trauma has attached to the womb and to genital penetration, may have fared less well but the idea of corrosive and enervating primal anxiety remains at the core of much current thinking.

It is assumed by those who are sympathetic to this view that, though sensitive obstetric care may reduce birth trauma, it can do no more than that: however ideal the delivery and normal the baby, anxieties are inevitably created, and can only be discharged by reliving these fateful moments with the insight of an adult and the help of others. Some therapists, like Leonard Orr, simulate birth conditions as far as is practicably possible – which means, in his case, submerging clients face downwards in a warm bath (which substitutes for the womb) whilst they breathe deeply through a snorkel. Presently, it is claimed, memories of the womb and birth surge back into consciousness, recreating the fear, isolation and anxiety of that time. But, as soon as this happens, the client is taken from the bath to be cossetted and comforted: positive feelings of the 'rebirth' replacing the sense of alienation and anxiety which had persisted from the original event. It may take several sessions to achieve it, and a number of other physical interventions such as massage and breathing exercises, but 'rebirthers' are supposed to be able to achieve positive mental health this way.

'Primal Integration' sessions take place on the ground and in groups – where the rebirther, in foetal position, is pressed down upon by others with cushions. The struggle to escape is accompanied by paradoxical fears: dread of being suffocated in the 'womb' being opposed by an equivalent terror at the prospect of leaving it, to be forever alone. As with Orr's technique, the re-creation is followed by a counter-conditioning experience of relief and satisfaction; the aims and outcomes being apparently identical.

But perhaps the best known of these approaches is Arthur Janov's 'Primal Therapy'; a much more comprehensive psychological treatment, concerned with a broader spectrum of stored pain. It begins with three days of oral and sexual abstinence, during which the client lives in relative isolation. Physical measures of cardiovascular, EEG and other vegetative functions are then made in order to assess the amount of 'pain' stored in the body. Once this has been done, psychotherapy begins – with an emphasis upon uncovering sources of infantile fear, particularly the birth trauma. Regression and acting out of baby-like behaviour are encouraged, with the aim of unlocking repressed memories and discharging the locked-in tension through a cathartic scream – the *Primal Scream* of his celebrated book.

'Primalling' is, however, concerned with more than the traumas of parturition: after all, shock and emotional pains may begin then, but they continue for the rest of our lives. Adopting this premise, Janov's approach is therefore very much the same whether the pain being exorcized dates from birth, childhood, or adult life. In each case, physical 'letting go' through regressive behaviour, crying and screaming is used as a way of liberating the mind from tensions which have become locked not only into it, but into the body also.

If Janov is correct, our mental lives are impoverished in two ways as a result of repressed traumas: firstly, psychic energy must be diverted from more useful employment to retain unacceptable memories in the unconscious (this is an orthodox psychoanalytic view); secondly, repression leads to physical tensions which also sap energy while diminishing the body's capacity to provide the joy, élan, grace and self-confidence which can make or mar the quality of our lives. In almost every respect, it is quite clear that both rebirthing and primal therapy owe a great deal to the influence of psychoanalysis in general and Wilhelm Reich in particular.

Perhaps because his early roots were so deeply set in Freudian psychosexual theory, Reich's own ideas were always powerfully influenced by a belief that sexual conflict is the most important fact of mental development. In fact, though, his own misgivings about the potential psychological and social harm which may come from unsatisfied physical desire led to an even more radical point of view than Freud's. Both saw the enormous sociological as well as psychological ramifications of the sex drive but, whereas Freud regarded its repression or stringent regulation by other means as necessary and desirable, Reich considered such repression personally and politically injurious.

During the early 1930s, Reich travelled around Germany promoting his 'Sexual Politics Association', arguing that the proletariat were being exploited by a 'capitalist morality' which forced people to marry in order to express their sexuality, then sprang an economic trap which held them as slaves thereafter. He attacked attempts to limit birth control, to make sex a joyless and guilt-ridden area of ignorance and taboo, and impose the ultimate absurdity – monogamy. His avowed aim was to undermine the family, which he regarded as an institution which not only creates sexual and emotional dissatisfaction for the couples concerned, but also leads on to a self-perpetuating and faulty model for future generations. His fellow communists, who were at first attracted by a movement determined to bring down capitalism and bourgeois standards by means of the proletarian sexual revolution, soon became alarmed at a rebellion which might just as easily spread and loosen their own grip on youth. Reich and his theories were denounced.

The rising Nazi party was even more antagonistic towards such ideas, as were orthodox psychoanalysts. He had affronted or threatened the morality and authority of all factions and most public opinion: as an 'unfrocked' communist and psychoanalyst, and a

German Jew who had given up his religion, there was only one thing to do – start again elsewhere, and quickly. In due course, his travels led him to the United States where, despite rather more tolerance for his ideas, he still met much opposition and contrived to die in prison as a result of his quite unnecessary skirmishes with authority. But despite this sad end, and a period when his ideas were more unknown than unpopular, Reich's time as an American were productive and provided an opportunity to plant the seeds of a normal psychology of body-mind which have since blossomed so profusely in that country.

The origin of Reich's views about the ways in which apparently healthy bodies and minds can interact with one another to the detriment of both lay in the observation that neurotic females never experience vaginal orgasm; and neurotic males, though they may have absolutely no problem with erection or ejaculation, are equally incapable of full and satisfying orgasm. Of course, many modern researchers would now regard the notion of a specifically vaginal orgasm as physiologically unsound anyway, but Reich was here following Freud's curious distinction, and one which was difficult to study in detail at that time. Nevertheless, Reich regarded clitoral orgasm alone (and even this was often elusive or absent) as immature and inhibited; it being the equivalent of males experiencing only genital excitement during intercourse. Each was, in his view, the sign of 'orgastic incompetence', and was likely to result in boredom and post-coital revulsion. More seriously, when undischarged tensions remained and conventional outlets were unattractive and unsatisfying, personally and socially damaging redirections of energy might lead to such things as masochistic or sadistic impulses, or to other neuroses and irrational behaviours. In any case, if these normal bodily energies are unable to find the satisfactory outlet, physical symptoms would ensue: indeed, Reich regarded them as part of the neurosis itself, rather than just an indicator. So, it was argued, the presence and nature of neuroses can not only be seen through their affects on the body, it follows that they can be treated, at least in part, by means of appropriate physical therapy.

In essence, what Reich proposed was that if what he called 'life energy' (virtually interchangeable with sexual drive) was dammed up and prevented from discharge, it would give rise to a tension or 'stasis anxiety' which provides the energy and impetus for neurotic activities. No one can be completely and permanently free of stasis as, unlike simpler forms of animal life, human existence does not permit the immediate discharge of sexual urges. Consequently, Reichian theories and methods are held to be just as relevant to normal healthy people as they are to those whose stasis anxiety is such as to give rise to florid hysterical or psychosomatic disorder. Use of the term 'therapy' should therefore not be interpreted to suggest that Reich's work only concerns abnormal conditions: quite healthy bodies and minds can be subject to tensions which, when removed, create improvements in the quality of life. All bodies and minds are, on this view, in a more or less constant state of reciprocal activity: anxieties and inhibitions giving rise to physical tensions which, in turn, give rise to further psychological strains, and so on.

A personality which is marred by inhibitions and fears is said to develop a 'character armour'; a controlled and defensive attitude towards others which, though it may represent a socially successful adjustment, nevertheless segregates the individual within his armour and adds further to his anxieties. Collaterally, the body too creates a 'muscular armour' which consists of areas of stiffness and rigidity, within which are locked the sources of psychic tension. All areas of the body can be involved but particularly the head and neck, chest and diaphragm. However, as many energy blocks occur in relation to sexual conflicts, it is not surprising that reports of marked tension in the lower abdominal area should also be common. For example, muscular armouring often causes considerable tightening of the musculature in thighs, buttocks, belly and lower back, inhibiting pelvic thrusts in intercourse and making a full orgasmic discharge of energy even less likely.

The solution, according to Reich, was partly along more or less conventional psychotherapeutic lines but also – and this was a revolutionary break with psychoanalysis and all previous forms of therapy – to work on the body itself. Generally working from the head downwards, areas of tension are identified, muscles palpated, and manual pressure applied to appropriate parts of the body at relevant stages in the therapy. The result is often a combination of intense pain and profound relief; the theory being that a block or log jam in the flow of energy has been destroyed, allowing pent-up dynamism to surge through the body again.

Rather foreseeably, and very unfortunately, descriptions of this process were sometimes interpreted as the therapist masturbating his or her client. The misconception is understandable enough in view of the way both problem and process are outlined, but the release brought about by Reichian therapists is emotional not organic, even though it is intended to facilitate the client's later sexual behaviour. Indeed, the key objective of the entire treatment is seen as attaining 'orgastic potency' – the capacity to surrender completely to the involuntary physical processes of orgasm, discharging all dammed-up sexual excitation in a mutually tender embrace with one's partner. Once achieved or restored, both muscular and character armour can be discarded, and mental and physical health should be enormously improved. Reich was always absolutely emphatic and totally uncompromising in his assertion that a thoroughly balanced and healthy mind must always finally depend upon orgastic potency.

Few today would accept this overwhelming sexual emphasis, but innumerable 'neo-Reichian' transformations and refinements of his theories have burgeoned during recent years. Of these, by far the most influential, and most fully worked out, is Alexander Lowen's 'bioenergetics'. That this should be so is not entirely surprising as Lowen was not only one of Reich's students in New York, he was also treated by him, and more or less simultaneously trained in what Reich called his 'vegetotherapy'. In most respects, Lowen continues to accept and promulgate his teacher's original ideas: bioenergetics is not so much a revision of Reich's theories as a major expansion of them. The point of growth came in Lower's realization that, though many neuroses and much mental and physical disease does originate in the way Reich explained it, a great deal more has quite different antecedents.

Both, however, are equally emphatic that mental problems are apparent in the body; that psychological armouring is always transformed into muscular armouring, so that the health of the mind depends upon restoring flexibility to the body and allowing energy to flow freely again. We create armour to protect our self-esteem, to inhibit what we see as our own risky impulses, and to keep others at a distance. But defensive postures are, in many ways, quite incompatible with freedom and spontaneity: the choice is between an illusory impregnability and living a full and exuberant life. That at least is how the alternatives are put, and suggests the objectives of this particular form of 'growth' or 'human potential' activity.

Of course, most people are quite unaware of their armour: it is adopted quite unconsciously as a response to stress, but readily persists long after circumstances have changed. Lowen has given innumerable examples of the ways in which emotions may be frozen into the body itself including, for example, the way anger can be seen in the clamped set of a jaw, the thrust of a face, in posture, or in facial expression. Sometimes it results in a feeling like a 'lump' in the throat, or may be experienced as a tight or leaden sensation which, because it affects the musculature of neck, diaphragm and chest, is also often apparent in speech. Fears and anxiety give rise to their own characteristic forms of body tension and are apparent from such things as raised shoulders, or drawn-in head, fearful glances or habitual avoidance of steady eye contacts, voice quality, and so on. Patterns are idiosyncratic, but Lowen regards all bodily tensions as equally important in so far as their existence uses energy, and their persistence blocks its flow.

Because of the emphasis placed on removing these blocks, it is sometimes supposed that bioenergetics is essentially a form of somatic manipulation: that exercise and massage alone will lead to mental release and growth. Body-work is certainly characteristic of the approach, but it is only a part: the system remains rooted in its origins, an analytic concern with the unconscious. Psychoanalysis began by addressing itself to the more obvious and distressing problems of how the unconscious mind gives rise to such hysterical symptoms as paralysis, anaesthesias, or blindness, and only much later did it turn its attention towards the more mundane psychosomatic disorders. Reich and Lowen have simply extended this enquiry to include apparently perfectly healthy and normally functioning people, but their commitment to psychotherapeutic methods and certain psychoanalytic concepts remains very much a part of the whole enterprise.

Exercise, massage, improved ways of breathing and a cathartic acting out of anger or hatred are some of the basic techniques used to dislodge emotions blocked up in the body, but psychological procedures are regarded as being of fundamental importance for identifying and ensuring the permanent removal of these obstructions to the free flow of energy. Lowen was always interested in sport, calisthenics and outdoor activities but he has never supposed that they alone are sufficient to ensure mental health. Were this the case, athletes and the physically most fit and supple would also be the most mentally sound and vigorous.

Despite his assertion that 'the energetic processes of the body determine what goes on in the mind just as they determine what goes on in the body', their influence is only seen as part of a much broader determination. Of course, on this view, an individual with excellent body awareness and a finely regulated constitution will have certain advantages over those who are less healthy. However, it has been Lowen's experience that though dancers, athletes and exercise addicts may be extremely healthy and tuned to their chosen physical activity, they frequently have very poorly developed body feelings. Instead of experiencing their body as themselves, and as an elemental part of the natural order, such people are often remarkably alienated from their physical selves. Treating the body as a machine – an instrument of the ego by means of which one can compete with or impress others, make a living, or work out an inferiority complex – has only limited psychological advantages. Sport and exercise can alleviate stress effects by improving health and breathing, thus increasing vitality: they can even be useful in diverting energy from ruminative thoughts which would otherwise add to existing tension. But, though they help, they are not enough.

Lowen, no less than Reich, accepts that sexual tensions are omnipresent in most of us and can be highly disruptive of mental processes unless they can be satisfactorily discharged. Among the most troublesome consequences, tend to be the shame, guilt and consequent repression brought about by lust and fantasies; these being the natural mental representations of blocked physical drives. Unlike Reich, though, Lowen realized that discharging blocks created by sexual repression only dissipates these particular obstructions, and sex is only one of the pressures which leads to armouring. Modern living, with its traffic and hustle, competitiveness and obligation to be efficient; even coercions to leave one's home and family to follow work and attain status, contributes its share. Wars, illness, ageing and death have always been present or in prospect, as have the problems encountered in relating to other people – whether as child, parent or adult. But when all of these are taken together, their enormously increased stress potential is obvious, and almost anyone can create the sort of energy blocks described by both Reich and Lowen.

Virtually every form of human relationship is capable of creating tensions which can be locked into the body. But some, like husband/wife, parent/child, or boss/subordinate, are particularly likely to do so because the relationships are long-term, unavoidable, and often do not allow expression of one's real feelings. Anger may have to be suppressed and concealed behind a mask of assent, or even disguised by a smile. Yet emotions seethe within and, if they cannot be adequately discharged, frustration and damaged self-esteem may require their banishment from consciousness. The resulting metamorphosis may very well be, according to Lowen, anger stored in the throat as a lump or strangulating tension which expresses an unconscious 'frozen' scream or shout of rage.

Lowen is certainly not advocating the spontaneous discharge of all such emotions when they occur: that could only make matters worse and lead to social chaos, but he is arguing we should use body consciousness to become aware of these inevitable, and physically stored, unresolved problems of living. But, in addition to body awareness which indicates *where* tensions reside, bioenergetic methods also involve psychological probing to reveal *why* they occurred in the first place. A combination of psychotherapy, physical manipulation in the area of the blocks, giving expression to repressed feelings by actually shouting, hitting or screaming during therapy, and participating in a more general programme of exercises created to improve the flow of energy, is then used not only to remove conflicts and their symptoms, but positively to enhance people's approach and response to life.

Lowen has always regarded conventional forms of psychotherapy as too 'head orientated'; too likely to intellectualize and discuss feelings rather than deal with them directly. Talk alone allows people to dissemble and rationalize, but the body's deceits are more apparent and transparent when, for example, massage pressures release great burdens of pent-up emotion in sobs or shrieks. Only by shedding dammed-up tears or expressing the anger or fear locked in taut muscles can people get in touch with their real feelings and deal with them. This, at least, is the argument. Quite clearly, such methods have many therapeutic applications with those whose mental state is such as to require professional treatment, but their major influence continues to be in normal psychology rather than psychiatry. Bioenergetics is very much about self-improvement and attaining a state of calm but efficient harmony, not just the alleviation of malaise or distress.

Frustration and tension are an inevitable part of life, whether we spend it in the frenetic bustle of a city or an altogether quieter physical environment. The important thing is how we respond to stresses we cannot avoid, and how we disburden those we cannot readily shed. The bioenergetic solution is through a careful balance of mental and physical procedures: psychological interchange is used to provide insight into which things lead or have led to stored tension, while work on attitudes and adjustive strategies helps prepare the individual to face future sources of stress more effectually. Body work is not only used to dissipate stress feelings which get through and become locked in, but also has its part to play in increasing resistance and preventing it happening in the first place.

Exercises which improve breathing and body tone are held to be particularly useful in raising psychic and somatic energy levels, and so furthering the basic bioenergetic objective of attaining equilibrium and harmony between physical processes, consciousness and the unconscious. Lowen's method does not claim it is possible to make the unconscious conscious, but the discharge of stored anxiety and greater familiarity with its workings can make its manifestations far less disturbing. The whole process is, in many respects, philosophical. In fact, it is a journey of self-discovery which involves creating a picture of one's past and present, overcoming dualistic thinking, and unifying body and mind consciousness.

Tension blocks feelings so, only by getting rid of it is it possible to 'let go' and experience ecstasy or pure unrestrained happiness. If the body remains an obdurate jailer of the past, none of this is possible: diseased bodies give rise to diseased minds. We may not be able to avoid stress and its effects on our body, but it is possible to learn how to discharge it effectively: to become an efficient channel rather than a repository. Lowen's techniques are extremely varied but 'grounding' (the opposite of being 'hung-up') is of fundamental importance.

The process of grounding involves literally restoring a feeling of contact with the ground beneath our feet. One of the main exercises used to achieve this entails rising on to the balls of the feet, the trunk arched backwards and the hands reaching behind to rest on a stool-top, while the belly is thrust forward and the knees bent. It is a most difficult posture to maintain but, if one can hold it, it results in trembling and vibratory responses which run up through the body, unblocking muscle tensions, allowing energy to stream through the system, enhancing body awareness, the ability to feel and awareness of one's being truly a part of the natural order. More specifically, it is claimed this newfound sense of ground contact confers a greater sense of poise and ability to 'hold one's ground' with others, and allows the individual to handle and discharge high levels of tension. Rather like attaching a lightning conductor to a building, it allows the channelling away of dangerous energy charges.

Bioenergetics is certainly the most comprehensive form of body-mind analysis and treatment presently available, but it is by no means the only one. Others, like Ida Rolf's *Structural Integration*, owe a similar debt to Reich, and indeed to Lowen, but differ in so far as they place a greater relative emphasis upon body work than psychological analysis, and are more inclined to be 'treatments' given than procedures actively undertaken.

Dr Rolf's theories and practice take as their starting point a conception of ideal posture. Standing sideways, this is defined by an imaginary straight line passing downwards from the centre of the ear, through the shoulder, hip and knee, to the ankle. In practice, few of us have this perfect stance: poor habits or other causes have resulted in head or shoulders tilted or held forward, spine curved inwards and hips inclined down, or whatever. Structural integration is concerned with correcting these deviations by a particularly vigorous form of massage and, in so doing, liberating the energy wasted in maintaining bad posture, allowing it to be redirected along more constructive lines.

In addition to misalignments of stance, 'Rolfers' are also very much concerned with rectifying unduly taut muscles, displaced bones and even stilted behaviour – it being assumed that, however small the actual locus of awkwardness, its consequence is likely to be all-pervasive. Some chronic muscular tensions and deformations of structure may be psychosomatic, but others are a straightforward consequence of adopting poor postural habits. For example, the long-term effect of sitting awkwardly can readily lead to the deterioration of certain back muscles and connective tissue, whilst creating additional demands elsewhere. Together, these set up patterns of strain which have far-reaching effects on carriage and co-ordination, producing pain and fatigue which can dominate body and mind. Anyone who has ever suffered with chronic back troubles will need little convincing of this.

Sometimes, unnatural posture is the result of a choice which ceases to be open once the body has had time to adapt. Modelling ourselves on a stereotype – whether it be the military 'ramrod', the gang's slouch, or the bearing and movements of a starlet – may lead to irrevocable habits. The stresses and strains created by these different styles are, or course, extremely variable and dependent upon our particular constitution but any postural abnormality can give rise to unusual demands or changes in tissue tone which drain an individual's potential for bodily and mental vigour.

'Rolfing', or 'postural integration' techniques, must surely be among the more painful forms of treatment for which normal people are prepared to pay and submit cheerfully. They involve massage sessions in which the whole body is subjected to torturing attacks involving fingers, knuckles, fists and elbows: the aim being not only restoration of the natural vertical alignment of head, trunk and legs, but also to ensure that all tissues are loosened and freed to do the work for which they were designed. Muscles that have become shortened are stretched, and the overstretched allowed to relax. Tight bunches of muscle fibre and other connective tissues are separated and slackened, thus reducing unproductive energy consumption while allowing for greater mobility and the more efficient functioning of such vital body processes as respiration and circulation.

But, as Reich and Lowen had already discovered, many postural habits and areas of unusual muscular tension indicate repressed unconscious attitudes or stifled emotions. Unblocking them, whether by the techniques of bioenergetics or 'Rolfing' is therefore likely to liberate powerful emotions and call for psychological help in handling them. By no means all practitioners of structural integration wish, or are prepared, to go beyond the restoration of good postural habits and the generalized aim of improving mental poise and vitality. Yet the process may allow very little choice in the matter: not all muscular tension is due to poor habits and, if Lowen is correct, there can be very few individuals who do not store some emotional pain in their bodies.

In *Bodymind*, Ken Dychtwald describes his own experiences with 'Rolfing' at the Esalen Institute in California, and his growing recognition that not only are emotions almost invariably locked into people's physical structures, but they tend to be stored in quite specific places. This became apparent as work on the same part of the bodies of different individuals regularly gave rise to memories, fantasies and emotional responses of a similar kind. For example, unlocking tension in the jaw typically resulted in the expression of unhappiness whilst the upper back seemed to store rage, the chest feelings connected with being neglected, the hips sexual themes, the shoulders burdening responsibility, and so on.

Dychtwald's observations were based on hundreds of cases, including participation in the group's attempts to help one another express, and come to terms with, the emotions liberated in the body work. But, despite an overall extremely favourable attitude towards 'Rolfing', he nevertheless concluded that the psychological aspects receive too little systematic attention. For those whose bodies are unfit and in greatest need of toning and reintegration, this is considered an excellent technique. But, where there are also deeply seated and obstinate emotional problems to be dealt with, the more thoroughly developed psychotherapeutic methods of bioenergetics might be needed to resolve the conflicts uncovered, and prevent the mental stresses from once again becoming locked back into the body and mind.

An alternative method favoured by some is 'Shiatsu', an oriental form of massage in which finger pressure is applied to acupuncture meridians in order to unblock and redirect the flow of energy. In combination with exercises and careful diet, often of the macrobiotic variety, it is claimed that both bodily and mental ailments and distress can be relieved and psychic energy greatly increased. However, not all procedures concerned with mental and physical health are concerned with unlocking and treating psychological distress. Many, like the 'Alexander Technique', are very little involved in purifying or enhancing people's mental states, except in so far as improved postural and breathing habits may have a beneficial effect on vitality and self-confidence.

The Alexander technique is also very different from such systems as bioenergetics and postural integration in that insight and gradual change, rather than sudden cathartic discharge of energy and pain are seen as being the most important instruments of somatic reform and psychological benefit. Instead of being the object of someone else's manipulation, individuals are counselled and helped to achieve a more keen subjective understanding of the habits which maintain misalignment of their body or inhibit such key activities as breathing. It is claimed that increased self-awareness and the adoption of new patterns of walking, sitting and moving are alone sufficient not only to improve strength, stamina and poise, but additionally to greatly enhance self-confidence, calm and other aspects of mental balance.

Similar aims and consequences are also claimed for a whole range of oriental practices, particularly those deriving from Zen and Taoism. As a matter of fact, some of these exercise derivatives are surprisingly closely related to Reichian and bioenergetic methods, especially in so far as breath control, grounding and the development of bodily poise are concerned. Among the better known of these are the 'martial arts' of Aikido, Karate and Judo. Known more for their sporting and combative potential in the West, they are nevertheless also closely connected with attempts at mental and spiritual growth. Physical development is, of course, the starting point; though the fitness, strength, speed and co-ordination which come with intensive exercise have quite obvious psychological consequences, particularly with respect to self-confidence. But an equally important alternative or additional aim which can be pursued through these same techniques of bodily control is the channelling of 'ki' or 'chi', vital energy, in such a way that the practitioner transcends the experience of all contradictions in his thoughts, and the appearance of all opposites or disunities in nature.

The grandeur of these objectives may be somewhat shadowed by the sight of people practising the kicks, chops and throws which are so demonstrably effective in killing, maiming or hurting others. Non-initiates may therefore be forgiven if they have some difficulty in reconciling such apparent opposites, and express some reservations about this particular route towards cosmic consciousness. Nevertheless, like Zen archery, it is possible to see that such things might be helpful in teaching the habits of poise, restraint, concentration and self-awareness, so that even the process of thinking becomes more focused and decisive, thereby reducing confusion, irresolution and conflict. Such at least are the benefits claimed and widely accepted by Lowen and other prominent workers in the field of Western body-mind work. Indeed, Lowen makes the point that many of his patients find *t'ai chi ch'uan* exercises – that is, the Taoist techniques which underly Aikido, Karate, Kung Fu and Judo – a useful accompaniment to bioenergetic therapy.

Both major elements of t'ai chi – controlled rhythmic exercise and careful breath control – are said to have prophylactic value through balancing the flow of chi energy throughout the body. By contrast, acupuncture and Shiatsu are more distinctly therapeutic techniques, treating disturbances and unblocking obstructions to the natural flow of this vital energy. But, in each case, breath control is basic: it is the one element which most clearly typifies virtually every attempt, Eastern or Western, to achieve mental goals through physical practices. Postural control is a close runner-up: inevitably so, as breath control can never be independent of posture, but it is the correct flow of breath that is almost invariably regarded as most fundamental to physical vitality and mental equanimity.

Aware of this, and the many other similarities and common links between say Zen, Yoga, t'ai chi, bioenergetics, and even athletics, Lowen has pointed out that, though considerable benefits may accrue from whichever method is chosen, each system depends upon a different philosophy and each has implicit features which lead its practitioners towards a different goal. Sometimes, two systems may seem to have a remarkable amount in common, yet their objectives can be almost diametrically opposite. For example, Reich's vegetotherapy and some forms of Tantric Yoga not only place the highest possible emphasis on developing breath control and body consciousness, both also consider copulation and superb orgasmic technique the royal road to a harmonious and truly contented state of mind.

But though each system shares a number of basic beliefs about the need to concentrate and release energy through intercourse, the Tantric objective goes much further. Whereas Reich's way is concerned with achieving tension reduction in order to overcome problems of a mainly interpersonal origin and significance, the objectives of Tantra are a good deal more introverted and private. In their case, the aim is to elevate, concentrate and appropriate already highly energized sensual feelings, combining and directing them in such a way as to create a sort of 'spiritual guided missile' with which to fight a personal battle for 'enlightenment'.

Most comparisons are far less striking though Kundalini Yoga, referred to in Chapter seven, is also frequently described as closely similar to Reichian or bioenergetic methods in that each is fundamentally concerned with freeing the flow of energy blocked at various sites in the body. Yet, despite the many points of similarity in beliefs about the desirable mental effects of diet, exercise, posture, breath and other forms of bodily control, the resemblance is nevertheless superficial. A great gulf created by their quite different objectives separates almost all Eastern body-mind practices from Western ones.

Unfortunately, the consequences of this rift are not always realized or foreseen by those who set off to pursue the goal of psychological harmony and growth through body-based disciplines. Lowen feels that many young Westerners take to yogic or other exotic practices rather than counterparts in their own culture, at least in part, in the spirit of rebellion against the mechanism and materialism characteristic of their own society. However, there may come a point at which alien, and perhaps ultimately incredible, belief systems create new conflicts, adding to the adjustive problems their devotees hoped to solve. And, as almost all the techniques discussed so far are even more part of a voyage of self-discovery than they are about just feeling better, inability to accept implicit values or creeds can hamper this process a good deal.

Such may be the risks involved for a Westerner taking up yoga in a serious way, but a system which liberates and intensifies energy flow without providing an adequate psychological framework, or sense of purpose or meaning, can be equally harmful. So, though a healthy body is generally an advantage in the search for mental health and growth, care and circumspection about the psychological *context* within which this physical tuning takes place is no less important.

But for each person who becomes seriously involved with yoga, bioenergetics, or some other intensive body-mind practice, many more follow a much less demanding path. Most who pursue the ancient conjoint goal of mental and physical excellence do so through one or other of the many heterogeneous packages now being fashioned to suit contemporary tastes for something which is simple to understand, requires only limited time, and seems compatible with familiar medical and dietetic doctrines.

Consequently, luminaries of these contemporary common-sense approaches are seldom very concerned with the mystical perfection of mind sought through systems like yoga or Buddhism; or with the therapeutic discharge or easing of somatopsychic tensions which so much occupied Reich, Lowen, Rolf and Alexander. Instead, emphasis is more definitely focused upon care of the body as such: mental benefits being assumed, though definite goals are seldom stated. Most characteristic of this approach is the popularized form of yoga promoted by people like Richard Hittleman, whose own books and television programmes alone reach literally millions. And he is only one of a vast number of popularizers currently presenting practical guidance on how to optimize body-mind functioning or, more realistically, how to minimize mental stresses whilst maximizing physical fitness.

Whatever else it has achieved, massculture yoga seems to have made all of us more aware of the positive value of steady deep breathing and postural control. Together with diet, it has become one of the foremost means of reducing weight, toning the body, improving balance and developing physical poise. Its goals and effects may not resemble those of authentic yoga too closely but, though different, significant mental benefits may nevertheless accrue. Even at the most modest level, a trim and supple figure can bring great comfort and aid to self-assurance, whilst the calming effects of slow and considered exercises might reasonably be expected to offset stress, reduce mental tension, and create a refreshing mental quietude in which clear and equable thinking becomes at least more possible.

Participation in popular yoga activities may be mainly, or even completely, motivated by a simple concern for physical health or the desire to be slimmer and more attractive. If so, more conventional forms of exercise – like tennis, weight training or cycling – might seem capable of serving these ends equally well. Yet every form of physical exercise, and every claimed route towards health and vigour, has its own unique characteristics – whether these involve modifying breathing habits or posture, developing stamina, improving reflexes, or whatever. It would therefore be most unwise to assume that people's original motivations are too important in determining outcomes: after all, the relationship between breathing and feelings of anxiety or relaxation is well established, so even the most Westernized forms of yogic practice may automatically produce the sort of benefits which something like weight training would be most unlikely to create.

Of course, formal programmes of exercise or body care may be helpful but they are by no means always necessary to attain or maintain good physical health. For many people, a robust constitution and sound health are gifts which even a good deal of neglect or abuse may not seem to affect. In fact, good health is normal: optimal fitness, vitality and body functioning may require more than a passive stewardship, but illness or disturbances which seem capable of adversely affecting mental functioning are exceptional. So perhaps it is appropriate to look again at the original problem of whether a healthy body gives rise to a healthy mind, and consider whether it might not actually comprise two rather different questions – one concerning the outcome of particular physical activities, the other relating to the consequence of deviations from normal good health.

Previous chapters have already dealt with examples of ways in which the effects of age, disease and other malfunctions can limit or distort normal adjustment, so the evidence that physical disorder *can* be a negative influence on mental health has already had a good airing. Finding and describing these links, though not easy, is at least a very much simpler affair than attempting to show how good physical health relates to positive mental health. The problem is in no small part one of definition and criteria, it being much easier to obtain agreement on what constitutes negative mental states than positive ones.

Furthermore, any attempt to define positive mental health inevitably involves value judgements, and this is something all scientists try to avoid as far as possible. Psychiatrists and clinical psychologists cannot evade making such judgements; they are inevitable if one is to direct change, but even clinicians are usually extremely uneasy about making their implicit values explicit. As a result, positive mental health is seldom dealt with directly and, even on the relatively rare occasions when it is, discussion readily slides into the use of negative terms. The very concept 'mental health' has, like physical health, come to mean very little more than the absence of disease or distress: research dealing with it in any other way is therefore extremely sparse.

Nevertheless, if we are to discuss positive mental health at all, the question of whether good physical health contributes to it or not remains to be answered. If it does, the correlation is obviously far from simple or perfect, otherwise athletes would always have the highest level of mental health, and those with old or disordered bodies would have the worst. That this is patently not the case hardly needs saying: no doubt we could all think of plenty of examples where marked physical illness or deterioration is accompanied by vigorous mental health, or a healthy body coexists with a demonstrably diseased or disordered mind. However, though it would obviously be quite unjustifiable to say that mental and physical health are necessarily related, there is plenty of *prima facie* evidence to show that they tend to be; each facilitating, though not ensuring, the other.

For example, superior co-ordination, strength endurance, or sensory functioning are quite patently advantageous in a great many occupational and social situations; and the quality of one's life is likely to be much better and less stressed if there is no need to compensate and even overcompensate in the battle against ill-health, weakness, fatigue, or an otherwise malfunctioning system. Of course, even the fittest individual can be driven to despair or into neurosis if their inner life and relationships are in disarray, but a robust constitution may reduce the chances of this happening if it provides higher energy levels to pursue and sustain psychologically important occupational activities and social relationships. Good health may not be necessary to experience joy, ease, success and positive self-feelings but, all else being equal, there seems no doubt it can help.

Substantiating such a conclusion is, however, another matter. For the most part, beliefs about the connection between positive bodily and mental health are just that – beliefs, convictions, or opinions. To be sure, they may be based upon considerable personal experience and wide-ranging observations, but it is rare indeed that they can be validated within a rigorously scientific framework.

Bioenergetics, Reichian therapy, or any of the other body-mind procedures developed to improve physical as well as mental health can all cite an impressive number of cases where rectification or enhancement of physical functioning led to remarkable improvements in mental balance or performance. But, because almost all the case material published so far has failed to meet even the most basic scientific requirements of sampling, standardization of procedures, control of variables and objectivity in data analysis, it still tends to be regarded as little more than anecdotal: suggestive, though certainly not proof of the claims made. The same applies, but with even greater force, to the health body/healthy mind claims made by practitioners of physical exercise, yoga, martial arts and all the other techniques discussed. For the most part, though, those involved are not at all dismayed by the lack of scientific verification. For them 'faith validity' is enough, and they seem little inclined to become involved with tedious experimental studies, particularly when this might interrupt or otherwise upset their primary concern with therapy or the pursuit of health and mental growth.

Given so many difficulties, it may never be possible to produce a strictly scientific account of the relationship between bodily and mental health. As with so much in psychotherapy, criterion problems and the quintessentially unobservable nature of mental activity preclude anything much beyond a personal or professional evaluation of any changes which might take place. Nevertheless, between our own experiences and those reported by the vast number of people now involved with one or other of the specialized body-mind techniques discussed, there exist impressive reasons why we should take the proposed connection between positive physical and mental health seriously. We may have to acknowledge that, as a scientific theory, the connection remains unproven. But, as a working hypothesis, I suspect that very few of us, whether scientist or layman, would wish to give it up entirely.

CODA

We hear a great deal nowadays about the need to be conscious and careful about our physical world. We are all, it is said, the passengers and crew of 'Spaceship Earth'; all on a single craft, all sharing the same journey, and all totally dependent upon each other's concern and care for our vehicle. The metaphor is extremely apt, and ecologists and conservationists are doing a fine job of alerting us to the crucial significance of our global environment. But each of us also travels on this larger spaceship in his or her own individual capsule: we are born within it, live within it, and die when if finally fails. Some would say we and this little craft are one. Either way though, unlike real space travellers, we can never step outside our personal shell – its basic functions, limitations and possibilities for action being highly restrictive – despite the fact that particulars of design, manufacture and fitting out may vary from person to person and from time to time.

Like any craft, we too depend upon others for attention and servicing – though our needs go beyond physical care to include the provision of psychologically enriching opportunities. And, like other craft, one of our most important inputs is feedback from outside: in our own case, perhaps the most important being the sympathetic regard and approval of others. Only with this sort of data can we judge our course and status accurately. To borrow the jargon of space flight again, we depend upon it to know whether we are 'looking good' and can therefore settle back to enjoy the journey, or whether we would be well advised to adjust our flight controls in order to make the desired destination.

It would, of course, be quite easy to push the analogy a good deal further, but the point at which these voguish comparisons become totally platitudinous may already have been reached, or passed. Nevertheless, the comparison seems to me entirely appropriate in so far as it underlines the need to adopt some sort of bio-social systems approach, with physical realities very much in mind. A person who neglects the proper maintenance and monitoring of the body; a society in which people do not help others to feel they are 'looking good'; and a psychology which underestimates the great importance of the physical self in social and psychological activities are all seriously deficient.

Unfortunately though, just as it now appears we had all been taking far too limited a view of the biosystem in our appraisal of mankind's present and likely future, a similar miscalculation seems to have been made by almost all students of personality in their analysis of individual behaviour. For, strange as it may seem to a non-psychologist, many still begin and end their studies entirely within the abstract realms of learning theory and group differences. A far smaller number correlate the effects of some chosen segment or property of the body on behavioural criteria, but even they seldom treat the physical self as of basic psychological significance.

Throughout the book, innumerable examples have been given of ways in which different theorists have explained personality development and adjustment with reference to the physical self, yet a more robust statement that we are our bodies and that the history of our bodies is largely coextensive with our mental histories, is seldom to be found. Quite possibly many of those mentioned would have had no difficulty accepting the body's fundamental role, but their particular interests seem to have prevented them from being so direct, or adopting so general a point of view. Freud and Sheldon stand out as the great exceptions, though even Freud's thoroughgoing biological system became virtually obsessed with the mouth, anus, genitals and instincts to the detriment of all other bodily features, and Sheldon devoted far more time to his correlations than he allowed for developing the equally necessary explanatory theories.

As a result, our understanding of the relationship between personality and the physical self must still be judged as rudimentary, with evidence for few if any clear, direct and invariable links to bind the two. But this is only partly due to our present lack of research effort: the problem is that the interaction of mental and physical factors takes place within a matrix of awesome complexity and scale. The total picture defies simplification, so approximations like the *Schema* in Figure 2 can do no more than suggest an outline and make tentative proposals about the likely scope and workings of this matrix. Yet, as with a jigsaw, without a picture on the box

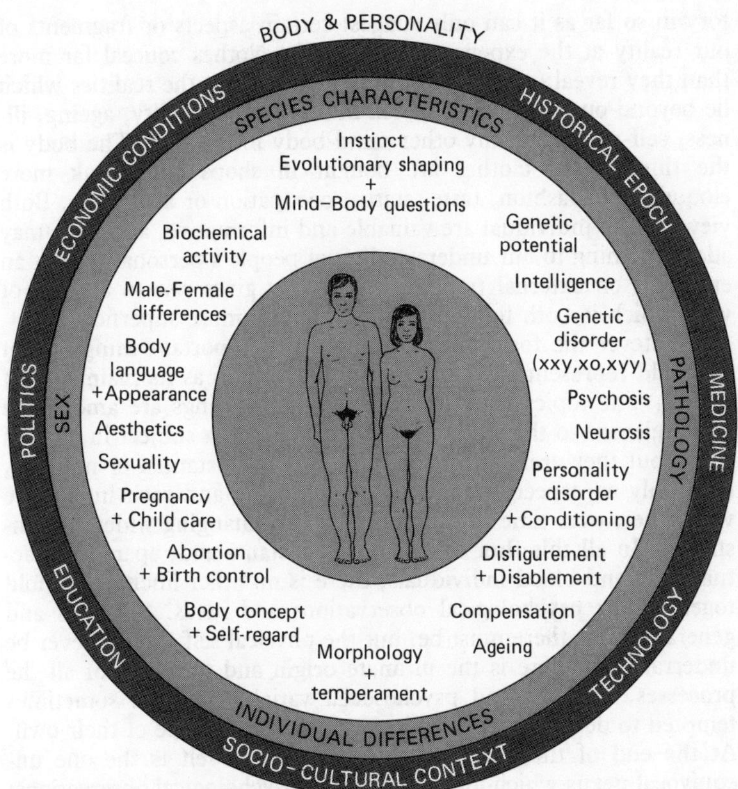

Fig. 2 Schema for body and personality

even the simplest puzzles can be difficult to solve and really complicated ones can lead to a miserable amount of trial and error activity before the pattern becomes apparent and more rapid progress can be made. Of course, the problems here are far more intricate than any conceivable jigsaw, but the schema is offered to fulfil a similar purpose, however rough-hewn a portrayal it may be of the elements and relationships which must somehow be pieced together in our attempts to solve the puzzle of personality.

At the centre, I have set two naked people; their nudity underscoring the fact that, whatever else we may be, human beings are also members of the animal kingdom. The choice may not have been everyone's, but any concrete image is bound to be unsatisfactory in so far as it can only suggest certain aspects or fragments of our reality at the expense of others. Yet clothes conceal far more than they reveal; covering not only modesty but the realities which lie beyond our discussions of sex differences, sexuality, ageing, illness, self-regard, or any other mind-body interaction. The body is the thing itself: clothes are bought in shops and speak more eloquently of fashion, taste, status, occupation or aspiration. Both views of the individual are valuable and informative, and both may add something to our understanding of people's personality, but an emphasis on external trappings inevitably gives rise to a point of view which is both figuratively and literally more superficial.

Whatever the focal image, though, the important thing is that it should represent solid and mortal individuals as its main subject matter. The topics listed in the surrounding rings are among the most relevant to the study of personality, each a subject in its own right, but they are still for the most part insubstantial or notional, each only an aspect or function of our being and each interactive with others over time and in unpredictably changing wider circumstances. In all this flux there are no constants and, apart from actual flesh-and-blood individuals, there is no other linchpin to hold together our psychological observations and ideas. Statistics and generalizations there must be, but the physical self should never be underrated for here is the ultimate origin and terminus of all the processes, qualities and psychosocial variables we are sometimes tempted to deal with as though they had an existence of their own. At the end of the day, though, the physical self is the one unequivocal nexus which joins together all psychological observations: it is the ultimate stuff of any empirically based science.

But, though the physical self has been set firmly at the centre of this suggested schema, there is absolutely no implication that the content of surrounding rings is to be regarded as any the less important. On the contrary, the immense contribution of such things as social learning to the development of personality could hardly be overstated. However, they are only part of the story and what this book has set out to do is show that any account of human similarities and variation would be equally incomplete without the inputs of such things as evolutionary theory, genetics, gerontology and other of the medical sciences. Together, both social and biological elements comprise the matrix of mind and personality, but the physical self is inevitably the point of intersect. Any attempt to look at abstract psychological phenomena in isolation from the body has always seemed to me rather like Lewis Carroll's wonderful piece of nonsense, in which Alice continued to observe the Cheshire Cat's smile even after the rest of it had disappeared.

Throughout the course of this book, each of the topics listed in the schema's inner circle has received a certain amount of discussion; sometimes only passingly, though some subjects have been dealth with at considerable length. In some cases, possible interactions were also explored but, because the combinations and permutations involved are almost infinite in extent, it was hardly feasible to do more than point out a little of what might be involved. One of the subject areas which recurred in several contexts was 'Male-Female Differences', it being discussed in relation to 'Evolutionary Shaping', 'Sexuality', 'Body Concept and Self-Regard', as well as many other categories. Yet, as is now widely recognized and the schema illustrates, the matrix within which sex differences develop has many more ramifications than have so far been mentioned.

So, taking 'Male-Female Differences' as a familiar and convenient example, it should be clear from the schema that the man or woman who stands at its centre is the product, and to some extent the originator, of highly idiosyncratic combinations of events taking place between the individual and their milieu. It goes without saying that genetically determined sexual characteristics are the prime cause of whatever gender differences duly occur but many of the psychological, and most prominently, personality differences between males and females are determined by moulding forces which only begin with whatever physical and perhaps dispositional, characteristics typify boys and girls at birth. From the onwards not only will biochemical and morphological differences have their progressive effects as infants pass towards old age, but the whole process of reproductive specialization and responsibilities is likely to shape markedly different life styles. And these are still only the primitive bases from which characteristic personality differences develop.

The outer ring summarizes other aspects of the matrix, indicating the extent to which social and cultural factors may be involved in intensifying or diminishing the effect of physical differences. Each category draws our attention to something which might add to our wider understanding of the way events unfold, but even these are only part of a still wider, interactive, whole. For example, when prevailing technological and economic circumstances are such that the means of production or defence depend largely on muscular strength, the division of sex roles is likely to be most marked, particularly as pregnancy and nursing are seldom compatible with fighting or heavy physical labour. But, when the most prestigious occupations do not make demands which favour one sex rather than the other; where medical advances introduce effective contraception, and religion and politics allow them; and where social, political and educational processes combine to reduce discriminations and promote equal opportunity, distinctions between men's and women's lives will be minimized and their psychological differences inevitably lessened.

Of course, this does not necessarily imply that all dissimilarities can be ironed out by social learning: important biological differences remain and these may well sustain considerable psychological differentiations in spite of all attempts to get rid of them. At present, marked characteristic differences between the sexes persist, and it remains to be seen how far convergences will go, but it is evident that psychological correlates of even the most conspicuous of mankind's mental and physical antitheses depend very heavily upon context. If what has gone before shows anything at all, it must surely be that neither a strictly biological nor an exclusively psychosocial model will explain any but the most superficial human differences. Whatever the particular characteristics under scrutiny, the key to understanding them always lies in the product of physical and mental interactions, not in their sum, and never in just one or the other.

Had the starting point of our chosen example been 'Ageing', 'Psychosis', 'Disablement', or any of several other categories shown in the schema, much the same sort of case might have been made: the psychological consequences of these conditions also being very much a matter of when, where and with whom they occur. Indeed, so dependent are we on prevailing social circumstances and the genetic or other fortunes of birth, that it is not uncommon to hear people speak of the 'game of life' as though what we become is virtually a matter of chance. But, though accidents and our physical constitution may add further to the things over which we have little control, it is quite evident that the game of life resembles bridge much more than it does roulette: it may still be a game of chance, but it is decidedly one of skill also. So far as our bodies are concerned, fate deals the cards – to ourselves, our partners and whoever else we encounter in the game – we may or may not be dealt a good hand, but the important thing is how we play it, and how we help others to play theirs.

In the end though, just as a game and its players are one, so too are the body and the personality. We may be able to conceptualize apparatus, activity and game rules separately, but only at the cost of dividing things which are in reality indivisible. Such a point of view would, until quite recently, have been far less widely admissible but times are changing and they now seem to favour allowing the body a much greater prominence in most areas of psychology. Indeed, as spirit and soul are no longer acceptable as concepts to unify our view of man, the mind having proved too metaphysical and the brain too limited as a substitute, the total physical self is now beginning to emerge as the only scientifically viable alternative. Certainly the body seems to me to be a natural point of departure for all those concerned with achieving a unified, and even coherent, view of human personality. So, with this in mind, the foregoing has been written in the hope that it may help advance these still very tentative attempts at conceptual unification.

REFERENCES AND FURTHER READING

CHAPTER 1: FORM, BEARING AND PERSONALITY

ALLPORT, G. W., *Personality: A Psychological Interpretation*. Holt: New York, 1946.

ALLPORT, G. W., *Pattern and Growth in Personality*. Holt: London, 1967.

ARGYLE, M., *Bodily Communication*. Methuen: London, 1975.

ARGYLE, M. and COOK, M., *Gaze and Mutual Gaze*. Cambridge University Press: Cambridge, 1975.

BIRDWHISTELL, R., *Kinesics and Context*. Allen Lane: London, 1971.

BROPHY, J., *The Human Face Reconsidered*. Harrap: London, 1962.

CARTER, J. L., 'The contributions of somatotyping to kinanthropy', in M. Ostyn, G. Bearner, & J. Simons (eds), *Kinanthropometry*. University Park Press: Baltimore, 1980.

DARWIN, C., *The Expression of the Emotions in Man and Animals*. University of Chicago Press: Chicago, 1965.

DeROPP, R. S., *The Master Game*. Dell: New York, 1969.

EYSENCK, H. J., *The Structure of Human Personality*. Methuen: London, 1970.

FISHER, S., *Body Consciousness*. Fontana/Collins: London, 1976.

FREUD, S., *The Psychopathology of Everyday Life*. Penguin: Harmondsworth, 1975.

GOFFMAN, E., *The Presentation of Self in Everyday Life*. Penguin: Harmondsworth, 1971.

HALL, C. S. and LINDZEY, G., *Theories of Personality*. Wiley: New York, 1978.

HAMILTON, D. L. (ed.), *Cognitive Processes in Stereotyping and Intergroup Behavior*. Erlbaum: Hillsdale, New Jersey, 1981.

HENLEY, N., *Body Politics*. Prentice Hall: Englewood Cliffs, New Jersey, 1977.

KRETSCHMER, E., *Physique and Character*. Harcourt Brace and World: New York, 1925.

LINDZEY, G., 'Behavior and Morphological Variation', in J. N. Spuhler (ed.), *Genetic Diversity and Human Behavior*. Aldine: Chicago, 1976.

MEHRABIAN, A., *Nonverbal Communication*. Aldine: Chicago, 1972.

MORRIS, D., *Manwatching*. Panther: London, 1978.

OBUDHO, C. (ed.), *Human Non-Verbal Behavior: An Annotated Bibliography*. Greenwood Press: Westport, Conn., 1980.

PARNELL, R. W., *Behavior and Physique*. Arnold: London, 1958.

POLHEMUS, T. (ed.), *Social Aspects of the Human Body: A Reader of Key Texts*. Penguin: Harmondsworth, 1978.

SHELDON, W. H., HARTL, E. M. and MCDERMOTT, E., *Varieties of Delinquent Youth: An Introduction to Constitutional Psychiatry*. Harper & Row: New York, 1949.

SHELDON, W. H. and STEVENS, S. S., *The Varieties of Temperament: A Psychology of Constitutional Differences*. Harper & Row: New York, 1942.

TANNER, J. M., *The Physique of the Olympic Athlete*. Allen & Unwin: London, 1964.

TURGENEV, I., *The Portrait Game*. Horizon: New York, 1973.

WELLS, B. W. P., *Personality and Heredity*. Longman: London, 1980.

WOLFF, C., *The Human Hand*. Methuen: London, 1949.

CHAPTER 2: BODY IMAGE AND SELF-ESTEEM

ADLER, A., *The Science of Living*. Anchor/Doubleday: New York, 1969.

ADLER, A., *Understanding Human Nature*. Fawcett Premier: New York, 1954.

APTON, A. B., *Your Mind and Appearance*. Citadel Press: New York, 1951.

BRUCHE, H., *Eating Disorders: Obesity, Anorexia Nervosa and the Person Within*. Routledge & Kegan Paul: London, 1973.

BURNS, R. B., *The Self Concept*. Longman: London, 1979.

FISHER, S., *Body Consciousness*. Fontana/Collins: London, 1976.

FISHER, S. and CLEVELAND, S. E., *Body Image and Personality*.

Dover: New York, 1969.

GOFFMAN, E., *Stigma: Notes on the Management of Spoiled Identity*. Aronson: New York, 1978.

KNAPP, M. L., *Nonverbal Communication in Human Interaction*. Holt, Rinehart & Winston: New York, 1978.

KUBIZEK, A., *Young Hitler*. George Mann: Maidstone, Kent, 1973.

MacLEOD, S., *Art of Starvation: Adolescence Observed*. Virago: London, 1981.

NIETZSCHE, F. W., *Thus Spoke Zarathustra*. Gordon Press: New York, 1974.

NIETZSCHE, F. W., *Beyond Good and Evil*. Penguin: Harmondsworth, 1975.

ORGLER, H., *Alfred Adler, The Man and His Work: Triumph Over the Inferiority Complex*. Sidgwick & Jackson: London, 1973.

PALMER, R. L., *Anorexia Nervosa*. Penguin: Harmondsworth, 1980.

SCHILDER, P., *The Image and Appearance of the Human Body: Studies in the Constructive Energies in the Psyche*. International Universities Press: New York, 1935.

SHAKESPEARE, R., *The Psychology of Handicap*. Methuen: London, 1979.

STALLIBRASS, A., *Self Respecting Child*. Penguin: Harmondsworth, 1978.

WAY, L., *Alfred Adler: An Introduction to his Psychology*. Penguin: Harmondsworth, 1956.

CHAPTER 3: SEX AND SEXUALITY: GENERAL

ARDREY, R., *The Hunting Hypothesis*. Fontana/Collins: London, 1976.

DE BEAUVOIR, S., *The Second Sex*. Penguin: Harmondsworth, 1972.

CLEUGH, J., *Love Locked Out: A Survey of Love, License and Restriction in the Middle Ages*. Blond: London, 1963.

COOK, M. and MCHENRY, R., *Sexual Attraction*. Pergamon: Oxford, 1978.

DARWIN, C., *The Expression of the Emotions in Man and Animals*. Murray: London, 1872.

DAWKINS, R., *The Selfish Gene*. Granada/Paladin: London, 1978.

ELLIS, A. and ABARBANEL, A., *The Encyclopaedia of Sexual Behaviour*. Aronson: New York, 1978.

ELLIS, H., *The Evolution of Modesty: Studies in the Psychology of Sex*. 3rd Revised edn, Vol. 1, Pt. 1. Random House: New York, 1936.

FISHER, S., *The Female Orgasm: Psychology, Physiology, Fantasy*. Basic Books: New York, 1973.

FRIEDAN, B., *The Feminine Mystique*. Dell: New York, 1977.

HUTT, C., *Males and Females*. Penguin: Harmondsworth, 1972.

LAVER, J., *Modesty in Dress*. Heinemann: London, 1969.

MORRIS, D., *The Naked Ape*. Mayflower: St Albans, 1977.

MORRIS, D., *Intimate Behaviour*. Panther: London, 1979.

SCHNEIDER, C. D., *Shame, Exposure and Privacy*. Beacon: Boston, 1977.

SHARPE, S., *'Just Like a Girl': How Girls Learn to be Women*. Penguin: Harmondsworth, 1977.

SHERFEY, M. J., *The Nature and Evolution of Human Sexuality*. Random House: New York, 1972.

WILSON, E. O., *On Human Nature*. Bantam Books: New York, 1980.

WILSON, G. and NIAS, D., *Love's Mystery: The Secrets of Sexual Attraction*. Fontana/Collins: London, 1977.

ZIMBARDO, P. G., *Shyness*. Addison-Wesley: London, 1977.

CHAPTER 4: SEX AND SEXUALITY: SPECIFICS

COMFORT, A., (ed.), *The Joy of Sex*: Quartet Books: New York, 1978.

EYSENCK, H. J., *Sex and Personality*. Abacus: London, 1978.

EYSENCK, H. J., *The Biological Basis of Personality*. C. C. Thomas: Springfield, Mass., 1967.

EYSENCK, H. J. and WILSON, G. D. (eds), *The Experimental Study of Freudian Theories*. Methuen: London, 1973.

ELLIS, H., *The Psychology of Sex*. Harcourt Brace, Jovanovich: New York, 1978.

FREUD, S., *On Sexuality*. Penguin: Harmondsworth, 1977.

FREUD, S., *Three Essays on the Theory of Sexuality*, in *The Standard Edition of the Complete Psychological Works of Sigmund Freud*. Hogarth Press and Institute of Psychoanalysis: London, 1974.

FRIDAY, N., *My Secret Garden: Women's Sexual Fantasies*. Trident Press: New York, 1973.

GREER, G., *The Female Eunuch*. Paladin: London, 1971.

HITE, S., *Hite Report: Nationwide study on Female Sexuality*. Dell:

New York, 1976.

HITE, S., *The Hite Report on Male Sexuality*. MacDonald Futura: London, 1981.

HOPSON, J. L., *Scent Signals: The Silent Language of Sex*. William Morrow: New York, 1979.

HUTT, C., *Males and Females*. Penguin: Harmondsworth, 1972.

KAPLAN, H. S., *The New Sex Therapy*. Penguin: Harmondsworth, 1981.

KINSEY, A. C., POMEROY, W. B. and MARTIN, C. E., *Sexual Behaviour in the Human Male*. Saunders: Philadelphia, 1948.

KINSEY, A. C., POMEROY, W. B., WARDELL, B., MARTIN, C. E., GEBHARD, E. and PAUL, H., *Sexual Behavior in the Human Female*. Saunders: Philadelphia, 1953.

KLINE, P., *Fact and Fantasy in Freudian Psychology*. Methuen: London, 1981.

LEACH, P., *The Wise Wound*: Menstruation and Everywoman. Penguin: Harmondsworth, 1979.

MASTERS, W. and JOHNSON, V. E., *Human Sexual Response*. Bantam Books: New York, 1980.

RAWSON, P., *Tantra: The Indian Cult of Ecstasy*. Thames & Hudson: London, 1973.

VATSYAYANA., *Kama Sutra*. Panther: London, 1963.

WELLS, B. W. P., *Social Aspects of Venereal Diseases*. British Social Biology Council: London, 1968.

WILSON, C., *Origins of the Sexual Impulse*. Panther: London, 1970.

CHAPTER 5: PERSONALITY AND PHYSICAL MALFUNCTION

ADLER, A., *The Science of Living*. Allen & Unwin: London, 1930.

ALEXANDER, M., *The Dance Goes On*. Leader Books: Kingsley, Hants, 1980.

AYALAH, D. and WEINSTOCK, I. J., *Breasts: Women Speak About Their Breasts and Their Lives*. Summit Books: New York, 1979.

DEELEY, T. J., *Attitudes to Cancer*. SPCK: London, 1979.

ENBY, G., *Let There Be Love: Sex and the Handicapped*. Pemberton: London, 1975.

EYSENCK, H. J., *Crime and Personality*. Routledge & Kegan Paul: London, 1977.

EYSENCK, H. J., *You and Neurosis*. Collins/Fontana: London, 1978.

FAULDER, C., *Breast Cancer*. Pan: London, 1979.

GYLLENSKÖLD, K., *Breast Cancer: The Psychological Effects of the Disease and its Treatment*. Methuen: London, 1981.

JEFFERSON, J. W. and MARSHALL, J. R., *Neuropsychiatric Features of Medical Disorder*. Plenum: New York, 1981.

KELLER, H., *The Story of My Life*. Doubleday: New York, 1954.

LINDEMANN, J. E., *Psychological and Behavioural Aspects of Physical Disability*. Plenum: New York, 1981.

MASLOW, A., *The Farther Reaches of Human Nature*. Penguin: Harmondsworth, 1976.

ORNSTEIN, R. E., *The Psychology of Consciousness*. Harcourt Brace Jovanovich: New York, 1977.

ORTON, C., *Learning to Live with Skin Disorders*. Souvenir Press: London, 1981.

REIFF, P., *The Triumph of the Therapeutic: Uses of Faith after Freud*. Penguin: Harmondsworth, 1973.

SCHREIBER, F. R., *Sybil: The Story of a Woman Possessed by Sixteen Separate Personalities*. Penguin: Harmondsworth, 1975.

Sexuality and Disability: A journal devoted to the study of sex in physical and mental illness. Human Sciences Press: New York.

SUTHERLAND, A. T., *Disabled We Stand*. Souvenir Press: London, 1981.

The Task Force on Concerns of Physically Disabled Women. Towards Intimacy. Human Sciences Press: New York, 1978.

TWISTINGTON-HIGGINS, E., *Still Life*. Mowbray: London, 1970.

WELLS, B. W. P., *Personality and Heredity*. Longman: London, 1980.

WELLS, B. W. P., *Psychedelic Drugs*. Penguin: Baltimore, 1974.

WILLIAMS, M., *Brain Damage and the Mind*. Penguin: Harmondsworth, 1975.

CHAPTER 6: AGEING AND DYING

AIKEN, L., *The Psychology of Later Life*. Saunders: Philadelphia, 1978.

DE BEAUVOIR, S., *Old Age*. Penguin: Harmondsworth, 1977.

BIRREN, J. E. and SCHAIE, K. W., *Handbook of the Psychology of Aging*. Van Nostrand Reinhold: Princeton, 1977.

BROMLEY, D. B., *Psychology of Human Ageing*. Penguin: Harmondsworth, 1974.

CHESSER, E., *Living with Suicide*. Hutchison: London, 1967.

COMFORT, A., *The Biology of Senescence*. Churchill Livingstone:

Edinburgh, 1979.
FAULDER, C., *Breast Cancer*. Pan: London, 1979.
FRANKL, V. E., *Man's Search for Meaning*. Pocket Book: New York, 1976.
GEORGE, S., *How the Other Half Dies*. Penguin: Harmondsworth, 1976.
HINTON, J., *Dying*. Penguin: Harmondsworth, 1971.
JUNG, C. G., *The Stages of Life*, in *Collected Works*, Vol. 8, Routledge & Kegan Paul: London, 1978.
KÜBLER-ROSS, E. (ed.), *Death: The Final Stage of Growth*. Prentice Hall: New York, 1975.
KÜBLER-ROSS, E., *On Death and Dying*. Tavistock: London, 1973.
LAMARTON, R., *Care of the Dying*. Penguin: Harmondsworth, 1980.
LYNCH, J. J., *The Broken Heart: The Medical Consequences of Loneliness*. Harper & Row: New York, 1980.
NEALE, R., *The Art of Dying*. Harper & Row: New York, 1977.
REICHARD, S., LIVSON, F. and PETERSEN, P. G., *Aging and Personality*. Wiley: New York, 1962.
STODDARD, S., *Hospice Movement: A Better Way of Caring for the Dying*. Cape: London, 1979.
WEISMAN, A. D., *On Dying and Denying: Psychiatric Study of Terminality*. Human Sciences Press: New York, 1977.
YOUNG, J. Z., *An Introduction to the Study of Man*. Oxford University Press: Oxford, 1974.
ZARIT, S. H., *Readings in Aging and Death*. Harper and Row: New York, 1982.

CHAPTER 7: MIND OVER MATTER

BARBER, T. X., *LSD, Marihuana, Yoga and Hypnosis*. Aldine: Chicago, 1970.
BARKER, J. C., *Scared to Death*. Muller: London, 1968.
BLACK, S., *Mind and Body*. Kimber: London, 1969.
BREUER, J. and FREUD, S., *Studies on Hysteria*. Penguin: Harmondsworth, 1980.
BROOKS, C. H. *The Practice of Autosuggestion by the Method of Emile Coué*. Allen & Unwin, London, 1922.
BROWN, B. B., *Stress and the Art of Biofeedback*. Bantam Books: New York, 1977.
COXHEAD, N., *Mindpower*. Penguin: Harmondsworth, 1979.

DANSKIN, D. G. and CROW, M. A., *Biofeedback: An Introduction and Guide*. Mayfield: St Albans, 1981.

DAVID-NEIL, A., *Magic and Mystery in Tibet*. Souvenir Press: London, 1967.

DUNBAR, H. F., *Mind and Body: Psychosomatic Medicine*. Random House: New York, 1947.

DUNBAR, H. F., *Emotions and Bodily Changes: A Survey of Literature on Psychosomatic Interrelationships 1910–53*. Arno Press: New York, 1976.

FISCHER-WILLIAMS, M., NIGEL, A. J. and SOVINE, D. L., *Textbook of Biological Feedback*. Human Sciences Press: New York, 1981.

FRIEDMAN, M. and ROSENMAN, R. H., *Type A Behaviour and Your Heart*. Knopf: New York, 1974.

FUNDERBURK, J., *Science Studies Yoga: A Review of the Physiological Data*. Himalayan International Institute of Yoga Science and Philosophy of USA, 1977.

HEBB, D. O., *Essay on Mind*. Erlbaum: Hillsdale, New Jersey, 1980.

HILGARD, E. R. and HILGARD, J. R., *Hypnosis in the Relief of Pain*. W. Kaufmann: Los Altos, California, 1975.

MARCUSE, F. L., *Hypnosis: Fact and Fiction*. Penguin: Harmondsworth, 1982.

MARTIN, B., *Abnormal Psychology*. Holt, Rinehart & Winston: New York, 1981.

ORNSTEIN, R. (ed.), *The Nature of Human Consciousness: A Book of Readings*. Freeman: San Francisco, 1973.

PAVLOV, I. P., *Conditioned Reflexes and Psychiatry*. Translated and edited by W. H. Gantt. International Publishers: New York, 1941.

RAY, W. J., RACZYNSKI, J. M., ROGERS, T. and KIMBALL, W. H., *Evaluation of Clinical Biofeedback*. Plenum: New York, 1979.

RUSSELL, P., *The Transcendental Meditation Technique*. Routledge & Kegan Paul: London, 1978.

SCHULTZ, J. H. and LUTHE, W., *Autogenic Methods*. Grune & Stratton: New York, 1969.

TART, C. T., *Altered States of Consciousness*. Wiley: New York, 1969.

TESTER, M., *Healing Touch*. Psychic Press: London, 1976.

THURSTON, H., *The Physical Phenomenon of Mysticism*. (Posthumously ed. J. H. Crehan.) Burns Oates: London, 1952.

WEST, D., *Psychical Research Today*. Penguin: Harmondsworth, 1962.

YATES, A. J., *Biofeedback and the Modification of Behaviour*. Plenum: New York, 1980.

YOGENDRA, VIJAYDEV (ed.), *Mind-Made Disease*. Heinemann (India), 1981.

CHAPTER 8: HEALTHY BODY AND HEALTHY MIND

DALTON, K., *Once a Month: Menstrual Syndrome, Its Causes and Consequences*. Fontana/Collins: London, 1982.

DYCHTWALD, K., *Bodymind*. Jove Books: New York, 1978.

FELDENKRAIS, M., *Awareness Through Movement*. Penguin: Baltimore, 1980.

FLUGEL, J. C., *The Psychology of Clothes*. Hogarth Press: London, 1930.

GITTELSON, B., *Biorhythm: A Personal Science*. McDonald Futura: London, 1981.

HITTLEMAN, R., *Guide to Yoga Meditation*. Bantam: New York, 1981.

HUNTINGTON, H. S., *Defense of Nudism*. McBride: New York, 1958.

JANOV, A., *The Primal Scream*. Sphere: London, 1973.

KIRSCHNER, M. J., *Yoga for Health and Vitality*. Unwin: London, 1977.

KURTZ, R. and PRESTERA, H., *Body Reveals: Illustrated Guide to the Psychology of the Body*. Harper & Row: New York, 1979.

LEBOYER, F., *Birth Without Violence*. Fontana/Collins: London, 1977.

LOWEN, A., *Betrayal of the Body*. Collier-MacMillan: London, 1969.

LOWEN, A., *Bioenergetics*. Penguin: Harmondsworth, 1979.

LUCE, G. G., *Body Time*. Paladin: London, 1974.

McDOUGALL, W., *An Introduction to Social Psychology*. Methuen: London, 1960.

ORR, L. and RAY, S., *Rebirthing in the New Age*. Celestial Arts: Millbrae, 1978.

RANK, O., *The Trauma of Birth*. Harper & Row: New York, 1973.

RANK, O., *Will Therapy and Truth and Reality*. Knopf: New York, 1945.

REICH, W., *The Function of the Orgasm*. Farrar, Strauss and Giroux: New York, 1973.

ROLF, I., *Rolfing: The Integration of Human Structures*. Dennis-Landman: Santa Monica, 1977.

RYCROFT, C., *Reich*. Fontana/Collins: London, 1971.

SANTA MARIA, J., *Anna Yoga: The Yoga of Food*. Rider: London, 1978.

INDEX

Acupuncture, 232–3
addictive activities, 48–9
Alder, A., theory of compensation, 39–42, 45–7, 137–8, 144
adolescents, *see* young people
ageing, 146–58: adjustments to, 153–5; attitudes to, 47–8, 53–4, 149–52, 154–8; and body type, 3, 16; causes, 147–8, 150; health and, 53, 146–8, 150–1; self-esteem, 47–8; *see also* middle age, old age *and* young people
Aikido, 232–3
All India Institute of Medical Sciences, New Delhi, yogic studies, 202
ambiverts, 115
amnesia, hysterical, 46, 179
anal sex, 110
anal stage of development, 108–9, 111
androstenol, chemical attractant, 102–3
anorexia nervosa, 50–1, 213
armouring, psychological, 224–5
armpit odours, 100, 104
asthenic body type: characteristics, 2–4; and ectomorphy, 6–7; and mental disorder, 2–4
athletic body type: characteristics, 3, 6; and mental disorder, 3; and mesomorphy, 6
athletics: educational ideals, 205–7; physical health, 148, 204–7, 233, 235–8, in Germany, 206–8, in other countries, 206; *see also* mesomorphy
attractiveness, physical: body image, 62; face, 59; sexual appeal, 82–4, 116–17; stereotypes, 16, 48, 52, 84–8
behaviour therapy, psychosomatic disorders, 196–200
behaviourist theories, 112–13
Belgian Academy of Medicine, investigation of stigmata, 174
bereavement, and grief, 156–7, 165–9
biochemical processes, sexual behaviour, 64, 106, 113–14, 151
bioenergetics, 225–9, 231–5, 237
biofeedback techniques, 197–200
biorhythms, 214–19: and birth, 124; circadian, 214–15; lunatic, 215–18; ultradian, 215
birth: defect, 124; trauma, 34, 219–22, therapy for, 221–2; *see also* infants
blindness: combined with deafness, 136; problems, 125–6, 130
blushing: circumstances causing, 78–80; clue to emotional state, 31–2
body image; feedback data, 36–7, 126–8; and self-esteem, 34–62, 90
body movements, NVC, 23–32; *see also* expressions, facial, gestures, kinesics *and* postures
body typing theories: ancient Greece, 1; Kretschmer's, 2–7, 12, 18, 122; Sheldon's, 5–18; terminologies, various systems, 12
brain: damage, 119–22; psychotherapeutic surgery, 119–20; and sexual behaviour, 106
breast(s): cancer, psychological penalties, 132–4; erotic potential, 95; exposure, 89; puberty, 37
British Dental Association, concern for misshapen teeth and mouths, 59

Buddhism: macrobiotics, 212; spiritual practices, 95, 201, 235; *see also* Zen

castration: anxiety, 109; complex, 112
celibacy, *see* sexual abstinence
cells, replacement of dead, 147–8
cerebrotonia: definition, 9; and ectomorphy, 9, 14
children: death, 165; deformity, 54–5; development, stages of, 107–9, 111, 210; disabled, *see* disabled children; fantasies, parents, 108–9, 112; inferiority feelings, 40; nudism and, 209–10; parents attitudes to, 35–6; self-concept, 36–7, 126–8; *see also* infants *and* young people
Christian Science, mental control of illness, 188
Christianity, attitude to sexual behaviour, 72–8; *see also* Roman Catholic Church
clitoris: contact problems, 97; and sexual pleasure, 108, 223, *see also* orgasm; *see also* genitals
compensatory behaviour, inferiority feelings: 39–47, 60, 134–9, 144; direct, 42–4, 46; indirect, 43–6; miscellaneous, 46–7; named examples, 42–6, 134–8
conversion hysteria, 178–80
convulsive hysteria, 179–80
cyclothymia, mental characteristics, 4–5

deafness: and blindness, 136; old age, 156; problems, 125, 130
death and dying: attitudes to, 164–5, fear, 165; awareness of, 159–60; causes, 147–8, 151; children, 166; counselling, 165; instinct, 107; psychological problems, 158–69; rituals, 166–7; *see also* euthanasia, suicide *and* terminal illness
deformity: attitudes to, 53–5; consequences of, 54–6; and self-esteem, 36–7, 54, 58; treatment, 53, 55, 57–9; *see also* disabled adults *and* disabled children
development, stages of, 107–11, 210
diathesis stress, 123
diet: and body type, 7–8; control, for health, 148, 211–14; weight problems, 4, 7, 14, 48–50, 235
disabled adults: compensatory behaviour, 43–4, 134–8; conventional activities, 56, 141; education, 56, 141, 143; hierarchy of needs, 138–41; mobility, 141–3; pleasures, 130–1; psychological penalties, 53–7, 128–34, 137–41, 144–5; relationships, 129–30; self-concept, 54–8, 128–9, 136; transition from childhood, 128; treatment, 53, 55, 57–9, 141; work, 130–1, 141, 143; *see also* deformity
disabled children: attitudes to, 55, 124; care for, 124–6, 141; education, 124, 127–8; psychological penalties, 124–6; transition to adult life, 128; *see also* deformity
dissociative hysteria, 178–9
dying, *see* death and dying
dysplastic body type, 3

ectomorphy: and asthenic body type, 6–7; and cerebrotonia, 9, 14; mental and physical characteristics, 6–7, 10–12, 14–15, 37; problems, 14–15; university and career choices, 11
education: for disabled adults, 56, 141, 143; for disabled children, 124, 127–8; mental and physical ideals, 205–7; somatotype analysis, 11
endomorphy: mental and physical characteristics, 6–8, 12, 14–15, 37; problems, 14–15; and pyknic body type, 6; and viscerotonia, 9, 14
epilepsy: birth trauma and, 219; body types, 3; convulsive hysteria similar to, 179; and sexual relationships, 130
erogenous zones, 95, 106, 108–10: focus of fear and guilt, 110
eroticism, cultural differences, 95
Esalen Institute, California, 'Rolfing', 231
esteem needs, 139–41
euthanasia, and terminal illness, 164–5
exhibitionism, 96
expression, facial, 21–3, 26, 58: assumed, 27, 32; interpretation, 22–3, 29–32
extraversion: dimension of personality, 12, 114–15; and sexual behaviour, 115

eye contacts: blindness, and lack of, 125–6; uses and interpretation, 21, 25, 28, 31–2
Eysenck, Hans, on: psychological dimensions, 5, 12–13, 114–17, 194; sexual development, 106

face (facial): appearance, 21, 59–60; expressions, *see* expressions, facial; features, 16, 19–22; personality assessment, 17–23; textural aspect, 16; *see also* mouth
family: attitude to disabled members, 54, 125–6, 141, old people, 156–7; support and care of the dying, 159–60, 163–5; traditional links, 87
female(s): Church's attitude to, 74–6; -male differences, 63–9, 243; -male resemblance, 15–17; sexuality and sexual behaviour, 64–70, 73–4, 87, 92–8, 150–1; *see also* mothers
fire walking, 171–2
flushes, *see* blushing
foreplay, sexual, 94
Freud, Sigmund, on: compensatory behaviour, 39–40; sexuality and psychoanalytical theories, 23–4, 27, 46, 65–6, 68, 107–14, 117–18, 193–4, 216
frigidity: causes of, 92–3; hysteroid personalities, 178
frontal lobotomy (surgery), 199

gaze, *see* eye contacts
genital(s): anxiety, 92, 99; attacks, 91; damage to, 132; erogenous zones, 106, 108–10; exposure, 77–9, 89, 96, 99; odour, 100–1, 104; puberty and, 37; stage of development, 108–9, 111; *see also* clitoris, penis, vagina *and* testicles
gestures: assumed, 27–8; significance, 21, 25–9, 32
glances, *see* eye contacts
gynandromorphy, 15–16

hand: and personality assessment, 17–18; physical characteristics, 17–18; shakes, 26; sweaty, 18, 28, 60; *see also* gestures
handicapped, the, *see* disabled adults *and* disabled children
head, physical characteristics: and personality assessment, 17, 20; *see also* face (facial)
hierarchy of needs, Maslow's, 139–41
Hinduism, spiritual practices, 95
home care for: disabled children, 126; the dying, 163–5; old people, 156
homeostasis, 139
hormones and sexual behaviour, 64, 113–14, 151
hospices for the dying, 163–5
hospital(s): birth trauma, delivery in, 219; terminal illness in, 158–9, 163–4
hypnosis: hysteria and, 181–9; stigmata induced by, 174–5; and warts, 193–4
hysteria: categories, 178–80; diagnosis physical ills, 177–81, 186–7; group, 76, 186–7; hypnosis and, 181–9; sexually motivated, 76
hysterical symptoms: amnesia, 46, 179; categories, 178–80; causes, 46; malingering, 180–1; miraculous cures, 177–8; physical reality of, 177–8, 180–1; stigmata, 173, 181; wartime, 178–80
hysteroid personalities, 178

impotence, 92–3
infants: birth trauma, 34, 219–21; body image, 35; development stages, 108–9, 111; disabled, 124; inferiority feelings, 40, 46; *see also* children
inferiority feelings: compensatory behaviour, 39–47, 60, 134–9, 144; infants, 40, 46; and superiority complex, 42
Inquisition, the Holy, 75–6
introversion: dimension of personality, 114–16; and sexual behaviour, 115

Judaism, attitude to sex, 72
Judo, 232–3
Jung, Carl: developmental psychology, middle and old age, 152–3; theory of the collective unconscious, 167–9

Karate, 232–3
kinesics, 25–32: use of cine and video equipment, 25–6, 30; vocabulary, 26, 30
Kretschmer, Ernst, body typing theories, 2–7, 12, 18, 122
Kung Fu, 233

latency stage of development, 108
legislation and sexual behaviour, 71–2
Leidenfrost effect, 172
logotherapy, 162–3
London University Council for Psychical Investigation, demonstration of fire-walking, 171–2
looks, *see* eye contacts
love needs, 139–41
Lowen, Alexander, bioenergetics, 225–9, 231–5, 237
Lung-gom, 202–3

macrobiotic diet, 212–13
male: -female differences, 63–9, 243; -female resemblance, 15–17; 'menopause', 151; sexuality and sexual behaviour, 64–70, 87, 92–8
manic depression: body type, 2–4, 122–3; causes, 122–3
marriage: attitudes to, 65–7, 87; and conventions of modesty, 77; *see also* pair-bonding
martial arts, 232–3, 238
Maslow, Abraham, 137–8, 144: hierarchy of needs, 139–41
masturbation: breast stimulation and, 95; children, 108; for the disabled, 130–1; fantasies, 96–7, 130–1; physiological events, 98; problems, 96–8; and self-esteem, 96–7; and sin, 72–4, 97
media and: the disabled, 143–4; female orgasm, 97; nudity, 88–9, 99; old people, 156; stereotypes of physical attractiveness, 52, 85–9
men, *see* male
menarche, attitudes to, 105
menopause: attitudes to, 105; hormonal upsets, 151; 'male', 151
menstrual synchrony, 104
menstruation: attitudes to, 104–6; odours, 104; pre-menstrual tension, 218; puberty, 37, 105; taboos, 104–6
mental disorder, and body type, 2–4, 122–3
mental health, physical health and, 204–38
mesomorphy: and athletic body type, 6; mental and physical characteristics, 6–8, 12, 14–15, 37; problems, 14–15; and somatotonia, 9; university and career choices, 11
mid-life crises, 151–2
middle age: attitudes to, 149–52; developmental psychology, 152; disease in 146, 151, psychosomatic, 191; sexuality, 151; weight problems, 4; *see also* ageing
miraculous cures: by Jesus Christ, 176; at Lourdes, 177, Church's attitude to, 176–7
modesty: blushing and, 78–80; cultural conventions, 80–1, 88, 92; motivation, 76–80; old age, 158; religious conventions, 76–8
mortuary practices, 166
mothers: attitudes to disabled offspring, 124; duties, 68; and hospital delivery, 219; *see also* parents *and* pregnancy
mourning rituals, 166–7
mouth: deformity, 58–60, treatment, 59–60; and sex, 58, 100, 110; stage of development (oral), 108–9, 111

nakedness, *see* nudity
naturism, *see* nudism
Naturist Federation, International, 210
naturopathy, 213
neuroticism, dimension of personality, 12, 114–16, 194
non-verbal communication (NVC), 23–33: in animals, 25; conventions, 25
nudism, 207–11
nudity: attitudes to, 78, 80–2, 88–9; disclosure taboos, 80; ideology, 207–11; religious conventions, 72, 76–8; and sexual encounters, 79–81,

90–1, 99; and shame, 77–9; stripping attacks, 91
odours, body: anxieties about, 99–101; genital, 100–1, 104; menstrual, 104; NVC, 32; pheromones, 102–4, 117; and sexual attraction, 100–4, 117; sweating and, 100, 104
Oedipus complex, 108–9, 112
old age: developmental psychology, 152–3; family attitude to, 156–7; problems, 150, 154–8; shame, excretory activities, 156–8; *see also* ageing *and* death and dying
Open University, higher education for the disabled, 143
oral sex, 58, 110: and vaginal odours, 100
oral stage of development, 108–9, 111
orgasm: animals, 69; female, 68–9, 94, 97, 223; male, 69, 94, 223; reinforcement of motivation, 96; simulated, 94; Tantric Yoga and, 233–4; unsatisfactory, 68–9, 117, 223; *see also* masturbation *and* sexual intercourse
overweight problems, 48–9: dieting, 4, 7, 14, 48–9, 235; and self-esteem, 48–50; yoga, 235; *see also* pyknic body type

pair-bonding, survival and, 66, 79–80; *see also* marriage
pallor, clue to emotional state, 31–2
palmistry, 17–18
paralysis: hysterical, 46; sexual relationships and, 130; treatment, 121–2; *see also* disabled adults *and* disabled children
parents: attitudes towards offspring, 35–6, when disabled, 54, 124–6; children's fantasies about, 108–9, 112; role, 46, 65–6; *see also* mothers
penis: attitudes to, 91–3, envy, 109; erection difficulties, 92–3; and intercourse position, 97; and sexual pleasure, 106, 108, *see also* orgasm
phallic stage of development, 108–9
phallic worship, 92
pheromones: and menstruation, 104; as sex attractants, 102–3, 117
phrenology, 17, 20
physical health: athletics and, 148, 204–7, 233, 235–8; attitudes to, Germany, 206–8, other countries, 206; bioenergetics, 225–9, 232–5, 237; diet control and, 148, 211–14; educational ideals, 205–7; Graeco-Roman ideals, 204–5; martial arts and, 232–3; and mental health, 204–38; nudism and, 207–11; spiritual practices, 201–2, 233–6
physiognomy, 17–23; ancient Greece, 18
physiological needs, 139–40
postural integration techniques, 229–32
postures: assumed, 27–8; muscular tension and, 23; Rolf's theories, 229–32, 235; significance, 21, 25–9, 32
pre-menstrual tension, 218
pregnancy: frigidity due to fear of, 93; and self-esteem, 52–3
primal therapy, 221–2
psychedelic drugs, mental states induced by, 120, 123
psychic surgery: cures resulting from, 175–6; and trickery, 175–6
psychological characteristics: categories, 8–9; genetic element, 10–11
psychoses: causes, 122–3; correlation with body types, 2–4, 122–3
psychosomatic disorders: causes, 46–7, 189–94, fear, 191; examples, 190–4; personality types, 195–6; therapy, 196–200; wartime, 194
puberty: changes due to, 8, 37–8, 105–6; latency stage before, 108
pupil size and NVC, 31
pyknic body type: characteristics, 2, 4, 6; and endomorphy, 6; and mental disorder, 2–4

rape, 70–1, 91
rebirth therapies, 221–2
Reich, Wilhelm, therapy for muscular tensions, 23, 117, 210, 220, 222–7, 231–5, 237
religion: faith, in middle and old age, 152–3, in terminal illness, 153, 162, 165, 168–9; and sexual behaviour, 71–8; *see also individual religions*

retirement: age of, 149, 154–5; attitudes to, 153–5
Rolf, Ida, postural integration (Rolfing), 229–32, 235
Roman Catholic Church, attitude to: miraculous cures, 176–7, at Lourdes, 177; stigmata, 173–5; *see also* Christianity
Royal Free Hospital, London, group hysteria, 187

sadism, 91
safety needs, 139–40
'samadhi' (meditation), 202
scatological themes, and sex, 73–4, 99
schema for body and personality, 240–5
schizophrenia: body types, 2–4, 122–3; causes, 122–3; eye contact avoidance, 31
schizothymia, mental characteristics, 4–5
self-actualization needs, 139–40
self-esteem: and ageing, 47–8; body image and, 34–62, 90; deformity and disablement, 36–7, 54–8, 128–9, 136; encounter groups, support from, 61; masturbation and, 96–7; pregnancy, 52–3; sexual encounters, 90–3; transsexualism, 51–2; weight problems, 48–51
sex education texts and manuals, 94–5, 110
sex magazines, and chemical attractants, 102–3
sexual abstinence: Christian attitude to, 74–6; dreams and fantasies caused by, 74–6; neurotic defence mechanisms, 74–5, corporate, 76
sexual appeal (attraction): in middle age, 151; odours and, 100–4; and physical attractiveness, 82–4, 116–17
sexual drives, 109–10, 118, 223–4
sexual encounters: anxiety and, 81, 90; cultural conventions, 68, 80, 99, disabling and physical conditions affecting, 130–4; foreplay in, 94; motivation, 66–9, 118; nakedness and shame, 79–81, 90–1; and self-esteem, 90–3
sexual intercourse: association with excretion, 99; difficulties, 69, 92–4, 97, for the disabled, 129–30; modesty and, 78; physiological events, 70, 98; positions, 73, 97, 100; rape, 70–1, 91; and Tantric Yoga, 233–4; *see also* orgasm
sexual perversion, 96, 100, 110: ancient Rome, 72–3; attacks, 91
Sheldon, William: body typing theories, 5–18; body and the unconscious, 234
Shiatsu, 232–3
sin: disfigurement and, 131; sex and, 71–4, 77, 97
smells, *see* odours
sociobiology, treatment of sex and sexuality, 65–8
sodomy, 110
somatotonia: definition, 9; and mesomorphy, 9
somatotyping, 6–17: Sheldon's three-number code, 7
Spiritual Healers, National Federation of, 176
spiritual healing, 175–6
stability, dimension of personality, 114–16
stasis anxiety, 223–4
stigmata: Church's attitude to, 173–5; deception and, 173; hypnosis and, 174–5; hysterical symptoms, 173, 181
stigmatics, named examples, 173–5
stripping attacks, 91
suicide: obesity and depression, 49; old and young people, 157
superiority: complex, and inferiority, 42; striving for, 41; *see also* inferiority feelings
sweat(ing): clue to emotional state, 28, 31–2; hands, 18, 28, 60; odours, 100, 104

t'ai chi exercises, 233
Taoism, martial arts, 232–3
teeth deformities, 58–9: treatment, 58–9
temperament: components of, 9; physical characteristics, 9, scale, 9
tensions: bioenergetics (Lowen's therapy), 225–9; 231–5, 237; causes,

227; premenstrual, 218; Reichian therapy, 23, 117, 210, 220, 222–7, 231–5, 237; Rolfing, 229–32, 235
terminal illness, 155: family support in, 159, 163–5, guilt, 165; at home, 163–5; in hospices, 163–5; in hospital, 158–9, 163–4; religious faith and, 153, 162, 165; in underdeveloped countries, 163
textural aspect, the (Sheldon), 16
Three Faces of Eve, The (film), 179
transsexualism, 51–2
tremor, clue to emotional state, 28, 31–2
Tumo, 202–3

underweight problems, 50–1; *see also* asthenic body type

vagina: attacks on, 91; attitudes to, 106, 109; exposure, 78; odours, 100, 104; pleasure, 106, 223; problems, 93; *see also* genitals
vegans, 212
vegetarianism, 211–13
viscerotonia: characteristics, 14; definition, 9; and endomorphy, 9, 14

weight problems, *see* overweight problems *and* underweight problems
witch hunts, 76
women, *see* female(s)
World Health Organization (WHO), female attitude to menstruation, 105

Yoga, 201–3, 233–6, 238: Kundalini, 202, 234; Tantric, 233–4
young people: death, 146, 166, suicide, 157; puberty, 8, 37–8, 105–6, 108; *see also* children

Zen, 200–1, 203: 'Electric', 200; martial arts, 232–3; *see also* Buddhism